D1067374

FROM GALLUP

BLIND SPOT

The Global Rise of **UNHAPPINESS**
and How Leaders Missed It

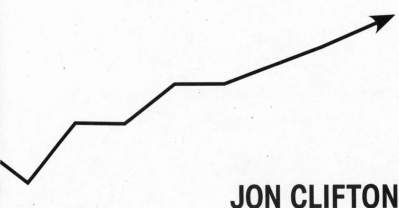

JON CLIFTON
CEO of Gallup

"There are 5 billion ways to lead a life, and we should study them all."

GEORGE GALLUP (1901-1984)

GALLUP PRESS
The Gallup Building
901 F Street, NW
Washington, D.C. 20004

Library of Congress Control Number: 2022931319
ISBN: 978-1-59562-245-7

First Printing: 2022
10 9 8 7 6 5 4 3 2 1

Printed in Canada by Friesens

Copyright © 2022 Gallup, Inc.
All rights reserved, including the right of reproduction in whole or in part in
any form.

Gallup®, CE³®, CliftonStrengths®, The Gallup Path®, The Gallup Poll®, Gallup Press®,
Q¹²®, and the 34 CliftonStrengths theme names are trademarks of Gallup, Inc. All
other trademarks are property of their respective owners.

The Q¹² items are Gallup proprietary information and are protected by law. You
may not administer a survey with the Q¹² items or reproduce them without written
consent from Gallup. Copyright © 1993-1998 Gallup, Inc. All rights reserved.

Table of Contents

INTRODUCTION

Every year, Gallup interviews people in over 140 countries to ask them how their lives are going. The following conversation — translated into English — is an exchange between a Vietnamese interviewer and a female shoe factory worker in Ho Chi Minh City.

Interviewer: Did you feel well-rested yesterday?

Woman: No. I am working 12 hours a day at the factory, but I still don't have enough money.

Interviewer: Were you treated with respect all day yesterday?

Woman: Don't know. I will get into fights if I don't finish my target.

Interviewer: Did you smile and laugh a lot all day yesterday?

Woman: [Silence]

Interviewer: Sis, are you still there?

Woman: [Struggles to answer]

Interviewer: You can talk to me if you have anything to share.

Woman: [Crying] No one ever asks me whether I'm happy or not, whether I'm well or sick.

This worker is struggling. You can feel her unhappiness. But how many people in the world feel just like her? In other words, how much unhappiness is there in the world?

If there was a definitive answer to that question, would leaders pay attention to it?

They sure pay attention when the economy contracts. If the stock market collapses, it makes headlines everywhere. And all leaders worry when unemployment increases. But what about when anger rises? Or stress? Or sadness? Do they even know it happened?

Imagine you are in a room with the leaders of the G-20: the president of the United States, the prime minister of India, the chancellor of Germany, the president of China, the king of Saudi Arabia, and the leaders of the other 15 largest economies in the world. You ask them: "What indicators do you follow most closely?"

All leaders use indicators to measure progress. For example, if you asked CEOs this question, they would probably say revenue growth or share price. With world leaders, it's harder to know. Would they say GDP? Unemployment? The poverty rate? Maybe the Saudi king would say oil prices.

I am not entirely sure what their answer would be, but I know what they would *not* say. None of them would say *happiness*.

As a result, none of them know just how much unhappiness there is in the world today. And that is concerning because unhappiness is now at a record high. According to Gallup, people feel more anger, sadness, pain, worry, and stress than ever before.

Now, I know what you're thinking: "I didn't need data to know that. The pandemic made everyone miserable. Why is that surprising?"

COVID-19 was bad for everyone, but we cannot blame the rise of unhappiness on the pandemic alone. Global misery was rising well before the pandemic. In fact, unhappiness has been steadily climbing for a decade — and its rise has been in the blind spot of almost every world leader.

The Global Rise of Unhappiness

Anger, Stress, Sadness, Physical Pain, and Worry Reach New Global High

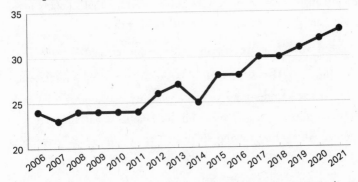

The Negative Experience Index is a composite measure of the five negative experiences (anger, stress, sadness, physical pain, and worry). Index scores range from zero to 100.

Source: Gallup

Experts know how to count almost everything: CO2 emissions, the size of urban slum populations, the contribution tourism makes to every country's economy, and even the number of trees in the Sahara desert. But while experts seem to count almost everything, they don't systematically measure how people feel.

Dear 7.7 Billion World Citizens, How Are Your Lives Going?

In 2006, Gallup began conducting global research on subjective wellbeing, which is used interchangeably with "happiness." The goal of the research was to definitively report — by country — how people's lives were going from *their* perspective. Was the world getting more stressed? Were people more hopeful? Were they getting angrier?

Thousands of interviewers have now sat with people in their homes or called them and asked them about their lives — just like the Vietnamese worker above. This work now represents more than

98% of the world's population and, as of this writing, includes over 5 million interviews.

It is remarkable how open people are about sharing their sadness, their pain, or their anger. But it's also concerning that so many more people are sharing these negative emotions with us.

But why? Why are so many more people feeling this way?

The answer has to do with an inequality the world is not familiar with. Leaders understand *income* inequality — the growing divide between the financial haves and have-nots. What they are not familiar with is the growing divide between the haves and have-nots of a *great life*. This is called *wellbeing* inequality.

At the beginning of every wellbeing survey, we ask people to tell us how good of a life they have. Here is the question verbatim:

> Please imagine a ladder with steps numbered from zero at the bottom to 10 at the top. The top of the ladder represents the *best possible life* for you and the bottom of the ladder represents the *worst possible life* for you. On which step of the ladder would you say you personally feel you stand at this time?[1] (emphasis added)

When we first asked the world this question in 2006, 3.4% of people told Gallup their lives were a 10 — the best possible life. And only 1.6% said their lives were a zero — the worst possible life.

After 15 years of tracking, those numbers have shifted significantly. The number of people living their best lives has more than doubled (to 7.4%), while the number people living their worst lives has more than quadrupled (to 7.6%). (See References for trend: Best and Worst Life Ratings.)

---

1 The Cantril Self-Anchoring Striving Scale (ladder scale) was originated by pioneering social researcher Hadley Cantril in his 1965 book *The Pattern of Human Concerns*.

But it gets worse.

If you isolate the 20% of people globally who rate their lives the best and compare them to the 20% of people who rate their lives the worst, you find just how unequal the world is becoming in terms of wellbeing and happiness.

In 2006, the 20% of the world who rated their lives the best had an average life rating of 8.3. The 20% who rated their lives the worst had an average life rating of 2.5.

Now look at 2021. The 20% who rated their lives the best had an average life rating of 8.9, and the 20% who rated their lives the worst had an average life rating of 1.2. The gap in those life ratings is now 7.7 points — the highest in the history of Gallup's tracking. The top 20% of the world could hardly be doing better, and the bottom 20% could hardly be doing worse.

Global Wellbeing Inequality

Average life evaluations for the lowest 20% and highest 20% ratings

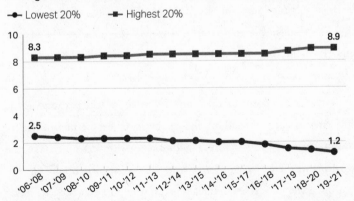

Average wellbeing scores for the 20% of people worldwide who rated their lives the best and the 20% who rated their lives the worst from 2006-2021. Wellbeing scores range from 0-10. Projection weighted.

Source: Gallup

7

You might think that income inequality explains wellbeing inequality and therefore rising unhappiness. That is certainly part of it. But a great life is more than just money. After studying the 20% of people who report having a great life, Gallup finds they have five things in common: They are fulfilled by their work, have little financial stress, live in great communities, have good physical health, and have loved ones they can turn to for help.

The 20% of people who rate their lives the worst have very little of any of those things. They don't have a quality job, their income is not enough to get by, they live in broken communities, they are hungry or malnourished, and they don't have anyone in their life they can count on for help. And the 20% who rate their lives this low are getting sadder, more stressed, and angrier than ever before.

One of our earliest advisers on this work was Nobel laureate Daniel Kahneman. He told us something over 15 years ago that he recently repeated on a podcast: "… we speak of happiness, the dimension is labeled by its positive pole. And that's very unfortunate because actually increasing happiness and reducing misery are very different things." He also said, "… I would not focus on the positive end. I would focus on the negative end, and I would say it is a responsibility of society to try to reduce misery."

That is the point of this book — to show where the world is suffering in each of Gallup's five elements of wellbeing and where it can improve. But before I address that, we cannot make the world better if we do not know how it is doing. The book starts by outlining the indicators that leaders can watch so that they are never surprised again by rising stress, sadness, or anger.

And lastly, please remember that subjective wellbeing ("happiness") is still fairly new compared with indicators such as GDP, which dates back almost 100 years. This research has led us to make some discoveries that we do not fully understand, nor can we fully explain. This book outlines four of those perplexing discoveries in the hopes that the world will help us better understand what is going on.

I hope this book makes you think differently about measuring happiness. And by the time you are done reading it, I hope you become more interested in understanding how people feel in your organization, your community, and your country.

Overview

Part I: The Leadership Blind Spot: Happiness and Wellbeing

The first part of this book outlines the problem: Global leaders have relied too heavily on objective indicators to the detriment of their constituencies. The book begins with examples of countries where their economies were growing but the subjective wellbeing of their citizens was declining — in some cases, dramatically.

Part II: Addressing the Blind Spot: Measuring Happiness and Wellbeing

The second part of this book offers a solution: Global leaders should closely follow wellbeing and happiness metrics to better understand how people's lives are going. Gallup has produced global statistics for wellbeing and happiness since 2006, and these metrics perfectly complement the objective indicators for human development that leaders already follow so closely.

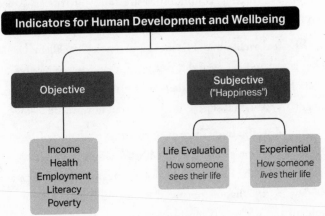

Part III: What Makes a Great Life?

Wellbeing and happiness metrics have helped us better understand what makes a great life. The third part of this book highlights the five elements of wellbeing — work, financial, community, physical, and social wellbeing — and where the world is struggling most in each of them.

Work wellbeing: The world is facing a global jobs crisis — but from the looks of global unemployment, you wouldn't know it. The jobs crisis is not just a lack of work, but a lack of *great* work. Of the 3.3 billion people who want a great job, only 300 million have one.

Financial wellbeing: The age-old question "Does money buy happiness?" has largely been answered. Money may not buy happiness, but it is hard to be happy without it — and roughly 2 billion people are struggling on their current income.

Community wellbeing: Living in a great community is fundamental to a great life. But over 1 billion people are so dissatisfied with their community that they want to leave it forever. Almost 2 billion would not even recommend their community to a friend. These broken communities are not just the result of crime and a lack of basic infrastructure; they also lack a *sense of community*. Thriving communities are built on trust and people who help each other.

Physical wellbeing: Having high physical wellbeing includes being active and eating right. But what about not being able to eat at all? For almost 30 years, the world was winning the war against hunger. In 2014, that started to change, and now we are losing.

Social wellbeing: There is a growing epidemic of loneliness. Over 300 million people do not have a single friend. Low social wellbeing is as bad for you as smoking nearly a pack of cigarettes per day. In the chapter on social wellbeing, I'll shed light on the problem and where it is most prevalent.

Part IV: Four Unanswered Questions

The fourth part of this book poses four questions from Gallup's wellbeing research that continue to confound experts. This section outlines what we have discovered and offers possible explanations. I invite you to share your own thoughts about these unanswered questions, because if we can find the answers, we can make a significant contribution to the world.

Part V: What Leaders Can Do to Improve How People's Lives Are Going

The fifth part of this book gives public and private sector leaders recommendations on what they can do to improve people's wellbeing. The list is by no means exhaustive, and with additional wellbeing research, we can continue to find even more solutions to better the lives of everyone on the planet.

PART I
The Leadership Blind Spot:
Happiness and Wellbeing

CHAPTER ONE
What Economic Models Miss

"It's the economy, stupid."

This is one of the most popular catchphrases in U.S. political history. But is it true?

Democratic strategist James Carville famously coined the phrase during Bill Clinton's 1992 presidential campaign. The economy was recovering too slowly from a recession under the Republican administration, and Carville knew the slow recovery would give the Democrats an advantage.

Carville wanted the slogan to be a significant focus of the campaign — he even posted it in Clinton's Little Rock, Arkansas, campaign headquarters. Ever since, those words have been used extensively in American politics.

But why did *that* catchphrase become so popular?

Maybe because it worked. Clinton won the White House that year, defeating incumbent President George H.W. Bush by 202 Electoral College votes.

Or maybe the slogan became popular because people think it's true. They think voters do, in fact, judge leaders based on the strength of the economy. Some political analysts and academics are so convinced of this that many now use economic models to predict the outcomes of elections all over the world.

But is a leader's job at risk if the economy is deteriorating? And does a leader have more job security if the economy is improving?

Eighteen years after Carville said, "It's the economy, stupid," another person halfway around the world shattered this conventional wisdom. And it happened in a country where the economy was expanding at an average of 5% for two straight decades.

But before I tell this person's story, look at how the economy was doing in his country from 1990-2010.

A Growing Economy

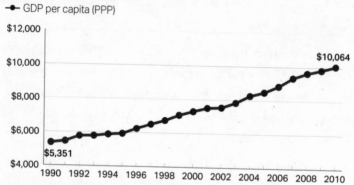

GDP per capita (PPP) estimates are from the International Monetary Fund's World Economic Outlook database, April 2021. Purchasing power parity; 2017 international dollars.

Source: International Monetary Fund

Based on this chart, how would you say people's lives were going in this country? If economic growth can be used as a proxy for how people's lives are going, then we could conclude that their lives were going well, right?

The last year of the trend is 2010. In 2011, the economy contracted. The cause of the 2011 economic contraction begins with the story of a young man named Mohamed.

As in many stories, the protagonist had a hard life. Mohamed was raised in a poor household, he never graduated from high school, and his father died when he was young.

At 26, Mohamed wanted what most young men want — to work and make money. He had a natural talent to negotiate, which he used to sell fruit. Mohamed's dream was to make enough money so that one day he could buy an Isuzu pickup truck. With a truck, he would no longer have to buy fruit at the market. He could buy it directly from the farmers and make even more money.

Starting your own business is hard anywhere, but it is especially hard in Mohamed's country. According to *Foreign Policy*, it takes "55 administrative steps totaling 142 days and fees amounting to some $3,233" to start a business. Mohamed did not have that kind of time or money, so registering a business was out of the question. And $3,233 might not seem like a lot of money in some countries, but it is a lot in his country. It is so much money that many businesses never get registered there. In fact, about half of the country's workers are employed by businesses that are not legally registered.

Yet operating without a license makes doing business risky — you never know when you will be the victim of a police shakedown. This kind of corruption is commonplace in Mohamed's country, but you may not have known that from the official statistics.

According to the World Bank's *Doing Business 2010* report, this country ranked 69th out of 183 countries for ease of doing business, improving four spots from the year before. And it ranked only seven spots below Spain, a far wealthier country. Yet the corruption in Mohamed's country did not go unnoticed by its people — a majority felt corruption was widespread in their government at that time.

On December 17, 2010, Mohamed came face to face with that corruption.

The night before, he had taken out an estimated $200 loan to buy fresh fruit that he would sell the next day. Because of the loan, Mohamed was low on cash and in debt.

On the morning of the 17th, Mohamed went to the center of town to sell fruit. And after a few hours, the police approached him.

What followed was a typical shakedown. First, the authorities charged Mohamed with an infraction. A customary bribe would usually make them go away, but he had nothing to offer. So they took his fruit and his expensive scale. Mohamed was frustrated — he no longer had anything to sell. He was worse off than he was the day before.

Then things got heated. There is debate about exactly what happened next, but most accounts agree that one of the police officers slapped Mohamed across the face. Now he was broke *and* humiliated.

Demoralized and enraged, he decided to fight. After the confrontation with the officer, Mohamed walked over to the local governor's office to demand that the police return his things. But the governor wanted no part of it. He refused to see Mohamed. Yet Mohamed persisted — he wanted to be heard. But the governor still refused to see him.

Even more frustrated, Mohamed left the governor's office and made his way to a local store. With the little money he had, he bought paint thinner. At 11:30 a.m., Mohamed walked back to the governor's office and stood in the middle of the street. Then, he poured the paint thinner all over himself and yelled, "How do you expect me to make a living?"

With the stroke of a match, Mohamed Bouazizi set himself on fire. In broad daylight and in front of the governor's office, a man so desperate to earn a living burned himself alive.

That single act triggered a revolution in his country — Tunisia. His defiance inspired people all over the Middle East and North Africa. Aided by social media, the *entire* region erupted in protest.

The Arab uprisings spanned 16 countries and toppled leaders in four of them.

In late January 2011, *The Economist* was reporting what was happening in Tunisia. The following paragraph describes what we thought we knew about the country:

> Tunisia has more solid foundations than many Arab states. Despite the country's paucity of natural resources, its 10.6m people enjoy relatively good standards of health, education, and other public services. It has a high level of home ownership and reasonably solid national accounts. *Its economy, integrated with the outside world as a magnet for investment in manufacturing, offshore services and tourism, has grown at an annual average of 5% for the past two decades.* (emphasis added)

This was surprising but true, as evidenced by the GDP trend I showed earlier and again below. The upward trend from 1990 to 2010 represents an average growth rate of 5%.

Tunisia: GDP per Capita 1990-2010

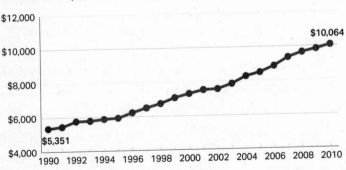

GDP per capita (PPP) estimates are from the International Monetary Fund's World Economic Outlook database, April 2021. Purchasing power parity; 2017 international dollars.

Source: International Monetary Fund

Had we used GDP growth as a proxy for how people's lives were going in Tunisia, it may have misled us to believe that its citizens' lives were getting better.

What did GDP look like in other countries that experienced revolts during the Arab uprisings?

Although the protests started in Tunisia, mental images of the Arab uprisings are often closely associated with the hundreds of thousands of people in Egypt's Tahrir Square who eventually ousted strongman President Hosni Mubarak.

As in Tunisia, Egypt's economy was growing before the Arab uprisings — increasing over 80% from 1990 to 2010.

Egypt: GDP per Capita 1990-2010

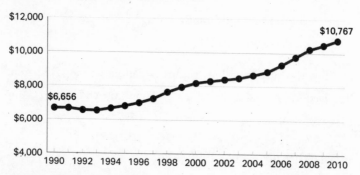

GDP per capita (PPP) estimates are from the International Monetary Fund's World Economic Outlook database, October 2021. Purchasing power parity; 2017 international dollars.

Source: International Monetary Fund

Yet the growing economies in Egypt and Tunisia masked a rising frustration in both countries. And GDP wasn't the only indicator that may have misled us about the prevailing mood.

Take, for example, the Human Development Index (HDI) produced by the United Nations. The HDI exists to "emphasize that people and their capabilities should be the ultimate criteria for assessing the development of a country, not economic growth alone," according to the United Nations Development Programme (UNDP).

How does the HDI focus on people and their capabilities? According to UNDP, the HDI is "a summary measure of average achievement in key dimensions of human development: a long and healthy life, being knowledgeable and have a decent standard of living." To produce a number for each of these, they use life expectancy for "a long and healthy life," expected years and mean years of education for "being knowledgeable," and gross national income per capita for "a decent standard of living."

The HDI trends for Tunisia and Egypt show that both countries were experiencing considerable progress leading up to the Arab uprisings.

Human Development Index (HDI): Tunisia and Egypt

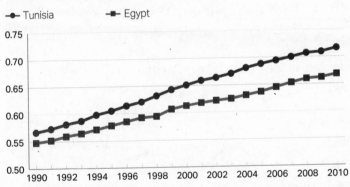

The Human Development Index is a composite index measuring average achievement in three basic dimensions of human development: a long and healthy life, knowledge, and a decent standard of living. Index scores range from 0 to 1.

Source: United Nations Development Programme

The World Economic Forum's Global Competitiveness Index also proved unhelpful in uncovering the nationwide discontent in Tunisia. Two months before Mohamed set himself on fire, the Forum released *The Global Competitiveness Report 2010–2011*, which ranked Tunisia 32nd out of 139 countries for competitiveness. Tunisia jumped eight spots from the previous year, making it the seventh country in the world for the most significant improvements on the index.

Most of these global indicators focus solely on economics or quantifying the transactions of life. Very few focus on how people feel. To better gauge how people feel about their lives, Gallup essentially asks them, "How is your life going?" Gallup asked Tunisians this question for the first time in 2008, then again in 2009 and 2010.

In 2008, 24% of Tunisians rated their lives high enough for Gallup to classify them as thriving. To put that in context, Tunisia's thriving rate was in line with the global average (24%) in 2008. By 2010, thriving in Tunisia dropped to 14%. This put Tunisia on par with the Palestinian Territories (14%), which consistently ranks among the lowest in the world for thriving.

Tunisia: Thriving and GDP per Capita

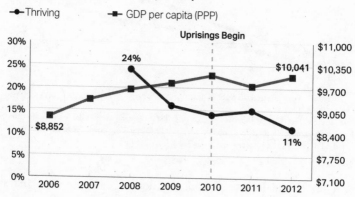

GDP per capita (PPP) estimates are from the International Monetary Fund's World Economic Outlook database, April 2021. Purchasing power parity; 2017 international dollars.

Source: Gallup and International Monetary Fund

Here is how Egyptians felt in the years leading up to the Arab uprisings:

Egypt: Thriving and GDP per Capita

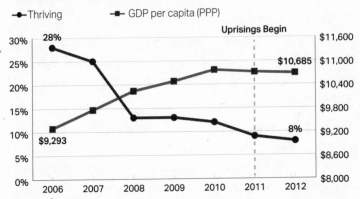

GDP per capita (PPP) estimates are from the International Monetary Fund's World Economic Outlook database, April 2021. Purchasing power parity; 2017 international dollars.

Source: Gallup and International Monetary Fund

With 28% of its population thriving in 2006, Egypt was slightly above the global average (25%). The 15-point decline by 2008 also put Egypt on par with the Palestinian Territories. In 2010, Egypt ranked 93rd out of 124 countries for thriving. The 9% in 2011 was captured after the Arab uprisings began in Egypt.

Imagine if these were unemployment trends. A 10-15-point swing in unemployment anywhere would be headline news everywhere.

Tunisia's 10-point drop meant that 800,000 adults who were thriving in 2008 were no longer thriving in 2010. The 15-point drop in Egypt meant that almost 9 million people who were thriving in 2006 were either struggling or suffering in 2008.

The most dramatic drop in thriving among the countries affected by the Arab uprisings was in Bahrain. Two years before the Arab uprisings, 40% of people there were thriving. That number fell to 27% in 2010 and 11% in 2011 — putting oil-rich Bahrain slightly below the Palestinian Territories.

The literature and popular commentary are now filled with examples of growing economies that are not necessarily improving everyone's lives. Consider when a prison is built in the middle of a community. Wages will rise, unemployment will decrease, and the economy will grow — but do people's lives get better? Economic modeling suggests they would, but a conversation with locals would tell you the opposite.

Even the "father of GDP," Simon Kuznets, warned the world about the metric being misused. In his famous testimony to Congress in 1934, he said, "The welfare of a nation can, therefore, scarcely be inferred from a measurement of national income."

Despite his warning, economic indicators still lead the conversation to determine if society is progressing. And absent from the conversation is the voice of the people.

GDP is still an incredibly important measure for leaders, and as I will discuss later, money significantly affects a person's life. But too much reliance on economic indicators created blind spots for leaders in Egypt and Tunisia. It also created blind spots for leaders in the U.S. and the U.K., as we will explore in the next chapter.

CHAPTER TWO
Unhappiness and Elections

One of the most memorable moments in American politics took place on October 28, 1980.

That night, incumbent President Jimmy Carter and Republican Party nominee Ronald Reagan had their first and only presidential debate. It was their last chance to pitch America on why they should be president.

Nearly 81 million Americans were watching. At the time, no debate had been watched by more viewers. It remains the second-most-watched presidential debate in American history — ranking behind the first debate between former Secretary of State Hillary Clinton and future President Donald Trump.

With so many people watching, every word mattered — especially the candidates' closing arguments. But it was Reagan's that was the most notable. He closed with a question, which many historians consider the defining moment of his campaign:

> Next Tuesday all of you will go to the polls, will stand there in the polling place and make a decision. I think when you make that decision, it might be well if you would ask yourself, *are you better off than you were four years ago?* (emphasis added)

Reagan won, and many pundits think voters did exactly what he said: They went to the polls, asked themselves if their lives were better than they were four years ago, determined they were *not better*, and voted for Reagan — who won 44 states in a landslide.

The impact of Reagan's closing remarks in the debate is probably exaggerated. But it poses a fascinating question: *Do people vote based on how their lives are going?*

If they did, it would put a new twist on James Carville's quote. Instead of "It's the economy, stupid," the sign that would hang in every campaign office would be "It's how people's lives are going, stupid."

Brexit, the Economy, and Wellbeing

"BRITISH STUN WORLD WITH VOTE TO LEAVE E.U." *The New York Times* wrote the morning of June 24, 2016.

The Financial Times Stock Exchange (FTSE) 100 dropped almost 9% that morning, and the British pound's value fell to levels not seen since 1985. The result also caught Prime Minister David Cameron off guard. He resigned that same morning. *The Guardian* said the decision was a "turning point in British history to rank alongside the two world wars of the 20th century."

Why was the world so surprised?

One reason might have been that people relied too much on traditional economic indicators to assess the mood in the U.K. According to most economic indicators, things seemed OK in the U.K.

The official statistics showed that the economy had continually expanded since the global economic downturn in 2008-2009. In the year leading up to Brexit, the economy had not only rebounded — it was larger than it was before the economic downturn. In fact, the year before the Brexit vote, the economy grew 2.5%.

The jobs market also appeared to be in good shape. Before Brexit, unemployment had dropped below 5% in the U.K. for the first time since the 2008 economic crisis. Some economists consider 5% to be the "natural rate" of unemployment. Meaning, if a country's unemployment rate drops below 5%, which happened in the U.K., the jobs market should be pretty healthy.

The 2016 HDI also showed that things were going well in the U.K. In 2015, the U.K. reached an index score of 0.909 (a perfect score is 1). This was the U.K.'s second-highest score in the HDI's 26-year history at that time. The U.K. also ranked high globally, tying for 16th place out of 188 countries.

As a reminder, the HDI consists of three components: life expectancy, education, and income. These are not solely economic indicators, but objective metrics nonetheless.

Much of this recent economic progress probably seemed like a good reason for the U.K. to stay in the EU — such a good reason, you could campaign on it.

The "remain" supporters encouraged the electorate *not* to vote for change precisely because it would worsen the economy. Cameron believed that being part of the EU was an economic benefit and that leaving would have dire consequences. Three weeks before the official EU referendum, he told BBC News that an EU exit would "put a bomb under our economy."

If elections are about the economy, then the "remain" side should have won the day, right?

Wrong. And wrong by over 1 million votes: 52% voted to leave and 48% voted to remain a member of the EU.

Official economic indicators told us things were going well, but how did people *feel*?

For the past 15 years, Gallup has asked Britons this simple two-part question:

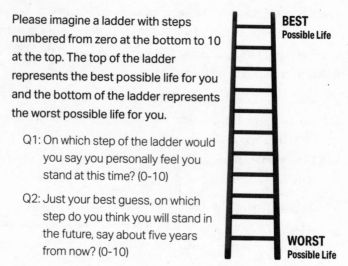

Please imagine a ladder with steps numbered from zero at the bottom to 10 at the top. The top of the ladder represents the best possible life for you and the bottom of the ladder represents the worst possible life for you.

BEST Possible Life

WORST Possible Life

Q1: On which step of the ladder would you say you personally feel you stand at this time? (0-10)

Q2: Just your best guess, on which step do you think you will stand in the future, say about five years from now? (0-10)

If a person answers the first question with a 7, 8, 9, or 10 and answers the second question with an 8, 9, or 10, Gallup considers them to be thriving. These cut points are not arbitrary. If someone rates their life high on both questions, they are also highly likely to tell us that life is going well on many other indicators. For example, they are also highly likely to say that they are eating well, have a roof over their head, have a good job with a solid paycheck, and have high physical and social wellbeing.

In 2013, 55% of Britons were thriving, which ranked the U.K. 16th out of 135 countries measured. Two years later, only 40% of Britons were thriving, ranking the U.K. 28th out of 142 countries measured. The 15-point shift is one of the most significant declines over a two-year period that Gallup has seen in any country since we started asking the question.

U.K.: Thriving and GDP per Capita

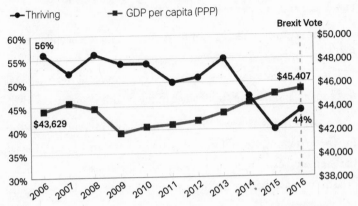

GDP per capita (PPP) estimates are from the International Monetary Fund's World Economic Outlook database, April 2021. Purchasing power parity; 2017 international dollars.

Source: Gallup and International Monetary Fund

Gallup was not alone in detecting this shift. Researchers at the University of Warwick used the Understanding Society dataset, which includes roughly 40,000 households per year and dates back to 1991. They analyzed the wellbeing of over 13,000 people who voted to leave the EU and concluded:

> When looking at overall life satisfaction only, the individual coefficients suggest that dissatisfied people are significantly more likely to favor Leave while the aggregate estimate implies that a higher relative dispersion of well-being across voting areas, which can be interpreted as a measure of life satisfaction inequality, has positive predictive power for the Leave support. Success rates of prediction are very similar whichever level of variation is considered.

With the Brexit vote in the rearview mirror, pundits are now offering a host of reasons why Britons wanted to leave the EU. The list includes threats to sovereignty, immigration, and lack of control over decisions in Brussels, but it should probably also include how people see and experience their lives.

Conservative pollster Lord Michael Ashcroft conducted a poll after Brexit and found that "small majorities of voters thought EU membership would be *better for the economy*, international investment, and the U.K.'s influence in the world." (emphasis added)

Most Britons believed that EU membership would be *better* for the economy, according to this poll — which is exactly what the "remain" campaign communicated: If we leave, it will have disastrous consequences for the economy (and the majority agreed). So why leave?

According to Lord Ashcroft's poll, "Leaving the EU was thought more likely to bring about a better immigration system, improved border controls, a fairer welfare system, *better quality of life*, and the ability to control our own laws." (emphasis added)

So most voters thought EU membership would be better for the economy but leaving the EU would bring about a better quality of life. How do you reconcile those?

This could be another example of a growing economy not benefitting the masses. For example, the U.K.'s membership in the EU may have been good for the overall economy, but not for everyone individually. One popular theory for why Brexit happened is that there is a specific segment of the population that feels "left behind" from the globalization that EU membership accelerates. Older, white, uneducated men who have not benefited from globalization were voting to stop it.

Maybe this is what caused Brexit — maybe not. It is hard to determine the exact cause or causes of Brexit. But regardless, we can conclude two things:

First, *the direction of the economy did not fully explain what happened.* GDP was rising, unemployment was falling, and leaders told fellow citizens that staying in the EU was beneficial to the U.K.'s economy. And, according to Lord Ashcroft's poll, most people believed that staying in the EU was an overall net economic benefit — yet Britons still wanted out.

Second, *wellbeing in the U.K. dropped considerably before the Brexit vote.* Gallup posed a question similar to the one that Reagan asked Americans in 1980. When asked if they were better off now than four years ago, many Britons said no. If someone feels like their life is getting worse, it may very well change their behavior at the polling booth.

But did the drop in wellbeing cause Britons to vote to leave the EU, or did the heated political debate around the issue itself cause the drop in wellbeing? The toxic nature of partisan politics can actually make people feel worse about their lives. In fact, we found evidence of this in the U.S.

Does Politics Make Us Miserable?

Every day in 2008 Gallup asked Americans how their lives were going. It was an election year, so at the beginning of each survey, we asked them who they intended to vote for — Barack Obama or John McCain — along with questions about their likelihood to vote and whether they approved of President George W. Bush's job performance.

After the election, we removed the political questions. Each survey started by asking people how their lives were going. When we removed the questions about politics, people rated their lives better.

We initially hypothesized that Obama's victory at the polls caused some people to rate their lives better. This did happen, especially with Black Americans, and that trend held for four years. But it was not just Obama's victory that caused the increase. People rated their lives better because we did not remind them about politics before asking how their lives were going.

Nobel laureate Sir Angus Deaton and Gallup's Chief Scientist Jim Harter discovered this phenomenon. According to Deaton:

> People appear to dislike politics and politicians so much that prompting them to think about them has a very large downward effect on their assessment of their own lives. ... The effect of asking the political questions on well-being is only a little less than the effect of someone becoming unemployed ...

This study suggests that politics dampens people's moods. Applying this to Brexit, the heated political environment could have been a contributing factor to the country's declining wellbeing.

But if toxic politics causes a decline in wellbeing, then we should have seen a national wellbeing decline during one of the most heated political environments in modern global history — the 2016 U.S. presidential election. Instead, we saw evidence that declining wellbeing at a much more local level may have contributed to the surprising election result.

Happiness and the 2016 U.S. Presidential Election

Leading up to the 2016 election, Gallup found that the percentage of thriving Americans was trending upward — from 52% in 2009 to 55% in 2016.

Americans' lives were getting better, but they still voted for change. Is this evidence that wellbeing *does not* predict the outcome of elections?

Remember that Hillary Clinton won the popular vote by almost 3 million votes (48.2% vs. 46.1% for Trump). A plurality of voters may have believed that their lives were going well, so they voted to keep the incumbent party in office.

But the story of wellbeing in the 2016 U.S. election is better told by the *county*-level trends than by the *country*-level trends.

As in the U.K., Gallup asked Americans to rate their current and future lives on a scale from zero to 10. But in the U.K., Gallup interviews only about 1,000 people per year. In the U.S., we interview far more. In the lead-up to the 2016 election, Gallup was interviewing roughly 300,000 Americans annually. Because we were talking to so many people, we could examine wellbeing at the U.S. congressional district and county levels.

We found that counties with the most significant increase in people voting for Democrats between 2012 and 2016 had the highest life satisfaction ratings. Counties with the largest increase in people voting for Republicans are where people rated their lives the worst. (See References for table: Shifts in Life Satisfaction in 2016 U.S. Presidential Election Relative to 2012 Election.)

A research team of scientists from Yale School of Medicine, Cincinnati Children's Hospital Medical Center, and Gallup concluded:

> The results of this analysis strongly suggest that current life satisfaction, future life optimism and experiencing positive daily emotions are all tied to shifts in voter preferences, with stronger or more greatly improving levels of each associated

with shifting toward the political party that was currently in the White House (e.g., voting more strongly Democratic in 2016 than in 2012). Lower or worsening well-being, in contrast, is associated with shifting away from the status quo (e.g., voting more strongly Republican in 2016 than in 2012).

Brexit and the 2016 U.S. election suggest a relationship between wellbeing and election outcomes. But how often does this relationship hold? Behavioral scientist George Ward attempted to answer this question in his paper *Happiness and Voting: Evidence from Four Decades of Elections in Europe.* In fact, an earlier version of the paper presented the central question as its title: *Is Happiness a Predictor of Election Results?*

To answer this question, Ward tapped into a massive survey known as the Eurobarometer — a study that now includes over 1 million respondents. Since 1974, the Eurobarometer has asked Europeans the following question translated into the preferred language of the respondent:

> On the whole, are you very satisfied, fairly satisfied, not very satisfied, or not at all satisfied with the life you lead?

What Ward wanted to know is: Do shifts in how people feel about their lives predict the outcome of elections?

His answer: Yes, they do.

According to his paper, "… the data suggest at the national level … that happiness measures are strongly predictive of the electoral fate of governing parties in general elections." Ward found that the health of the economy is also predictive of election outcomes, but not as predictive as wellbeing.

Predictors of Government Vote Share in Europe

Within-country R²

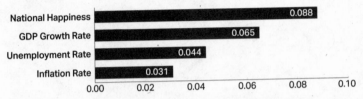

National Happiness	0.088
GDP Growth Rate	0.065
Unemployment Rate	0.044
Inflation Rate	0.031

0.00   0.02   0.04   0.06   0.08   0.10

Each bar represents the within-country R² value from a separate bivariate regression (with country fixed effects) of cabinet vote share on each of the four indicators. National Happiness is the country-mean of the life satisfaction question at the closest Eurobarometer survey prior to the election. Macroeconomic variables are drawn from the OECD and refer to the country-year of each election.

Source: Based on data from Ward (2020)

Ward's research gives credence to Reagan's famous question "Are you better off than you were four years ago?" But "predict" is a strong word. Declines in national wellbeing do not *always* predict that an incumbent will lose an election or that a leader will be ousted. For example, wellbeing had stagnated before Indian Prime Minister Narendra Modi was reelected in 2019. (See References for chart: India: Thriving and GDP per Capita.)

While a decline in national mood may not necessarily *predict* a leadership change, it can create the conditions for a leadership change. Sometimes, when the conditions are right, a trigger event needs to take place — such as when Mohamed Bouazizi set himself on fire. Other times, a trigger event may never happen.

Even if a decline in mood does not predict political change, this research demonstrates that wellbeing indicators help tell a more nuanced story about how people's lives are going that economics alone cannot tell.

PART II
Addressing the Blind Spot: Measuring Happiness and Wellbeing

"This is a practical joke, right?"

That was Alvin Wong's response to a phone call he received from a *New York Times* reporter on March 4, 2011. The reporter wanted the answer to this question: What does it feel like to be the happiest man in the United States?

Alvin received the phone call because there is no one like him in the U.S. You see, Alvin meets an unusual set of criteria. He appears to be the only person who is Asian American, married with children, a Hawaii resident, an observant Jew, a tall male, a business owner, over 65, and making more than $120,000 per year.

What do these characteristics have to do with happiness and wellbeing?

The New York Times was familiar with Gallup's wellbeing work in the U.S. They called Gallup and asked: What is the demographic profile of the happiest person in the United States?

So we looked at every demographic to see which groups give the highest score on wellbeing.

In which state do people rate their lives the highest? Hawaii.

The religious group? Judaism. The income group? $120,000+.

Men, tall people, Asian Americans, married people, parents, and business owners also topped their respective category. Put these characteristics together and who do you have? Alvin Wong.

That week, Alvin's story ran in *The New York Times*, and it went viral. Alvin became a global sensation — receiving phone calls from people all over the world. They all wanted the answer to the same question: What is the secret to happiness?

At first, Alvin found the question funny. He enjoyed telling people how happy he was and why. But after a while, it stopped being funny. He grew concerned about the people calling him. They wanted to know his secret to happiness, but for the wrong reason. They wanted a shortcut to happiness.

Alvin now has advice for these people: There are no shortcuts to happiness. The secret to happiness is, he said, "Like marriage or anything else, you've got to work at it."

Alvin is now a motivational speaker with his own website, *Alvin Wong: The Happiest Person in America*, where he shares his story and philosophies on happiness. He believes the most important elements of a great life are work, humility, family, and maintaining a positive attitude.

A few of Alvin's recommendations have solid statistical support (which I will explore later). But while America's happiest man offers good advice, there is one thing he said that people might not agree with. According to Alvin, "Happiness comes from within and it is possible for you to cultivate it in your own life."

But does happiness really come from within?

If you are a poor fruit vendor in Sidi Bouzid who lost everything to a system you perceive as corrupt, probably not. Happiness may not always come from within, but we can measure the happiness within people. That is why most major wellbeing studies use surveys — to fully understand someone's story, we need them to tell it to us.

CHAPTER THREE
The Happiest People in the World?

Finland is not the happiest country.

I don't really know why Finland always ranks top for happiness.

I don't feel very happy.

If that's true, I'd hate to see the other nations.

— Reactions from people in Finland after the release of the *World Happiness Report*

If I asked you, "Who are the happiest people in the world?" you might say people in Finland, Denmark, or "one of the Nordic countries." If so, it is probably because you are familiar with the most famous study on happiness: the *World Happiness Report* (*WHR*). If you guessed a country in Latin America, you are still right (which I will explain later).

In affiliation with the United Nations, the *WHR* is produced annually by the Sustainable Development Solutions Network (SDSN), a network of academics including Lord Richard Layard, John Helliwell, and Jeff Sachs. According to the authors, "The *World Happiness Report* is a landmark survey of the state of global happiness that ranks 156 countries by how happy their citizens perceive themselves to be."

The landmark survey the authors mention is conducted by Gallup. Known as the Gallup World Poll, this survey is the world's most extensive study on how people's lives are going. Each year, the World Poll covers roughly 140 different languages in over 140

43

countries. And to date, the World Poll has been conducted in over 160 countries and in 171 different languages. In Africa alone, we have interviewed in 82 different languages.

The *WHR*'s conclusion that the happiest people live in the Nordic countries is supported by prominent academics, robust data, and the U.N.'s imprimatur. But is it right?

That depends on how you define happiness. The *WHR* measures happiness using the results of one question that Gallup poses to the world:

> Please imagine a ladder with steps numbered from zero at the bottom to 10 at the top. The top of the ladder represents the best possible life for you and the bottom of the ladder represents the worst possible life for you. On which step of the ladder would you say you personally feel you stand at this time?

Does that question measure happiness — or contentment?

It measures contentment according to Minna Tervamäki, nominated as the most positive person in Finland. "I have very contradictory feelings about the happiness survey. Finnish people read it and laugh, like 'What? Us?' What comes to my mind is that Finnish people are content more than happy," she told BBC Travel.

The world-famous happiness rankings are probably not a reflection of happiness, but what if the report was called the *World Contentment Report*? Would you read it? Probably not.

In the 2012 *WHR*, the authors admitted that they used the word "happiness" to get more attention:

> "Subjective well-being" is the general expression used to cover a range of individual self-reports of moods and life assessments. The word "happiness" is often used in an equally general way,

as in the title of this report. It does help to focus thinking, *and attracts attention more quickly than does "subjective well-being." But there is a risk of confusion.* (emphasis added)

The authors agree that "subjective wellbeing" is the most accurate terminology, but they "nonetheless wrote their own books with 'happiness' in the title because they or their editors [knew] that happiness [would] draw more reader interest than does subjective well-being," according to the 2015 *WHR*.

But not everyone likes using the word "happiness" for this kind of research. The father of positive psychology, Martin Seligman, once said, "My original view was closest to Aristotle's — that everything we do is done in order to make us happy — but I actually detest the word *happiness*, which is so overused that it has become almost meaningless. It is an unworkable term for science, or for any practical goal such as education, therapy, public policy, or just changing your personal life."

He is probably right, but it is still the word that gets people's attention. So, for the purposes of this book, I am using "happiness" just like the *WHR* uses it: "Happiness" is shorthand for "subjective wellbeing." The only difference is that Gallup takes a broader approach to measuring it. The following chapter shows how we measure subjective wellbeing — or "happiness."

CHAPTER FOUR
How on Earth Do You Measure Happiness?

How do you measure the life of a woman or a man?

— "Seasons of Love" from the musical *Rent*,
by Jonathan Larson

When someone's father dies, most governments in the world record the time of his death and the cause of his death. These records are called *objective* indicators because whether someone dies is not a matter of opinion.

But what about the pain his death caused his family, friends, and community? Those emotions are captured through *subjective* indicators of wellbeing.

This chart shows the distinction between these indicators that help us better understand how humanity is doing.

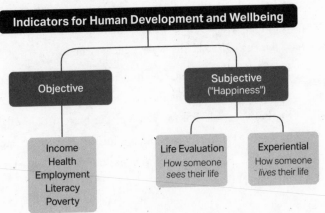

Indicators for Human Development and Wellbeing

Objective

Income
Health
Employment
Literacy
Poverty

Subjective
("Happiness")

Life Evaluation
How someone
sees their life

Experiential
How someone
lives their life

Subjective wellbeing is divided into two constructs: how someone *sees* their life and how they *live* their life. The first part is an overall assessment of their life; the second is how they experience their life each day.

Both aspects are critical because they measure different things. For example, look at two middle-aged Americans, one with young children and one without. How do they *see* life, and how do they *experience* life? Both rate their lives similarly, but they experience life differently. The person with young children experiences more positive *and* negative emotions. Meaning, the person with children is more likely to experience stress, sadness, and anger; they are also more likely to experience joy and laughter.

Another reason why both constructs are so important to measure has to do with income. Money plays a significant role in how people *see* their lives but makes far less of an impact on how people *live* their lives. More money makes you see your life better, but it will not necessarily buy you less stress or more laughter. I will discuss this more thoroughly in Chapter Nine.

How People See Their Lives (Life Evaluation)

The first component of wellbeing is evaluative wellbeing, which measures how someone sees their life. People are asked to evaluate or rate their lives using the ladder scale, which, again, is:

> Please imagine a ladder with steps numbered from zero at the bottom to 10 at the top. The top of the ladder represents the best possible life for you and the bottom of the ladder represents the worst possible life for you. On which step of the ladder would you say you personally feel you stand at this time?

We also ask a follow-up question to measure how much hope people have about the future:

> Just your best guess, on which step do you think you will stand in the future, say about five years from now?

Globally, people rate their lives a 5.3. Most of the world believes that life will be better in five years — rating their future lives a 6.7.

As I mentioned earlier, the *World Happiness Report* (*WHR*) uses only the first item for its rankings. This is why Finns are "the happiest people in the world" — they rate their lives the highest; Afghans rate their lives the worst.

Highest and Lowest Life Ratings

Highest ratings

Rank	Country	Rating
1	Finland	7.8
2	Denmark	7.6
	Iceland	7.6
4	Switzerland	7.5
5	Netherlands	7.4
	Luxembourg	7.4
	Sweden	7.4
	Israel	7.4
	Norway	7.4
10	New Zealand	7.2
	Austria	7.2
	Australia	7.2

Lowest ratings

Rank	Country	Rating
146	Afghanistan	2.3
145	Lebanon	3.0
	Zimbabwe	3.0
143	Rwanda	3.3
142	Botswana	3.5
	Lesotho	3.5
140	Sierra Leone	3.6
139	India	3.7
	Tanzania	3.7
	Zambia	3.7
	Malawi	3.7

Respondents' perceptions of where they stand "at this time." Life ratings range from 0-10. Averaged over 2019-2021.

Source: Gallup

If you were expecting Denmark to be No. 1, it is because they used to be No. 1. In fact, they were No. 1 for four years in a row. Denmark may still be No. 1 because the statistical difference between Denmark and Finland is not meaningful — they are in a statistical tie.

Haiti is often on the list of countries where people rate their lives the worst, but we have not conducted a survey there since 2018. In that survey, Haitians' average life rating was 3.6 — the 136th lowest life ratings out of 143 countries we measured in 2018.

Lebanon's presence on the lowest life ratings list is a more recent phenomenon. From 2006 to 2018, Lebanese rated their lives about a 5 on average. But starting in 2019, those ratings collapsed — falling to 4 in 2019, 2.6 in 2020, and 2.2 in 2021. Gallup's 2019 survey in Lebanon was conducted one month following the October 17 revolution, and the 2020 survey was conducted two months after the Beirut explosion.

How Gallup Reports Evaluative Wellbeing

As I mentioned previously, Gallup reports life evaluation differently than the *WHR* does. Gallup combines responses to both questions (*rate your life today* and *rate your life in five years*) to classify respondents as thriving, struggling, or suffering. If someone rates their life as a 7 or higher today *and* an 8 or higher in the next five years, we consider them to be thriving. If they rate their life as a 4 or lower today *and* a 4 or lower in the next five years, we consider them to be suffering. Anything in between, we classify them as struggling. The Arab uprisings and Brexit trends I discussed earlier use these indexes.

If you look at the countries with the highest thriving and highest suffering scores, you'll see that the results are similar to the individual life evaluation scores.

Life Evaluation Index Rankings

Highest **thriving** scores

Rank	Country	Thriving
1	Finland	72%
2	Denmark	71%
3	Iceland	70%
4	Netherlands	65%
5	Sweden	63%
6	Switzerland	62%
7	Norway	61%
	Israel	61%
9	Luxembourg	59%
10	New Zealand	57%
	Canada	57%

Highest **suffering** scores

Rank	Country	Suffering
146	Afghanistan	91%
145	Lebanon	51%
144	Rwanda	37%
143	Zimbabwe	34%
142	India	32%
141	Chad	30%
140	Pakistan	29%
139	Yemen	28%
	Lesotho	28%
137	Tanzania	25%
	Turkey	25%
	Mauritania	25%

The Life Evaluation Index measures respondents' perceptions of where they stand now and in the future. Averaged over 2019-2021.

Source: Gallup

Between 2019 and 2021, only 17 out of 146 countries were home to a majority of people who were thriving, according to their own life evaluations. During that same time period, only two countries had a majority of people who were suffering: Afghanistan and Lebanon.

Ninety-one percent of people were suffering in Afghanistan between 2019 and 2021. In fact, of the 2,684 interviews we conducted in 2019 and 2021, only two people rated their lives high enough to be considered thriving (which would mean national thriving in Afghanistan was less than 0.5%).

The 2021 measurement alone was the highest suffering rate Gallup has ever seen in the history of our database. Ninety-four percent of Afghans were suffering at the time of the survey, which took place from August to September and coincided with the U.S. troop withdrawal.

All-Time Highest Suffering Scores

All-time rank	Country	Year	Suffering
1	Afghanistan	2021	94%
2	Afghanistan	2019	87%
3	Afghanistan	2018	85%
4	Afghanistan	2017	73%
5	Lebanon	2021	66%
6	Afghanistan	2014	61%
7	Afghanistan	2013	55%
8	Lebanon	2020	48%
	Zimbabwe	2007	48%
10	South Sudan	2016	47%
	Tanzania	2009	47%
	Bulgaria	2009	47%
13	South Sudan	2017	46%
14	Bulgaria	2011	45%
	Yemen	2018	45%
16	Zimbabwe	2006	44%
	Haiti	2015	44%
18	Haiti	2016	43%
19	Zimbabwe	2019	42%
20	Bulgaria	2013	41%
	Yemen	2015	41%

Source: Gallup

When we look at the all-time rankings of where people are most likely to be thriving, Nordic countries make up the *entire* list — with the exception of Ireland in 2008 and New Zealand in 2007 (only 46% and 56% were thriving in those countries, respectively, in 2021).

All-Time Highest Thriving Scores

All-time rank	Country	Year	Thriving
1	Denmark	2006	83%
2	Denmark	2008	82%
3	Finland	2008	75%
	Denmark	2007	75%
5	Denmark	2011	74%
	Iceland	2012	74%
	Denmark	2019	74%
8	Finland	2018	73%
	Finland	2020	73%
	Denmark	2018	73%
11	Denmark	2010	72%
	Ireland	2008	72%
	Denmark	2009	72%
14	Denmark	2021	71%
	New Zealand	2007	71%
	Finland	2019	71%
	Iceland	2020	71%
	Denmark	2012	71%
19	Finland	2017	70%
	Finland	2021	70%
	Denmark	2013	70%

Source: Gallup

No matter how you look at life evaluation data, no one in the world *sees* their lives better than people living in Nordic countries. And conflict-ridden or impoverished countries like Afghanistan or Haiti are often where people *see* their lives the worst.

So, that is how people globally see their lives, but how do they live their lives? And how do you measure how people live their lives?

How People Live Their Lives (Experiential Wellbeing)

The second component of wellbeing is experiential wellbeing, which measures how someone lives their life. It quantifies how much people experience laughter, anger, sadness, and intellectual stimulation.

Asking millions of people about their daily emotions is a massive linguistic undertaking. The process is more complicated than just translating concepts into over roughly 140 languages. This is what makes it hard to ask about *every* emotion.

Take love, for example. It would be fascinating to know where in the world people feel the most loved and why. But love is hard to translate. We tried quantifying love by asking: Did you experience a lot of love all day yesterday?

We found that 70% of the world felt loved — with the most love reported in the Philippines (93%), Rwanda (92%), and Puerto Rico (89%). We found the least amount of love in Armenia (28%), Mongolia (30%), and Uzbekistan (31%).

Feelings of Love

Most love

Rank	Country	Yes
1	Philippines	93%
2	Rwanda	92%
3	Puerto Rico	89%
4	Hungary	88%
5	Trinidad & Tobago	87%
	Cyprus	87%
7	Paraguay	86%
8	Costa Rica	84%
	Lebanon	84%
10	Nigeria	83%

Least love

Rank	Country	Yes
130	Armenia	28%
129	Mongolia	30%
128	Uzbekistan	31%
127	Kyrgyzstan	33%
126	Belarus	39%
125	Georgia	41%
124	Kazakhstan	42%
123	Ukraine	43%
	Azerbaijan	43%
	Tajikistan	43%

Did you experience the following feelings during a lot of the day yesterday? How about love? Averaged over 2006-2007.

Source: Gallup

However, these rankings probably aren't right. In the West, respondents interpreted "love" as we intended: "an intense feeling of deep affection." But that was not how people everywhere understood it. In some cultures, respondents did not interpret it as emotional love, but instead as physical love. You can ask anything you want and get a response, but it does not mean you are measuring the same thing in every country.

Another example is the word "risk." As part of the Lloyd's Register Foundation World Risk Poll, we asked, "When you hear the word 'risk,' do you think more about opportunity or danger?" Globally, 60% think danger, and 21% think opportunity (8% say both and 11% say neither, don't know, or refused to answer).

But then look at the results by the language the survey was administered in. If you ask native Spanish speakers about risk (*riesgo*), 85% hear the word and think danger (12% think opportunity). If you ask someone whose native language is English, 67% who hear the word think danger, and 27% think opportunity. Here is how people responded to this question in six of the world's most commonly spoken languages.

Risk: Opportunity or Danger, by Survey Language

■ % Opportunity　■ % Danger　■ % Both
▨ % Neither　▨ % Do not know/refused

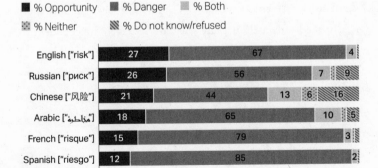

When you hear the word "risk," do you think more about opportunity or danger? Due to rounding, percentages may sum to 100% +/- 1%.

Source: The Lloyd's Register Foundation World Risk Poll 2019

The differences in perceived risk may not even be a linguistic issue — they might be more of a cultural influence. But the point remains: Language matters when you are conducting global surveys.

The last and most relevant example has to do with the word "happy." You might be wondering: Why doesn't Gallup just ask people how happy they are?

We tried it. We asked Americans if they experienced happiness during a lot of the day yesterday. Eighty-nine percent of Americans said they did — North Dakotans were the most likely to report feeling happy (93%); West Virginians were the least likely (86%).

But the question does not work globally. "Happy" does not translate well across languages and dialects. According to Australian National University linguist Anna Wierzbicka, "It is an illusion ... to think that the English words *happy* and *happiness* have exact semantic equivalents in Chinese or, for that matter, in other European languages."

Measuring Joy, Respect, Sadness, and Anger

When measuring emotions, negative and positive emotions must be quantified separately because they are relatively independent of each other, according to research by University of Chicago Provost Norman Bradburn in the 1960s. The absence of negative emotions does not necessarily mean a person is experiencing a lot of positive emotions. Conversely, the absence of positive emotions does not mean they are experiencing negative emotions.

People can also feel very little of either positive or negative emotions. Or, they can feel a lot of both. For example, imagine attending a funeral for your grandfather who died of old age. Think of the emotions you would experience that day. You are sad because you miss him, but you feel happy remembering the good times with him. Plus, you are surrounded by loved ones. You experience sadness, happiness, love, and maybe a little loneliness all in the same day.

After testing the names of a number of emotions, we found 10 that work across cultures: five that measure positive experiences and five that measure negative experiences. The five positive experiences are enjoyment, learning or doing something interesting, feeling well-rested, smiling and laughing, and feeling treated with respect. The five negative experiences are anger, stress, sadness, physical pain, and worry.

These are the questions we ask globally and the results.

Positive Experience Index

86% Were you treated with respect all day yesterday?

73% Did you smile and laugh a lot yesterday?

71% Did you experience the following feelings during a lot of the day yesterday? How about enjoyment?

70% Did you feel well-rested yesterday?

50% Did you learn or do something interesting yesterday?

Negative Experience Index

Did you experience the following feelings during a lot of the day yesterday?

41% How about worry?

38% How about stress?

30% How about physical pain?

27% How about sadness?

23% How about anger?

Averaged over 2019-2021.

Despite all the challenges facing the world, it is amazing to see that so many people still find a way to have fun: 73% report smiling and laughing a lot, and 71% experience a lot of enjoyment. They also feel a lot of respect (86%). Of the 10 experiences we measure, respect was the one people reported feeling the most.

But today's global wellbeing problem is not about positive emotions. It is about the rise in negative emotions. All five negative emotions have increased since we began tracking them. And Gallup's Negative Experience Index is up 10 points since 2007, with most of the increase taking place since 2014.

I will explore what drives positive and negative emotions more fully in Part III. In the rest of this chapter, we'll look at where people experience the most positive and most negative emotions in the world.

Positive Emotions Worldwide

Most positive experiences

Rank	Country	Score
1	Panama	85
2	Guatemala	84
3	El Salvador	83
4	Paraguay	82
	Honduras	82
	Nicaragua	82
	Indonesia	82
8	Philippines	81
9	Colombia	80
	Costa Rica	80
	Denmark	80
12	Senegal	79

Least positive experiences

Rank	Country	Score
146	Afghanistan	34
145	Lebanon	43
144	Turkey	45
143	Nepal	54
142	Northern Cyprus	55
141	Yemen	56
140	Tunisia	57
	Egypt	57
	Bangladesh	57
137	Ethiopia	58
	Chad	58

The Positive Experience Index is a composite measure of the five positive experiences (enjoyment, learning or doing something interesting, feeling well-rested, smiling and laughing, and feeling treated with respect). Index scores range from zero to 100. Averaged over 2019-2021.

Source: Gallup

Gallup's positive experiences list is dominated by Latin American countries, which has been true every year in our tracking. But the most remarkable thing about this list is how little it correlates with income. For example, Guatemala and El Salvador rank in the bottom half of the world for income — yet they are among the most likely in the world to report positive experiences.

And notice how different this list is from the life evaluation rankings (which are mostly Nordic countries). So are Latin Americans the happiest people in the world instead of the Finns and Danes? Before jumping to that conclusion, look at the countries where people experience the most negative emotions.

Negative Emotions Worldwide

Most negative experiences

Rank	Country	Score
1	Afghanistan	56
2	Lebanon	53
3	Iraq	52
4	Sierra Leone	49
	Rwanda	49
6	Chad	48
	Jordan	48
8	Iran	44
	Togo	44
	Gambia	44
	Tunisia	44

Least negative experiences

Rank	Country	Score
146	Taiwan, Province of China	14
145	Kazakhstan	15
144	Azerbaijan	16
143	Turkmenistan	17
142	Mauritius	18
141	Estonia	19
	Singapore	19
139	Mongolia	20
	Kyrgyzstan	20
	Russia	20
	Belarus	20

The Negative Experience Index is a composite measure of the five negative experiences (anger, stress, sadness, physical pain, and worry). Index scores range from zero to 100. Averaged over 2019-2021.

Source: Gallup

The No. 1 region is — by far — the Middle East and North Africa. This may not be surprising considering the sanctions and war that the region faces. Countries such as Iraq and Iran are on Gallup's "most negative countries in the world" list almost every year. And while the scores above are a three-year average, Afghanistan's score in 2021 alone was 63, which is the highest score we have ever recorded for negative emotions.

The second-highest Negative Experience Index score in our history was 61, in the civil-war-torn Central African Republic in 2017. We were unable to interview in 40% of the country due to security concerns, but had we been able to conduct interviews in those areas, this score may have been even higher. Because of the ongoing conflict, we have not been back to any part of the Central African Republic since.

The region that ranks right behind the Middle East and North Africa in negative emotions is Latin America. But Latin America is also No. 1 in positive emotions. This re-emphasizes why measuring positive *and* negative emotions is so important — you can experience a lot of both.

So then where is the happiest place on Earth? The answer depends on how you define happiness.

If you think happiness is how people *see* their lives, then Finns are the happiest people in the world. If you think happiness is defined by how people *live* their lives through positive experiences such as joy and laughter, then the happiest people in the world are Latin Americans.

CHAPTER FIVE
Do People Know How Happy They Are?

No man is happy who does not think himself so.

— Publilius Syrus, first century B.C. Latin writer

On a fall day in 2009, my morning started in a conference room in a midtown Manhattan office. You could see the famous Radio City Music Hall sign from the 23rd-floor window.

I was there to meet with a foundation Gallup was working with to study hunger in Africa. The foundation had retained a university professor to advise us on the study, and he was there as well.

Everything went as planned and nothing about the meeting was particularly noteworthy, except for one thing — an exchange between the professor and me.

For months, I had encouraged the foundation to include questions about wellbeing in their hunger survey. I brought it up again in this meeting, hoping they would finally use these items. The professor — who had never liked the idea — reiterated that they did not want to ask wellbeing questions in the survey. I still could not figure out why, so I asked him.

He didn't think twice about the question and replied, "We want to make sure that Africans don't say they are happier than they really are."

There it was. The professor was concerned that Africans could not accurately describe how their lives are going.

Except Africans — and all people — *do* know how their lives are going. And they can accurately describe their lives to anyone who asks them. This is why we use surveys to measure wellbeing — to understand how people's lives are going, we need to hear from people themselves.

How Accurate Are Happiness Surveys?

Many people believe that surveys capture "soft" data and that the only reliable data are "hard" metrics such as unemployment. They blindly trust labor force statistics and never ask, "How is that information collected?"

If you ask people how they think unemployment data are collected, they say it is based on a headcount or by tallying the number of people receiving unemployment benefits. The U.S. Bureau of Labor Statistics (BLS), the agency responsible for these indicators, addresses those issues verbatim:

> Some people think that to get these figures on unemployment, the government uses the number of people collecting unemployment insurance (UI) benefits under state or federal government programs. ...

> Other people think that the government counts every unemployed person each month. ...

> Because unemployment insurance records relate only to people who have applied for such benefits, and since it is impractical to count every unemployed person each month, the government conducts a monthly survey called the Current Population Survey (CPS) to measure the extent of unemployment in the country.

So even many "hard" metrics such as unemployment are captured by a survey. Most countries conduct a labor force survey at least once per year; wealthier countries measure unemployment even more frequently. The survey is administered by a government agency or ministry, such as the BLS.

The BLS conducts a household survey of around 60,000 people every month. Interviews are conducted in person and over the phone, similar to how pollsters call people during elections to ask who they intend to vote for.

The measures are reliable. In fact, you can independently verify them using nongovernment statistics, such as Gallup's U.S. unemployment data, which are collected using a similar methodology. In 2016, *The Wall Street Journal* showed just how closely Gallup's daily tracking of U.S. unemployment follows the BLS' figures on unemployment.

A Matter of Measurement

One common concern about unemployment figures, that the government is fudging the numbers to make itself look good, seems to be refuted by independent third parties who find an unemployment rate similar to the federal one.

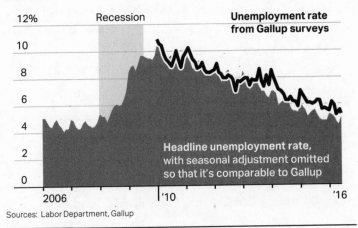

Sources: Labor Department, Gallup

Reprinted with permission from *The Wall Street Journal*.

Although they have methodological differences, both are still *surveys*. For wellbeing statistics, instead of asking people if they have a job, we simply ask them how their lives are going.

Many people trust survey methodology — it is the questions they do not like. They think asking if someone has a job is useful for leaders, but asking about policy on climate change or healthcare is not because people often are not fully informed on the issues.

Critics cite research that tests people's basic knowledge of civics. For example, Gallup once asked Americans: "As far as you know, from what country did America gain its independence following the Revolutionary War?" Nearly 20% of Americans did not know. We even conducted the survey not long before the Fourth of July. In fact, 13% of Americans were not even sure what the country celebrates on July Fourth.

Pundits denounce the "wisdom of crowds" based on this reasoning. If the public does not understand American history, why trust their judgment on issues like healthcare, immigration, or going to war?

But people's opinions still count — whether or not those opinions are informed. Additionally, people make decisions based on what they believe, so there is value in *knowing* what they believe, regardless of how well-informed they are.

Whatever the case, understanding a country's history or a country's plan for healthcare is different from *knowing your own life*. People may not be experts on history, science, or current events, but they *are* the best experts in the world on their own lives.

Former Gallup Regional Director Jihad Fakhreddine once interviewed a man in Lebanon and asked him how his life was going. The man replied, "A survey about my life! It is tar!" (He used the Arabic word *zeft*.) For Lebanese, "tar" or "asphalt" is a term that means things cannot be any darker — he is living the worst life imaginable. According to Jihad, the way this man described his life, coupled with his desperate facial expression, meant "No need to ask me dozens of questions to know how I am doing." The point is, that man knew how his life was going.

But if for some reason you do not believe this man, you can actually audit his wellbeing. Just ask the people he spends the most time with. Researchers began asking people's friends and family, "How would this person rate their life?" Time and time again, their friends and family knew.

The professor I mentioned earlier was probably not just wrong on philosophical or moral grounds, he is also statistically wrong. These metrics can also be audited using objective indicators. For example, life evaluation and life expectancy highly correlate, meaning countries where people rate their lives the highest are also where people live the longest.

How Gallup Asks the World About Wellbeing

Wellbeing *is* measurable. But it is not easy to measure it *everywhere*.

In some countries, it is too dangerous for us to do our work. That's because in most countries, Gallup conducts interviews in person. An interviewer literally knocks on someone's door and asks them a series of questions. If a country descends into war, experiences a disease outbreak, or suffers from a natural disaster, we may have to change how we interview or stop interviewing altogether. For example, in countries where it may be unsafe to go door to door, we can do phone interviews instead. In fact, in the roughly 40 countries where we do not conduct face-to-face interviews, we conduct interviews over the phone.

The people who conduct interviews in these countries are locals. Kenyans interview Kenyans; Brazilians interview Brazilians. The photograph below shows an interview being conducted in Indonesia.

The last major barrier to conducting surveys is politics. We have never conducted interviews in North Korea. Imagine Gallup approaching the Central Bureau of Statistics in North Korea to get permission to do a wellbeing survey. Even if Kim Jong Un approved such a study, Gallup would still not be able to conduct the survey. As a U.S.-based organization, we must follow U.S. laws, including the Trading with the Enemy Act of 1917, which says that if we have sanctions on a country such as North Korea, we cannot hire people there to conduct interviews.

So that is how Gallup collects wellbeing and happiness data worldwide. From the *World Happiness Report* to the Arab uprising trends we discussed earlier — they are all the same data, and we collect those data using the most robust methodologies in the world. See the Appendix for a more in-depth explanation on how Gallup conducts interviews globally.

CHAPTER SIX
Behavioral Economics and Measuring a Great Life

A few centuries ago, the world started counting everything we do — what we buy, how much money we make, and when and how we die. We have come a long way in figuring out how to measure and count everything. But we missed one thing. We forgot to measure how people feel.

And how people feel matters. Your feelings affect how you think and the decisions you make. Yet most people think decision-making is rational. In fact, much of economics is based on this premise. But decision-making is not always rational. It is often *emotional*.

This phenomenon led to the emergence of behavioral economics, a discipline that helps economists account for these emotional behaviors. Behavioral economics is "a method of economic analysis that applies psychological insights into human behavior to explain economic decision-making," according to Oxford Languages. In the words of one of the fathers of behavioral economics, Daniel Kahneman: "It seems that traditional economics and behavioral economics are describing two different species."

Here are two examples of how emotions guide decision-making and cognition:

The first is a basic marketing technique. A store wants to offer a promotion on a product — let's say a box of tissues. The store considers two kinds of promotions: buy two boxes at half price or buy one, get one free. Which promotion do you think will sell more tissues?

If people were robots and only thought rationally, then the decision between the two promotions does not matter. Economically, they are the same deal. Regardless of which promotion the store uses, the buyer pays the same amount. But because buying decisions are emotional, one of the promotions sells more boxes of tissues.

If you guessed "buy one, get one free" sells more tissues, you are right. That offer works better because of the presence of the word "free." Emotionally, people think they are getting something for nothing (instead of the first option, where they must buy two to get them half off). People change their purchasing behaviors simply based on how the store positions the offers.

The second example uses a behavioral nudge known as priming. Priming is so influential that the very presence of a random number influences how you guess a factual number.

One study asked participants to guess the number of African nations in the U.N. Before people guessed, researchers spun a wheel marked from 0 to 100 and asked participants to write down the number that the wheel stopped on. Having someone write down a number before they make an informed guess about the number of African nations in the U.N. should not influence their guess, yet it did.

The larger the number the wheel stopped on, the higher the participants' guesses were. The lower the number, the lower the guesses. Even if the person conducting the experiment reminded the group that the random number has nothing to do with the question, the random number *still* influenced their guess.

These behavioral influences are everywhere. If you have ever taken a course on negotiations, you learned about anchoring. Anchoring and priming are similar. Anchoring in negotiations encourages you to say an absurdly high number before your "ask."

This is based on people's emotional behavior — the presence of a larger number sets an arbitrary emotional benchmark that influences subsequent decision-making.

For example, if someone wants to buy a Toyota 4Runner for $45,000, the salesperson needs to figure out a way to say a higher price — *even if it has nothing to do with the 4Runner*. The behavioral objective is to make the $45,000 seem like less than it really is. If the salesperson is any good, they will say, "This 4Runner is a great selection. It does not cost anywhere near as much as the Mercedes-Benz G-Wagons, which are around $120,000. They run the same, but this one only costs you $45,000."

The buyer did not ask about G-Wagons; they want a 4Runner. But just hearing the $120,000 makes the $45,000 seem smaller emotionally.

Think about this: How can you make an objective figure such as $45,000 seem like less than it is? If people were strictly rational, the presence of a larger figure wouldn't matter. Our emotions — not our rational thoughts — guide our judgment.

Kahneman and fellow researcher Amos Tversky were the pioneers of behavioral economics. In 2002, Kahneman became the first person with a doctoral degree in psychology to win the Nobel Prize in Economic Sciences and the first awarded for behavioral economics.

Since then, the discipline has gone mainstream. Perhaps the best elucidation of how emotions influence our thinking is in Mark Manson's book *Everything Is F*cked: A Book About Hope*. He says the human brain is like two people in the front seat of a car. One is the rational mind, and the other is the emotional mind. Which one is driving? The emotional mind drives the car. The rational mind not only rides shotgun — it also provides the supporting evidence for the emotional mind's decisions.

How Behavioral Economics Is Revolutionizing Everything

The tighter bond between economics and psychology helped redefine everything — behavioral economics now influences government policy, the workplace, and the exact placement of products in stores.

Nobel Prize laureate Richard Thaler led one of the most famous experiments that eventually changed policy, and it involved organ donations.

In some countries, most people participate in organ donor programs; in others, most do not. Is the difference cultural? Religious? It turns out — neither. The difference is in how the program is presented. Some countries automatically enroll people as organ donors when they get a driver's license. They can opt out, but the default is participation. In countries with low participation rates, people had to *opt in*, so the default was *not* to participate.

The researchers claim that more people will participate if governments simply change how they present the program. By changing the default to participation, millions more people consent to be organ donors, benefiting thousands of people who need organ transplants.

Behavioral economics has also revolutionized workplaces. For example, if you have ever taken an employee engagement survey, your organization applies behavioral economics.

Historically, executives have believed that how people feel at work does not matter. People's emotions were not a workplace concern; workers should be treated like automatons or "rational actors."

Then, the behavioral concept of engagement changed the workplace. Behavioral researchers figured out that a worker's emotional attachment to their job mattered. Employees who are emotionally connected to their job work harder, are more innovative, and are less likely to leave. Conversely, the emotionally detached come into the office late, leave early, and don't really do anything exceptional.

The behavioral link between how someone feels about their job and their productivity might seem obvious — yet very few leaders have strategies to improve worker engagement.

Gross National Happiness

While behavioral economics has transformed everything from government policy to workplaces, unfortunately, it has not transformed global statistics. Most of today's indicators capture the rational transactions of life such as income or job status. Subjective wellbeing indicators were introduced to capture the mood, feelings, and emotions of people and societies.

The world has been tinkering with measuring national wellbeing for over 50 years. Perhaps the most famous call to "move beyond GDP" came from Bobby Kennedy in 1968. He said:

> … But even if we act to erase material poverty, there is another greater task. It is to confront the poverty of satisfaction — purpose and dignity — that afflicts us all.

> Too much and for too long, we seemed to have surrendered personal excellence and community values in the mere accumulation of material things. Our Gross National Product now is over $800 billion a year, but that Gross National Product — if we judge the United States of America by that — that Gross National Product counts air pollution and cigarette advertising and ambulances to clear our highways of carnage.

It counts special locks for our doors and the jails for the people who break them. It counts the destruction of the redwood and the loss of our natural wonder in chaotic sprawl.

It counts napalm and counts nuclear warheads and armored cars for the police to fight the riots in our cities. It counts Whitman's rifle and Speck's knife and the television programs which glorify violence in order to sell toys to our children.

Yet the Gross National Product does not allow for the health of our children, the quality of their education, or the joy of their play. It does not include the beauty of our poetry or the strength of our marriages, the intelligence of our public debate, or the integrity of our public officials.

It measures neither our wit nor our courage, neither our wisdom nor our learning, neither our compassion nor our devotion to our country. It measures everything, in short, except that which makes life worthwhile.

Kennedy poetically addressed how the U.S. needs to move beyond GDP; what he did not suggest is an alternative.

In the late 20th century, a scientific study emerged that would help provide an answer: positive psychology. This discipline is often defined similarly to Kennedy's words: the scientific study of "that which makes life worthwhile."

Abraham Maslow may have inspired the discipline in a chapter he wrote in his 1954 book *Motivation and Personality* titled "Toward a Positive Psychology." In it, he wrote:

> The science of psychology has been far more successful on the negative than on the positive side; it has revealed to us much about man's shortcomings, his illness, his sins, but little about

his potentialities, his virtues, his achievable aspirations, or his full psychological height. It is as if psychology has voluntarily restricted itself to only half its rightful jurisdiction, and that the darker, meaner half.

Or, as the grandfather of positive psychology, Don Clifton, asked, "What would happen if we studied what was *right* with people versus what's wrong with people?"

One of the pioneers of studying the positive side was George Gallup, who rose to national prominence in the early 1930s because of his political polling. But he was interested in more than politics.

Edward R. Murrow, one of the most respected broadcast journalists in American history, interviewed George Gallup in the 1950s. A few minutes into the interview, Murrow asked Gallup, "I know you've surveyed public opinion on a great many subjects. Any findings that particularly interest you, personally?"

George Gallup responded, "The most interesting survey that we ever made was one in which we tried to find out who the happiest people are in this country."

Like other social scientists, George Gallup was attempting to quantify how people's lives were going by simply asking them — letting people report their own happiness.

He found that religious people and those living near mountains were the happiest in the U.S.; the unhappiest people lived in cities and worked in factories. He even mentioned a study outside the U.S.: "We repeated that same survey in France ... the people who were the unhappiest were largely Communist, so you do see there is a relationship."

George Gallup was just scratching the surface of measuring national wellbeing. However, the very idea of quantifying the mood of a country was groundbreaking.

A few governments also began producing national statistics on wellbeing. The most famous is Bhutan, the South Asian country of less than 1 million people.

Bhutan is home to the world's first official government measure of Gross National Happiness (GNH). The chief architect was Bhutan's Fourth Dragon King, Jigme Singye Wangchuck. Before becoming king in 1972, Wangchuck had a revelation similar to Kennedy's — the world had become obsessed with economic growth and income. While this obsession helped make countries rich, it did not necessarily improve people's wellbeing. So, at the end of the 20th century, he announced that Bhutan would no longer be guided solely by economic growth (GDP). Instead, the country would also be governed using GNH.

Not everyone agrees with this course for Bhutan. Critics think it is a distraction from a stagnating economy. Bhutan's GDP per capita is less than $11,000, ranking it 136th globally. Others do not think Bhutan even "started" GNH, including many Europeans.

They believe it came from one of the founders of the European Union, Sicco Mansholt. According to Europe's Gross National Happiness Institute, on February 14, 1972, Mansholt sent a letter to the European Commission "suggesting the need to use an alternative measurement indicator to the Gross Domestic Product (GDP)" called *Bonheur National Brut (BNB)*, translated into English as Gross National Happiness (GNH).

The confusion about "who started GNH" also has to do with the concepts of happiness and wellbeing generally. Philosophers dating back to Socrates, Aristotle, and Plato were among the first to theorize what makes a great life and what makes people happy. But using happiness as a guiding principle for governments is more of a modern construct.

Americans are well-versed in these words from the Declaration of Independence: "We hold these truths to be self-evident, that all men are created equal, that they are endowed by their Creator with certain unalienable Rights, that among these are Life, Liberty and the pursuit of Happiness."

They are less familiar with the rest of the text, which doubles down on happiness — even recommending revolution if a government becomes destructive to a people's happiness:

> That to secure these rights, Governments are instituted among Men, deriving their just powers from the consent of the governed, — That whenever any Form of Government becomes destructive of these ends, it is the Right of the People to alter or to abolish it, and to institute new Government, laying its foundation on such principles and organizing its powers in such form, as to them shall seem most likely to effect their Safety and Happiness.

Wellbeing is becoming fashionable with 21st-century leaders too, such as former French President Nicolas Sarkozy. He brought top economists, statisticians, and psychologists together — creating the Stiglitz Commission — to develop a road map for the world to "move beyond GDP." The commission's recommendations were fully adopted by the Organisation for Economic Co-operation and Development (OECD), a Paris-based association with the goal to "shape policies that foster prosperity, equality, opportunity and well-being for all." The OECD now produces its own index known as the Better Life Index. It ranks 40 countries on 11 indicators, including one that is called "life satisfaction," which uses the Gallup World Poll.

Former U.K. Prime Minister David Cameron led the U.K. in building its own national statistics on wellbeing. Britain's Office for National Statistics measures wellbeing using these questions:

1. Overall, how satisfied are you with your life nowadays? (On a scale of 0 to 10, where 0 is "not at all" and 10 is "completely" satisfied.)

2. Overall, to what extent do you feel that the things you do in your life are worthwhile?

3. Overall, how happy did you feel yesterday?

4. On a scale where 0 is "not at all anxious" and 10 is "completely anxious," overall, how anxious did you feel yesterday?

Even the United Nations has taken an interest in wellbeing statistics. In July 2011, the U.N. passed a resolution encouraging all "… Member States to pursue the elaboration of additional measures that better capture the importance of the pursuit of happiness and well-being in development with a view to guiding their public policies."

Some countries created entire ministries for happiness. In 2016, Sheikh Mohammed bin Rashid Al Maktoum, the ruler of Dubai and vice president and prime minister of the United Arab Emirates, appointed the country's first Minister of State for Happiness.

New Zealand went even further. Under Prime Minister Jacinda Ardern, the entire focus of the government, including how it budgets, became the wellbeing of its citizenry. As if scripted by Bobby Kennedy, New Zealand's Finance Minister Grant Robertson said, "… many New Zealanders were not benefiting from a growing economy in their daily lives, and this year's budget had been designed to address the growing disparity between the haves and the have-nots."

While a few countries were creating their own wellbeing statistics, Gallup was building a tracker for the entire world. In 2006, Gallup began tracking how people's lives were going in as many countries as possible. This allowed for comparisons across countries over time, which helped us better understand where people are living the best lives and why their lives are going so well.

Now that these indicators exist, what exactly makes a great life? What can leaders do to help improve people's lives — and how can we curb the rise of unhappiness and close the widening gap of wellbeing inequality?

PART III
What Makes a Great Life?

The answer to "What makes a great life?" is inherently subjective. If I asked you to rate your life on a scale of zero to 10, where zero is the worst possible life and 10 is the best possible life, what comes to mind when you hear "best possible life"?

Your answer probably is not the same as my answer — and I'll bet it is not the same as a woman we interviewed in Kyrgyzstan.

In the summer of 2012, Neli Esipova, then a Gallup World Poll regional director, found herself in Kyrgyzstan. She and a Gallup interviewer were conducting interviews in Bishkek, the country's capital. They approached a randomly selected house and knocked on the door. A woman answered. They asked the woman if she would participate in our survey. She agreed and invited them into her home.[2]

Reading from a handheld device, Neli's colleague began the interview, "On a scale of zero to 10, where zero is the worst possible life and 10 is the best possible life, where do you think you stood five years ago?"

The woman looked at the interviewer and said, "Two."

The interviewer moved on to the next question: "Now, please rate your life on a scale of zero to 10. Where do you stand today?"

Again, the woman said, "Two."

---

2 Just because this woman answered the door does not mean we automatically interviewed her. We randomly select a person who lives in the house (which might be the person who answered the door). On this day, the woman who answered the door was also the person we selected to participate in our survey.

It's important to note that this interview never made it into our final database. Neli's presence could have affected how the woman answered the questions. These exercises are for testing purposes. But the qualitative information, like this story, are incredibly important to help us understand and interpret our final data.

Then the interviewer asked, "Where do you think you will stand in the next five years?"

The woman paused, thought for a second, and said, "10."

This jump is surprising. The woman just said her life was awful. A rating of two is terrible anywhere. Why would her life be a 10 in five years?

At the end of the interview, Neli looked at the woman and said, "You said your life was a two five years ago, a two today, yet a 10 in five years — what changed?"

The woman signaled to her belly and said, "I'm pregnant. Soon I'll be giving birth to my son."

For this woman, the very definition of a great life includes the birth of her son. That is how *she* sees a great life. This might be different from how a businessman in Kenya sees a great life — or how a farmer in Nebraska sees a great life. But despite how differently people may perceive a great life, there are commonalities.

CHAPTER SEVEN
The Five Elements of a Great Life

If there are rules for living long — and it seems that there are — they would include these: Don't be fussy about your food, and never, never overeat. Don't worry. Work at a job you love, and if it gives you physical exercise, so much the better; if not, be sure to get your exercise — and lots of it — some other way.

— George Gallup and Evan Hill,
   The Saturday Evening Post, 1959

This was George Gallup's conclusion about the secrets to a long life. To uncover them, he and his colleagues studied more than 500 people who lived to be 95 and older. These nonagenarians and centenarians also described their life partners and children as their "comfort and pride." Most of them rarely worried about money, and perhaps surprisingly, half of them said that more income would not have made them any happier.

George Gallup discovered what leads to a *long* life, but his findings also point to what makes a *great* life.

While there are many different things that contribute to a great life, Gallup finds that there are five aspects all people have in common: their work, finances, physical health, communities, and relationships with family and friends. If you are excelling in each of these elements of wellbeing, it is highly unusual for you not to be thriving in life.

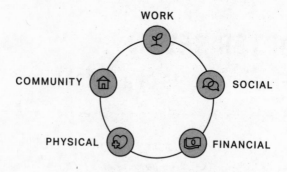

To discover these five elements, Gallup began by reviewing much of the vast literature on happiness and wellbeing. Search "wellbeing" on Google Scholar, and you will find over 1.9 million academic articles; "happiness" yields over 2.7 million articles. One person could not read every article in a lifetime, so we focused on meta-analyses — which combine the results of multiple studies — and the studies that had the greatest impact on the field of wellbeing research.

Then, we conducted surveys. Lots of them. To date, we have conducted about 5 million surveys in almost 170 countries — roughly 2 million interviews in the U.S. and 3 million globally. We also conducted panel studies, which allow us to track the same people over time so we can better understand what causes changes in wellbeing, such as an economic collapse, a job loss, or the death of a spouse.

The global nature of this work is crucial. Research conducted *only* in the West comes under a great deal of scrutiny — for good reason. These studies often include people who do not represent the entire world.

For example, the people who are recruited to participate in U.S. academic research are usually college students. This is problematic because U.S. college students are not representative of the world. In fact, they are not even representative of young people across the U.S.

This kind of research is called "WEIRD," which is an acronym for Western, Educated, Industrialized, Rich, and Democratic. Many U.S. academic studies rely solely on participants who fit these characteristics — but often claim that the conclusions from the research apply to all people. The authors of this concept — Joe Henrich, Steven Heine, and Ara Norenzayan — caution, "We need to be less cavalier in addressing questions of human nature on the basis of data drawn from this particularly thin, and rather unusual, slice of humanity."

Gallup's wellbeing research is truly global, covering over 98% of the world's adult population. It includes almost every ethnic group, religion, and income level and virtually every kind of human experience worldwide.

In every survey, we ask people how they *see* and *live* their lives. Their answers become the outcomes of interest in our analysis — meaning, we look at other variables to see what would help us explain how their lives are going. When someone says, "My life is a 10" or "I laughed and smiled a lot all day yesterday," what else do they tell us? Are they physically active? Do they love their job? Do they have a lot of friends? Or some combination of all three?

Gallup's research as well as research by the global community of wellbeing practitioners has produced hundreds, if not thousands, of discoveries.

One of the most famous discoveries is the U-curve of happiness, which shows how age is associated with wellbeing. Young people rate their lives high, and so do older people. But middle-aged people rate their lives the lowest. This trend holds every year in almost every country in the world. It is nicknamed the "U-curve" of happiness because when you look at the graph, it looks like a "U." Some jokingly say that the chart is smiling.

Average Life Satisfaction by Age

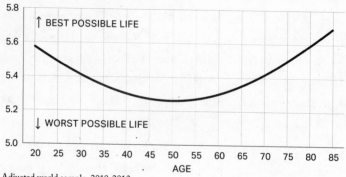

Adjusted world sample, 2010-2012.

Source: Brookings Institution and Gallup

Some discoveries are astonishing; others feel like they reveal a "blandly sophomoric secret," as George Gallup referred to some of his longevity findings. For example, you could argue that the U-curve of happiness simply quantifies conventional wisdom — that people have midlife crises.

Here are a few of the discoveries that are truly compelling:

- People who love their jobs do not hate Mondays.
- Education-related debt can cause an emotional scar that remains even after you pay off the debt.
- Volunteering is not just good for the people you are helping; it is also good for you.
- Exercising is better at eliminating fatigue than prescription drugs.
- Loneliness can double your risk of dying from heart disease.

We could list every insight ever produced from this research and encourage leaders to work on all of them. Instead, we took another approach. Using all these insights from across the industry combined with our surveys and analysis, we created the five elements of wellbeing. And our ongoing global research confirms that the five elements of wellbeing are significant drivers of a great life everywhere.

Wellbeing research by other organizations has produced similar results. A 2021 study by the Pew Research Center spanning 17 countries found that the top answers people gave when asked what makes life meaningful were: family and children, occupation and career, material wellbeing (wealth), friends and community, and physical and mental health.

But while Gallup's five elements of wellbeing explain a lot of what makes a great life, they do not explain *all* of what makes a great life. Pablo Diego-Rosell, my colleague in Spain, looked at how much the five elements of wellbeing predict a great life. He found that they predict at least 50% of a great life globally.

Genetics is another major factor. Research (including several studies of twins) finds that genetics plays a significant role in someone's wellbeing. Studies estimate that 30% to 50% of someone's emotional state was built in the day they were born.

This is often called the happiness set point: No matter what happens to you in your life, you revert to your genetically determined set point. For example, let's say you rate your life a 7 today; tomorrow, you move into a big new house. After the move, you rate your life a 10. The happiness set point theory suggests that the emotional bounce you got from moving into the new house will eventually wear off. In a year or two, your life rating will revert to a 7 (your set point) — your rating before moving into the new house.

The same is true if something awful happens, such as getting into an accident. You were a 7 before the accident, but after the accident, you rate your life a 2. Despite the trauma, later in life you revert to a 7. However, more recent research finds that people often do not have a *complete* rebound from a traumatic experience — if something awful happens, you may still improve, but not to where you were originally.

A theory similar to the happiness set point is the "hedonic treadmill," which says that by nature, people are always running toward a better life, but no matter what happens, their happiness always remains in the same place.

But if people are born with a predetermined level of happiness, why are happiness levels so different by country, and why are they changing globally?

How someone's life is going is undoubtedly influenced by their genetics, but external factors also play a large part. And we can examine those factors through the lens of the five elements of wellbeing.

The next five chapters will focus on the five elements of wellbeing and where the world is struggling in each of them. I chose to focus on where humanity is performing the worst because of the advice Gallup received from Daniel Kahneman when we were developing the Gallup World Poll.

Kahneman believes that the focus of leadership should not be on perfecting people's lives but on reducing global misery. Here is what he wrote in 2005 to the late Gale Muller, chief architect of the Gallup World Poll:

> I know this is not quite in the Gallup spirit, but I would strongly recommend that you look at the bottom end of your questions with special care. Most people in most places are fairly satisfied. The percentage of people who are very satisfied

or very happy is not very relevant as a policy statistic. Much more relevant to policy is the percentage of people who are very unhappy, very worried, or very dissatisfied. Furthermore, those measures are likely to show proportionately larger changes: an increase from 3% to 6% in the proportion of dissatisfied people is a doubling!

Kahneman probably did not anticipate that wellbeing inequality would widen or that negative emotions would increase so dramatically in our first 15 years of tracking. But to his point, imagine if we brought down global stress from 38% to 33% or decreased global sadness from 27% to 22%. If we did, it would mean that 270 million people would be experiencing a lot less stress and sadness. That alone would be worth our efforts.

CHAPTER EIGHT
The Global Great Jobs Crisis

*Your work is going to fill a large part of your life, and
the only way to be truly satisfied is to do what you
believe is great work.*

— Apple Co-Founder Steve Jobs at the 2005
Stanford University Commencement Address

The world is facing a jobs crisis. But you would never know it by
looking at the world's official unemployment rate. According to the
International Labour Organization (ILO), global unemployment has
remained around 5% to 6% for the past decade — a figure that hardly
indicates a crisis.

The official unemployment figure hides actual unemployment
because of how it is calculated. Real global unemployment may be
over 30%. Although this is very concerning, there is an even bigger
problem — the alarming scarcity of *great jobs*. Of the roughly 3.3
billion people who want a great job, only 300 million have one. This
is the real global jobs crisis.

The global unemployment rate should be replaced with a
new metric — the *great jobs rate*. This metric would hold leaders
accountable for what really helps improve people's lives — a great job.

The Wrong Jobs Metric

Official global unemployment was 5.4% in 2019, according to the
ILO. (The pandemic pushed global unemployment to only 6.6%
in 2020 and 6.2% in 2021). This would be a staggering figure if it

applied to the entire global population (7.7 billion people), but that is not how unemployment statistics work. Unemployment applies only to the people in the labor force.

The global labor force includes people who are working and people who are looking for work; it does not include children, retired people, students, homemakers, or people who are not looking for work. The global labor force totals 3.3 billion people. A 5.4% unemployment rate means that less than 200 million people are unemployed. A massive number, for sure. But is it a global crisis?

Compared with other global crises, maybe not. Roughly 2 billion people suffer from food insecurity, 1 billion people live in slums or informal settlements, and 2.2 billion people lack safely managed drinking water. In light of these figures, there doesn't seem to be a problem in the global jobs market. Yet there is — you just can't see it in the official unemployment figure.

When thinking of global unemployment rates, you might assume that rich countries have low unemployment rates and poor countries have high unemployment rates. Well, not according to the official unemployment numbers. Developing countries like Niger and Laos have some of the lowest unemployment rates in the world (0.6% and 0.9%, respectively) — and wealthier countries like France have much higher unemployment rates (8.4%). The unemployment rate for all low-income countries is 4.6%; it is 7.6% for the euro area. When we look at the statistical relationship of GDP per capita and the official unemployment rate for more than 200 countries, they do not correlate. (See References for chart: GDP per Capita (PPP) and Unemployment.)

The countries with the lowest unemployment rates in the world (in 2019) include many developing countries that collectively lack decent work for millions of people. Yet the unemployment rate in each of those countries implies that they all have healthy job markets.

Countries With Lowest Unemployment Rates

Country	Unemployment rate
Qatar	0.1%
Cambodia	0.1%
Myanmar	0.5%
Niger	0.6%
Thailand	0.7%
Solomon Islands	0.8%
Laos	0.9%
Rwanda	1.1%
Chad	1.1%
Bahrain	1.2%
Benin	1.5%
Burundi	1.6%
Cuba	1.7%

Modeled ILO estimate. 2019.
Source: The World Bank

Undercounting the Unemployed

Most countries collect labor force statistics using long surveys administered to tens of thousands of people. These surveys ask individuals how many hours they worked in the past week and whether it was for an employer or for themselves. If they are not employed, people are asked whether they are looking for work. If they did not work any hours and claim that they are looking for work, they are considered unemployed. The resulting data are the official employment statistics for the country.

Now, imagine posing these questions to a subsistence farmer in Africa or someone selling trinkets on the street in India. "Did you work 30 hours or more in the previous week?" Of course they did. Although their work does not meet their basic needs, they still have what global agencies define as work. They are officially "self-employed," meaning they are not "unemployed."

This is why unemployment rates are so low in some of the poorest countries in the world. Millions who are truly unemployed are considered self-employed, and their painful work arrangement is evident when you look at their wellbeing. In a previous Gallup analysis, my colleague Jenny Marlar and I found that the self-employed in poor countries reported the lowest wellbeing in the world, even lower than the unemployed.

Some people even believe that unemployment is a "luxury" in lower-income countries because the poor in those countries cannot afford to spend time looking for the right job; only the rich can do that. Additionally, many lower-income governments do not have enough money to assist the unemployed. According to *The Economist*:

> In many developing countries, unemployment is low simply because few people can afford it. Even when they are available, benefits may not be worth the bother. In Thailand, for example, payments last six months and range from 1,650 baht per month ($52) to 15,000. To be eligible, a Thai worker must register with the social-security office. But only one in three does so ... Many remain outside the formal economy, where they are denied benefits but also spared taxes.

If you live in a wealthy country like the U.S., the term "self-employed" often connotes small-business ownership or entrepreneurship. But again, this is not the reality for many of the self-employed in most countries. In fact, 30% of people who are self-employed globally live in extreme poverty (less than $1.90 per day).

Real Unemployment?

Gallup regularly tracks global employment using a survey that closely follows the standards set by the ILO. It is comparable to the official unemployment rates in many countries, and as I previously reported, it tracks closely with the U.S. BLS data. Our 2019-2021 results were:

- 44% employed full time for an employer
- 22% self-employed
- 13% part time, want full-time work
- 10% part time, do not want full-time work
- 11% unemployed

So, if 22% are self-employed, and 30% of the self-employed live in extreme poverty, we can estimate that at least 6% (30% of the 22%) of the total workforce is incorrectly categorized as "self-employed." They aren't entrepreneurs — they are people who desperately need meaningful work and are doing anything to get by. They are truly unemployed.

If you add 6% to the traditional unemployment figure that we found (11%), real global unemployment would be 17%. But even that is probably an underestimate. Living on less than $1.90 per day is *extreme* poverty, meaning the number of people who are categorized as self-employed but who are truly unemployed could be far higher.

Lastly, 13% of people have part-time work but want full-time work. Yet the headline unemployment figure ignores them precisely because they have *some* work. If they were also considered unemployed, then real global unemployment would be 30%.[3]

But sorting out who has some work and who has no work is not the core of the global jobs crisis. The real problem is the absence of metrics on the quality of someone's job.

---

3 Many statistics offices have a category that includes part-time workers in a broader unemployment statistic. The U.S. Bureau of Labor Statistics calls this "U-6" (which some call "underemployment"), and it includes the unemployed, the minimally employed, and the people who are employed part time for economic reasons. In December 2021, unemployment was 3.7% and U-6 was 7.3%.

Measuring Whether People Love or Hate Their Jobs

The unemployment metric is widely considered the single indicator to understand the health of the jobs market. But what metric captures how workers are feeling?

One of the most significant sources of global misery comes from work. Work is so miserable that when I Googled, "My job is …" the top four results were: "(My job is) too stressful, making me miserable, boring, killing me."

And work is literally killing people. Three million people die from occupational accidents and work-related diseases each year, according to the ILO. Even if work does not kill you, it can seriously hurt you. Nearly one in five workers — which translates to about 600 million people — say they have been seriously injured at some point while working.

But even if work does not injure or kill you, how much psychological damage does it cause? According to the official statistics, we don't know. Official labor statistics only tell us if people are working, not how they are doing at work.

One attempt to quantify how people are doing at work is a concept known as worker engagement. Or, as Daniel Kahneman said on Adam Grant's podcast, "My interpretation of (worker) engagement was fairly close to *wellbeing at work*." (emphasis added)

That day, Kahneman was referring to Gallup's measure for worker engagement, which quantifies wellbeing at work. We find that workers generally fall into three categories — people are either thriving at work (our technical term for it is "engaged"), indifferent ("not engaged"), or miserable ("actively disengaged").

People who are thriving at work are enthusiastic and passionate about what they do every day. They enjoy working with their colleagues, have development opportunities, and feel cared about as a person. People who are indifferent at work are psychologically detached from their jobs — they put in the time without energy or passion. Miserable employees are resentful that their needs are not being met and represent the nadir of worker unhappiness.

Whether someone is thriving, indifferent, or miserable at work is subjective. And everyone knows how they feel about their job and workplace. But understanding how workers are doing across large companies or even across countries requires having these conversations at scale.

After conducting millions of interviews with workers worldwide, Gallup identified 12 items (known as the Q^{12}) that help succinctly and scientifically measure worker wellbeing at scale. The Q^{12} allows workers to describe how they are doing at work from their perspective. Workers are asked how much they agree with each of the following statements on a 5-point scale. Their answers also predict future behaviors, such as turnover and productivity.

Gallup's Q^{12}

Q01. I know what is expected of me at work.

Q02. I have the materials and equipment I need to do my work right.

Q03. At work, I have the opportunity to do what I do best every day.

Q04. In the last seven days, I have received recognition or praise for doing good work.

Q05. My supervisor, or someone at work, seems to care about me as a person.

Q06. There is someone at work who encourages my development.

Q07. At work, my opinions seem to count.

Q08. The mission or purpose of my company makes me feel my job is important.

Q09. My associates or fellow employees are committed to doing quality work.

Q10. I have a best friend at work.

Q11. In the last six months, someone at work has talked to me about my progress.

Q12. This last year, I have had opportunities at work to learn and grow.

This list represents 12 of the most important emotional needs of a worker. Those needs include having the opportunity to learn and grow, getting meaningful recognition for doing good work, and even having a best friend at work — which is one of the single biggest predictors of whether someone will stay at a job.

But look at the first item — "I know what is expected of me at work." Half of workers do not strongly agree with that item. Imagine showing up to work every day and not knowing what you are supposed to do. It must be frustrating, confusing, or completely maddening, and that is how half of the world's workforce feels when they go to work every day.

Now look at the third item — "At work, I have the opportunity to do what I do best every day." Less than one-third of workers strongly agree with that item. They are doing a job that does not allow them to use their strengths. Again, imagine coming in to work every day and constantly being told to do things you are not very good at or that you don't like doing. This emotional detachment adds to the world's misery, and leaders miss it because they do not focus on how people feel in the workplace.

The World's Broken Workplace

Despite the importance of wellbeing at work, very few leaders make it a priority. After posing the Q^{12} to the world, Gallup finds that only 20% of all people are thriving at work, while 62% are indifferent and 18% are miserable.

And the misery that those 18% of workers feel consumes a massive part of their lives. According to one estimate, the average person spends 115,704 hours of their life at work. That is the equivalent of more than 13 years. The only thing we spend more time doing is sleeping (about 33 years).

If people truly spend that much time working, it's no surprise that how a person feels at work hugely affects their overall life. If you are thriving at work, you rate your overall life significantly higher compared with someone who is miserable at work. But thriving at work not only improves how you *see* your life, you also *live* a better life.

Gallup finds that if you are engaged and thriving at work, you experience far less stress, sadness, anger, pain, and worry every day compared with someone who hates their job. Thriving at work even enhances how much joy, laughter, respect, and intellectual stimulation you experience.

Having your emotional needs met at work changes everything. For instance, when we surveyed German working adults, 81% of engaged (thriving) workers reported having fun at work in the past week, compared with only 10% of actively disengaged (miserable) workers. The misery of the disengaged even follows them home. Fifty-nine percent of miserable workers say that in the past month, they had three or more days when the stress of work caused them to behave poorly with their family and friends.

Being miserable at work can even make your life worse than having no work at all. People who are miserable at work not only rate their lives worse than the unemployed, they *experience* worse lives. People who hate their jobs are more likely than the unemployed to report anger, stress, physical pain, and worry, and less likely to report positive experiences such as enjoyment, respect, intellectual stimulation, and laughing and smiling a lot.

A Great Job, a Miserable Job, and Unemployment — the Emotional Difference

	Great job (Engaged)	Indifferent at work (Not engaged)	Miserable job (Actively disengaged)	Unemployed
Negative experiences				
Sadness	24%	27%	42%	43%
Anger	16%	19%	29%	26%
Physical pain	31%	32%	42%	36%
Stress	28%	36%	50%	44%
Worry	37%	44%	59%	57%
Positive experiences				
Respect	95%	92%	81%	88%
Smile and laugh	87%	80%	64%	71%
Enjoyment	83%	75%	54%	62%
Well-rested	78%	71%	57%	70%
Learn	72%	61%	43%	50%

Averaged over 2019-2021.

Source: Gallup

The World's Official Statistics for Great Jobs

The official unemployment rate fails workers for two reasons: It doesn't capture real global unemployment, and it doesn't capture the misery in the workplace. The solution? Change the metric used for the health of the jobs market. Instead of working to lower the 5.4% global unemployment rate, world leaders should work on increasing the global great jobs rate, which today stands at 9%.

I'm going to show you how I calculated the global great jobs rate — and you may not fully agree with how I arrived at the number. But I hope this initial thinking will inspire someone to create a more perfect great jobs indicator.

First, let's define a good job and a great job. Gallup considers a good job to be steady work of at least 30 hours per week and a paycheck. A great job is steady work, a paycheck, *and* a job where the worker is engaged and thriving — they can use their strengths, their opinions count, and they have a manager who cares about their development.

Now, the math: There are about 7.7 billion people on the planet, and roughly 5.4 billion of them are adults. And 3.3 billion of those adults want a great job.

Out of the 3.3 billion who want a great job, roughly 1.5 billion have a *good* job (steady work and a paycheck). If 20% of those with a good job are engaged and thriving at work, that means about 300 million workers have a *great* job.

But that also means that out of the roughly 3.3 billion people who want a great job, 91% of them don't have one. *That* is the real global jobs crisis.

7.7 billion people on the planet

5.4 billion are adults

3.3 billion adults **want a great job**

1.5 billion adults **have a good job**

Only 300 million **have a great job**

---

3 billion
don't have a great job

The current global unemployment metric holds leaders accountable to the lowest common denominator for jobs. The message is: "Let's get the number of people with no work to the lowest percentage possible." Instead, the message should be: "Let's get the number of people with great jobs to the highest percentage possible."

Every week, *The Economist* publishes a page in the back of its magazine that is called "Economic data, commodities and markets."

The page lists the GDP, consumer prices, and unemployment rates from 40 of the world's largest economies.

But what if one day they just quit reporting those unemployment rates and instead reported only the great jobs rates? If they did, it would hold leaders responsible for getting everyone great work, which is what really makes a great life.

CHAPTER NINE
Does Money Buy Happiness?

*I wish for an increase in my wages because with my
meager salary I cannot afford to buy decent food
for my family. If the food and clothing problems were
solved, then I would feel at home and be satisfied.
Also if my wife were able to work, the two of us could
then feed the family and I am sure would have a
happy life and our worries would be over.*

— 30-year-old sweeper in India in 1965,
  monthly income approximately $13

So, *does* money buy happiness?

Here is Gallup's best attempt at answering this question: Money does not buy happiness, but it is hard to be happy without it.

The earliest research on the "Does money buy happiness?" question found that money can buy happiness, but only in a relative sense. This insight is rooted in a theory known as the relative income hypothesis by economist James Duesenberry. It assumes people's consumption habits have more to do with their neighbors' standard of living than their own.

Duesenberry's theory applied to what people bought, not how they felt about life. Economist Richard Easterlin advanced this research by answering this question: Do people also rate their lives based on how their neighbors' lives are going?

In his influential 1974 paper *Does Economic Growth Improve the Human Lot? Some Empirical Evidence*, Easterlin found that people *do* rate their lives based on how their neighbors' lives are going. He discovered that rich people rate their lives higher than poor people within the same country. However, when you compare how people rate their lives in rich countries with how people rate their lives in poor countries, you do not see much of a difference. He also found that as countries get richer, people do not get happier.

These findings present a paradox — known as the Easterlin paradox — regarding how money affects people's lives. The paradox is that economic growth does not make people happier; people are only happier if they have more money than other people in their own country.

These findings appear to statistically support the idea behind the early 20th-century comic strip *Keeping Up With the Joneses*. People don't rate their lives on a global scale; they assess how their lives are going based on how their neighbors are doing. Easterlin emphasized this point quoting Karl Marx: "A house may be large or small; as long as the neighboring houses are likewise small, it satisfies all social requirements for a residence. But let there arise next to the little house a palace, and the little house shrinks to a hut."

This finding raised critical questions for policymakers: How important is economic growth? How important is income? If your happiness is contingent on your neighbor's wealth, giving you both an extra $1,000 per month will not improve your life because your neighbor will still have more.

One of the limitations of Easterlin's work is that much of the data came from only a handful of countries. That changed in the 21st century, particularly with the Gallup World Poll. We now conduct wellbeing studies more frequently in far more countries.

One of the first global datasets from Gallup led to one of the most influential papers in the discourse of income and wealth. This paper, written by Angus Deaton, produced a finding that contradicted part of the Easterlin paradox. Deaton found that people in rich countries *do* rate their lives better than people in poor countries, which suggests that economic growth *does* cause people to see their lives better.

His analysis revealed a high positive correlation with life evaluation and GDP per capita. People in rich countries such as Denmark and Norway, on average, rate their lives higher than people in lesser developed places such as Togo and the Palestinian Territories.

People in Rich Countries Rate Their Lives Higher

Population (bigger circles = larger countries)

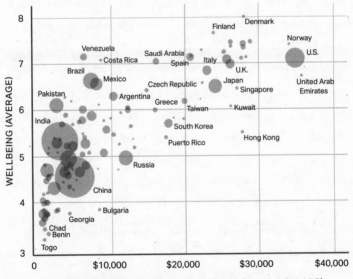

Gallup global research using the Cantril Self-Anchoring Striving Scale.

Source: Gallup and Angus Deaton

While this discovery appears to contradict one of Easterlin's conclusions, Deaton attempted to reconcile both findings. People's life ratings may still be relative. Instead of comparing their lives to their neighbors', they compare their lives to people's lives around the world. In his words, it is possible that "... Danes understand how bad life is in Togo and other poor places, and the Togolese, through television and newspapers, understand how good life is in Denmark or other high-income countries."

Are Danes high on life because they see global poverty and know they have it so much better? Or is Deaton's finding direct evidence that money does lead to a better life?

Happiness May Not Be Happiness

Here is where things get complicated. What many economists call "happiness" may not actually be "happiness." Most of the previous research focused on how people *see* their lives (life evaluation), not on how they *live* their lives (life experiences). In partnership with Kahneman, Deaton wrote another paper examining these differences.

In this study, they used Gallup's daily wellbeing survey in the U.S. Because we were calling 1,000 people every day, we had data on roughly 350,000 Americans each year. We asked people to rate their lives and to report how much they smiled and laughed a lot yesterday or whether they experienced a lot of stress, sadness, and anger. We also asked people how much money they make.

Using Gallup's income variable, Kahneman and Deaton found that the more money people make, the higher they rate their lives. In fact, there did not appear to be a satiation point. Meaning, money never stops affecting how well you *see* your life.

You might think, "There it is — money *does* buy happiness." That is true, but only if you believe that true "happiness" is defined by how you *see* your life. If you think happiness is how you *live* your life — how much you laugh and smile or how little anger you experience — then this study does not support the theory that money buys happiness.

When the authors looked at the relationship between income and reports of stress, anger, sadness, or enjoyment, they found a much weaker link. Beyond $75,000 of annual salary, income had almost no effect on how people *lived* their lives. Once your basic needs are met, money cannot buy laughter or a stress-free life.

Remember, this study was conducted in the U.S., and money may affect Americans differently. Although according to University of Michigan economists Betsey Stevenson and Justin Wolfers, Deaton and Kahneman's finding does apply globally. Looking at similar data across the world, the principle still holds: The more money people make, the higher they rate their lives. In fact, they believe that money's effect on life evaluation never satiates. "If there is a satiation point, we are yet to reach it," they say.

Academics at the University of Virginia and Purdue University disagree. Using the same Gallup World Poll data, they did a similar analysis but controlled for household size (an income of $95,000 may go further if you are single than if you have four kids). They also did not omit some of the highest incomes in the database.

They found that income's influence on life evaluation did satiate: Beyond $95,000 of annual income, people stop rating their lives better. If anything, incomes that are too high may cause people to see their lives worse in some parts of the world.

Why would more money make people rate their lives worse? According to the authors:

> Theoretically, it is presumably not the higher incomes themselves that drive reductions in [wellbeing], but the costs associated with them. High incomes are usually accompanied by high demands (time, workload, responsibility and so on) that might also limit opportunities for positive experiences (for example, leisure activities). Additional factors may play a role as well, such as an increase in materialistic values, additional material aspirations that may go unfulfilled, increased social comparisons or other life changes in reaction to greater income (for example, more children or living in more expensive neighborhoods). Importantly, the ill effects of the highest incomes may not just be present when one's maximum income is finally reached, but could also occur in the process of its attainment.

To summarize, money influences how people *see* their lives much more than how they *live* their lives, but only after their basic needs are met. While there is disagreement about how much it affects how they see their lives, everyone seems to agree — money matters. This is why one of the five elements of wellbeing is financial wellbeing.

To further emphasize the extent to which money influences how people see their lives, consider the effect of economic fluctuations on people's wellbeing.

People are loss averse. Or, as Los Angeles Dodgers broadcaster Vin Scully used to say, "Losing feels worse than winning feels good."

This is how loss aversion works: If you lose $20 and find $20 in the same day, economically, you are whole. But emotionally, you are not. Losing $20 causes pain that finding $20 does not make up for.

Loss aversion affects entire countries the same way it affects individuals. Oxford economist Jan-Emmanuel De Neve and his colleagues looked at how life evaluation fluctuates based on economic expansions and contractions. An economic contraction causes life ratings to drop far more than an economic boom causes life ratings to increase. According to the authors, "... life satisfaction of individuals is between two and eight times more sensitive to negative growth as compared to positive economic growth. People do not psychologically benefit from expansions nearly as much as they suffer from recessions."

Their recommendation? Policymakers should do everything they can to create slow, consistent growth — because the wild swings of economic busts and booms leave countries worse off emotionally. This is true even if those wild swings lead to greater national wealth than is created by slow consistent growth.

Of course, economic growth is distinct from personal financial growth. A growing economy may not benefit everyone. Additionally, money's impact on an individual is often examined through their income and not their overall financial situation, including their debt. Someone can make a lot of money, but that doesn't mean their finances are in good shape.

My colleagues Stephanie Marken and Andrew Dugan reviewed a massive Gallup survey of U.S. college graduates to answer one question: How does college debt affect people's wellbeing?

Not surprisingly, debt is bad. But college debt has lasting effects. Stephanie and Andrew found that college debt leaves an emotional scar on people *even after they pay off the debt*. Imagine a hardworking American who took out loans to pay for college. Then they graduated, got a good job, managed their finances perfectly, and finally paid off their debt. They are now in a good place financially, but they still have another deficit — an emotional one that may linger for a long time.

According to Stephanie and Andrew, "Studies show that high student debt can result in the deferral of major life events, such as marriage and homeownership. High student debt can also result in a graduate pursuing a career path he or she would not have taken otherwise."

How People Feel About the Money They Make

We know that money matters. So how is the world's financial wellbeing? According to more than 2 billion adults — not good.

Gallup asks the world:

> Which one of these phrases comes closest to your own feelings about your household income these days? Living comfortably on present income, getting by on present income, finding it difficult on present income, or finding it very difficult on present income.

From 2019-2021, 19% of people said they lived comfortably on their present household income, 41% said they were getting by, 23% said they found it difficult, and 16% found it very difficult. This translates into an estimated 1.2 billion people who find it difficult to get by on their current income and 860 million who find it *very* difficult — meaning there are over 2 billion people who are really struggling financially.

How People Feel About Their Income

Most likely to report finding it **very difficult** on present income

Rank	Country	%
1	Afghanistan	54%
2	Lebanon	48%
3	Zimbabwe	47%
4	Mozambique	41%
5	Zambia	40%
	Congo Brazzaville	40%
	Chad	40%
8	Uganda	39%
	Palestinian Territories	39%
10	Venezuela	37%
	Jordan	37%

Most likely to report **living comfortably** on present income

Rank	Country	%
1	Norway	68%
2	Denmark	59%
3	Iceland	57%
4	Sweden	56%
5	Netherlands	53%
	Luxembourg	53%
7	Switzerland	52%
8	Canada	49%
	New Zealand	49%
	United States	49%
11	Australia	47%
	United Kingdom	47%

Which one of these phrases comes closest to your own feelings about your household income these days? Living comfortably on present income, getting by on present income, finding it difficult on present income, or finding it very difficult on present income. Averaged over 2019-2021.

Source: Gallup

The U.S. ties for eighth globally for number of people who say they live comfortably on their present income. Despite being one of the highest countries on the list, the U.S. still has 6% of people who report the least satisfaction with their income — finding it very difficult to get by.

But are these 6% of Americans dissatisfied with their income because they cannot pay their bills — or are they unhappy with their income because it is low relative to other Americans' income? Or both?

Absolute Income vs. Income Inequality

According to the OECD, which analyzed Gallup World Poll data, "Income difficulties appear to be closer to an absolute than a relative equity measure, at least within the OECD." The OECD finds that while there is a significant relationship between income inequality and Gallup's subjective income question, the relationship is stronger between absolute household income and subjective income.

These correlations are true globally as well; "income difficulties" appear to correlate more strongly with absolute income than with income inequality. (See References for charts: Income Difficulties and Income Inequality and Income Difficulties and Median Income.)

But, according to my colleague Pablo Diego-Rosell, who has analyzed Gallup's subjective income measure more than anyone, the measure may be more nuanced. In his words, "This measure is the single most important driver of both life evaluations and experienced wellbeing. My hypothesis is that it is so important because it jointly accounts for all the direct and indirect effects of income, including income relative to others (social comparison) or to one's past income (habituation)." He further says, "Subjective material wellbeing and its objective determinants, including economic growth and income inequality, should remain at the center of the research and policy agenda."

Knowing the extent of income inequality and absolute income's influence on wellbeing better positions leaders to improve people's lives. If the source of a bad life comes a little more from absolute income than from income inequality, policy experiments such as a universal basic income (UBI) may be helpful to improve the lives of the more than 2 billion people who are struggling on their present income.

One of the most famous experiments involving UBI took place in Finland. The government tested a basic income with a group of people who were chronically unemployed. After following 2,000 participants for two years, the government found that the additional income made people rate their lives higher. This study has been replicated in at least 16 other studies globally with similar results, according to the Stanford Basic Income Lab.

UBI may have a positive impact on people's wellbeing, but that does not necessarily mean it is the best policy. Critics are understandably concerned about how UBI programs get funded and the potential impact on people's desire to work.

But regardless of the politics surrounding UBI, it is important to conduct policy experiments that attempt to improve people's financial wellbeing — precisely because of how much financial wellbeing affects a person's overall wellbeing.

CHAPTER TEN
The World's Broken Communities

Interviewer: In the next 12 months, are you likely or unlikely to move away from the city or area where you live?

Respondent: No. Although my town is underdeveloped, this town is where I was born, where my parents live. I will never leave this town

— Gallup World Poll respondent in Myanmar, 2020

Do you love where you live? What if I asked you: "Would you recommend the city or area where you live to a friend or associate as a place to live, or not?"

Thirty-five percent of the world says no. Roughly 1.9 billion people have such a negative impression of their community, they would tell a friend not to move there.

Widespread community detachment substantially contributes to negative emotions and wellbeing inequality. The communities that people love are getting better, and the broken communities are getting worse.

How much someone loves where they live is called community attachment or community wellbeing. We know that you love your city if you would recommend it to a friend (62% would), are satisfied with it as a place to live (82% are), and plan to continue living there (79% do). Gallup averages each of these measures in an index called the Community Attachment Index, although it very well could be called the "Loving Where You Live" index.

Loving Where You Live

Highest Community Attachment Index scores

Rank	Country	Score
1	Norway	93
2	Switzerland	92
3	Sweden	91
	Finland	91
	Denmark	91
	Netherlands	91
7	Slovenia	90
	Portugal	90
9	Luxembourg	89
	Austria	89
	Australia	89
	Uzbekistan	89
	Germany	89

Lowest Community Attachment Index scores

Rank	Country	Score
146	Afghanistan	47
145	Gabon	53
144	Congo Brazzaville	54
143	Togo	55
142	Namibia	58
141	Liberia	59
140	Sierra Leone	60
139	Morocco	61
	Tunisia	61
	Ivory Coast	61
136	Cameroon	62
	Zambia	62
	Algeria	62

The Community Attachment Index is the average of these three questions: Are you satisfied or dissatisfied with the city or area where you live? In the next 12 months, are you likely or unlikely to move away from the city or area where you live? Would you recommend the city or area where you live to a friend or associate as a place to live, or not? Index scores range from 0 to 100. Averaged over 2019-2021.

Source: Gallup

What Makes a Broken Community?

To better understand where communities are struggling most, let's look at the countries that perform the worst on the individual items.

Global Community Detachment

Most likely to move away		Most likely to not recommend		Most dissatisfied with where you live	
Country	%	Country	%	Country	%
Sierra Leone	51%	Indonesia	73%	Afghanistan	52%
Liberia	51%	Afghanistan	66%	Togo	50%
Congo Brazzaville	49%	China	47%	Gabon	49%
Gabon	47%	Cambodia	46%	Namibia	45%
Gambia	47%	Hong Kong S.A.R. of China	45%	Liberia	43%
Guinea	43%			Zambia	42%
Ivory Coast	43%	India	45%	Tunisia	40%
Namibia	43%	Mozambique	44%	Botswana	40%
Uganda	42%	Tunisia	44%	Lesotho	38%
Cameroon	41%	Lesotho	43%	Sierra Leone	38%
Kenya	41%	Albania	43%		
Zimbabwe	41%				

In the next 12 months, are you likely or unlikely to move away from the city or area where you live? Would you recommend the city or area where you live to a friend or associate as a place to live, or not? Are you satisfied or dissatisfied with the city or area where you live? Averaged over 2019-2021.

Source: Gallup

There are 14 countries where 40% or more people want to leave their community, including more than half of people in Sierra Leone and Liberia.

Over half of the population in Indonesia and Afghanistan would not recommend their community to a friend as a place to live. And interestingly, China and India are among the highest in the world for people who would not recommend their community to a friend. But dissatisfaction with your community does not necessarily mean dissatisfaction with your *country*.

For example, while 47% of Chinese would not recommend their community to a friend, only 4% want to leave their country permanently. And 45% of Indians would not recommend their community to a friend, but only 6% of Indians want to leave their country permanently.

The list of countries that are home to many struggling, broken communities have two fundamental things in common: widespread fear and a lack of basic infrastructure.

Broken Communities Are Built on Fear

The first step to building a great community is making sure people not only are safe, but *feel* safe.

To monitor crime, leaders often overly rely on traditional indicators that describe how much crime there is in a community. They use statistics such as crime reports (although not all crimes are reported), arrests (hiring more police increases arrests), and surveys on how many people have been victimized by various crimes that have not been reported. These indicators help describe how objectively safe a society is, but they do not tell leaders whether people *feel* safe — which is arguably more important.

For example, Egypt experienced a great deal of turmoil during the Arab uprisings. Although crime fell after protests in Tahrir Square, fear (not feeling safe walking alone at night) skyrocketed.

Fear and Crime in Egypt

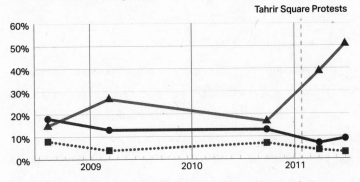

Within the last 12 months, have you had money or property stolen from you or another household member? Within the last 12 months, have you been assaulted or mugged? Do you feel safe walking alone at night in the city or area where you live?

Source: Gallup

Thefts fell from 18% before 2009 to less than 10% in 2011; muggings and assaults fell from 8% to 3%. While objectively, crime appears to have decreased in Egypt, fear did not decline simultaneously. In fact, after the uprisings in 2011, Egyptians expressed more fear than at any point in the history of our tracking. More than half of Egyptians (51%) said they do not feel safe walking alone at night, increasing from 17% just the year before. To contextualize this, in 2010, Egypt's global ranking for "fear of walking alone at night" was 103rd — in 2011, it jumped to 52nd.

On a national level, the widespread protests forced President Hosni Mubarak to resign, but fear did not completely subside. Even after Egypt held elections in 2012, which brought President Mohamed Morsi from the Muslim Brotherhood to power, fear *still* did not subside. In fact, in 2013, 55% of Egyptians said they did not feel safe walking alone at night in their community.

Morsi's tenure ended the next year as a result of a military coup. After the coup and another election, Abdel Fattah al-Sisi took office in May 2014. The next month, Gallup conducted another survey and found that fear had subsided. Egypt went from 55% of its citizens expressing fear in their communities — which ranked it 16th highest in the world — to only 25%, ranking it 105th.

Egypt is an example of where traditional crime statistics diverged from how people feel, further emphasizing the importance of monitoring people's emotions, especially with respect to fear.

World leaders are beginning to understand how important feeling safe is to a person's wellbeing. Look at the U.N.'s Sustainable Development Goals (SDGs), which are the world's blueprint to achieve global peace and prosperity for everyone. SDG Goal 16 exists to "promote peaceful and inclusive societies," and one of its underlying measures to determine progress is Indicator 16.1.4, which directs governments to improve the "proportion of population that *feel safe walking alone around the area they live.*" (emphasis added)

According to Gallup, 70% of people globally feel safe walking alone at night in their communities; 28% do not.

Feeling Safe in Your Community

Most likely to feel safe walking alone at night

Rank	Country	Yes
1	Singapore	96%
2	Norway	93%
	United Arab Emirates	93%
	Turkmenistan	93%
5	China	92%
6	Kuwait	90%
	Tajikistan	90%
	Slovenia	90%
9	Saudi Arabia	88%
10	Switzerland	87%
	Denmark	87%
	Luxembourg	87%

Least likely to feel safe walking alone at night

Rank	Country	Yes
145	Afghanistan	15%
144	Gabon	31%
	Venezuela	31%
142	Liberia	33%
141	South Africa	34%
	Lesotho	34%
139	Botswana	36%
138	Namibia	40%
	Dominican Republic	40%
136	Mexico	43%
	Cameroon	43%
	Madagascar	43%

Do you feel safe walking alone at night in the city or area where you live? Averaged over 2019-2021.

Source: Gallup

Almost everyone in Singapore, Norway, and the UAE feels safe walking alone at night. But in sub-Saharan Africa and Latin America, many people don't feel safe, especially in urban areas.

Broken Communities Lack Basic Infrastructure

Feeling safe where you live is foundational to a good community. But so is basic infrastructure. Globally, Gallup asks people whether they are satisfied with the public transportation systems, the roads and highways, the availability of good affordable housing, the educational system and schools, the availability of quality healthcare, and the quality of air and water in their community. These questions make up Gallup's Community Basics Index.

Gallup's Community Basics Index

Highest Community
Basics Index scores

Rank	Country	Score
1	Singapore	90
2	United Arab Emirates	85
3	Switzerland	84
4	Denmark	82
5	Tajikistan	81
6	Norway	80
	Cambodia	80
	Finland	80
	Saudi Arabia	80
10	Netherlands	78
	China	78
	Bangladesh	78
	Sweden	78
	Austria	78

Lowest Community
Basics Index scores

Rank	Country	Score
146	Venezuela	31
145	Gabon	35
144	Tunisia	36
143	Liberia	37
142	Lebanon	39
141	Mongolia	40
	Togo	40
139	Mauritania	41
138	Lesotho	42
137	Sierra Leone	43
	Guinea	43
135	Chad	44
	Algeria	44

The Community Basics Index evaluates everyday life in a community, including environment, housing, and infrastructure. Index scores range from 0 to 100. Averaged over 2019-2021.

Source: Gallup

Many countries on this list shouldn't be a surprise: Highly developed countries also have citizens who are very satisfied with their community's infrastructure. In fact, this index and the U.N.'s Human Development Index have a high positive correlation. But there are a few outliers, such as Tajikistan and Cambodia.

Gallup isolated the countries that looked like outliers and found that many of them are also considered the "least free" countries in the world, according to Freedom House. This finding suggests that people may have responded more positively about certain community services out of fear. We need further analysis on Gallup's Community Basics Index, but overall, people have a good understanding of the infrastructure in their communities.

The Difference Between a Good Community and a Great Community

A *good* community provides safety and basic infrastructure for its citizens, but that alone does not make a community great. A *great* community is more than the product of its roads, housing, and healthcare. What makes a community great is its people — people who trust and help each other. The good news is that there are many great communities, even where some of the community basics are missing.

Researchers try to measure whether there is an atmosphere of trust in a community by watching people's behavior. The best-known experiment to measure trust is known as the "wallet test." In this test, researchers fill a wallet with money and insert dummy identification with a return address. They take the wallet and drop it somewhere, such as a mall or a street corner. Then, from a distance, they watch what happens.

What do strangers do when they find the wallet? Do they keep it? Take it to the local police?

One researcher dropped more than 17,000 wallets in 40 different countries to see what would happen. Surprisingly, half of the wallets were returned. People polled in the same 40 countries thought only 25% would be returned. And when researchers put more money in the wallets, no one could predict the results: The more money in the wallets, the more likely they were to be returned.

In 2019, the Lloyd's Register Foundation and Gallup partnered to build on the wallet research. Our qualitative research found that the word "wallet" did not translate perfectly across languages; "a small bag that contained items of great financial value" worked better. We asked people in 142 countries these questions:

Suppose you lost a small bag that contained items of great financial value to you that had your name and address written on it. If it were found by each of the following people, in general, how likely is it that it would be returned to you with all of its contents? A neighbor? A stranger?

Globally, 78% of people think a neighbor would return the bag, whereas 18% think it is not at all likely that they would. But while people trust their neighbors, they are more skeptical of strangers. Nearly half (49%) think it is not at all likely that a stranger would return the bag, and 44% believe they would return it.

Although people do not express a great deal of trust in strangers in their communities, they may be underestimating their fellow citizens. Remember, in the 40-country wallet study, people greatly underestimated how many wallets would be returned. Strangers may be more trustworthy than their fellow citizens give them credit for.

And while people may not know precisely how trustworthy strangers are in their community, they usually have a pretty good idea. For example, 68% of Danes believe that a stranger would return a lost bag; in the wallet study, 80% *did* return a lost wallet. In Peru, only 23% of people believe that a lost bag would be returned; in the wallet study, only 10% were returned.

Danes and Peruvians may not know exactly what the likelihood is that a lost wallet will be returned, but Danes know that a lost wallet in Denmark has a high chance of being returned, and Peruvians know that a lost wallet in Peru is probably gone for good. (See References for tables: Do You Trust Your Neighbors? and Do You Trust Strangers?)

Trust is higher in some of the same countries where people rate their lives the best, including Norway, Finland, and Denmark (the three most consistently "happiest countries in the world," according to the *World Happiness Report*). Trust is much lower in Latin America (particularly in Central America) and Southeast Asia.

But how much does an environment of trust affect how your life is going? The short answer is — a lot. According to the *WHR*, people who trust their neighbors and who trust strangers are far more likely to rate their lives better. Trust is even more influential than doubling your income and the net loss of being unemployed. Additionally, research finds that communities with high trust are more resilient during severe economic contractions and natural disasters.

People Help Themselves When They Help Their Communities

While trust is a critical aspect of a great community, so is an environment where people support and help each other. Great communities are built on financial generosity, volunteering, and the willingness to help strangers. To measure each of these concepts, Gallup asks three questions:

Have you done any of the following in the past month? How about …?

- donated money to a charity?
- volunteered your time to an organization?
- helped a stranger or someone you didn't know who needed help?

Thirty-two percent of people worldwide report donating money to a charity, 24% report volunteering, and 55% report helping a stranger.

Where People Are Financially Generous

Financial generosity takes place even in the absence of wealth. Some of the world's most generous countries are also some of the poorest. For example, the Gambia ranks 209th globally in income per capita, yet it is tied for eighth in the world for donating to charity.

Global Giving

Most likely to donate

Rank	Country	Yes
1	Indonesia	84%
2	Myanmar	75%
3	United Kingdom	64%
4	Netherlands	62%
	Thailand	62%
6	Iceland	61%
7	Turkmenistan	60%
8	Australia	59%
	Gambia	59%
10	Kosovo	56%
	New Zealand	56%

Least likely to donate

Rank	Country	Yes
146	Morocco	4%
145	Yemen	6%
	Georgia	6%
	Lesotho	6%
142	Afghanistan	7%
141	Tunisia	8%
	Eswatini	8%
139	Botswana	9%
138	Azerbaijan	10%
137	Gabon	11%

Have you done any of the following in the past month? How about donated money to a charity? Averaged over 2019-2021.

Source: Gallup

Where People Volunteer

Volunteerism is another bright spot in the world, although people seem to be a little more generous with their money (32% donated) than their time (24% volunteered). This has been true every year in our global tracking. And just like donating money, the countries where people are the most likely to volunteer are not necessarily the richest.

Global Volunteering

Most likely to volunteer

Rank	Country	Yes
1	Indonesia	62%
2	Kenya	51%
	Liberia	51%
4	Tajikistan	44%
5	Comoros	43%
6	Sierra Leone	38%
7	Mongolia	37%
8	New Zealand	35%
9	Zambia	34%
10	Nigeria	33%
	Mozambique	33%
	Sri Lanka	33%
	United States	33%
	Ghana	33%

Least likely to volunteer

Rank	Country	Yes
146	Yemen	6%
	Egypt	6%
	Jordan	6%
143	Serbia	7%
	Bosnia and Herzegovina	7%
	Latvia	7%
140	Palestinian Territories	8%
	Romania	8%
	Albania	8%
	Azerbaijan	8%
	Belarus	8%
135	Armenia	9%
	Lebanon	9%
	Morocco	9%
	Cambodia	9%
	Hungary	9%

Have you done any of the following in the past month? How about volunteered your time to an organization? Averaged over 2019-2021.

Source: Gallup

Where People Help Strangers

More than half of the world readily lends a hand to people they do not know. Helping strangers is so widespread that a majority of people claimed to have helped someone they did not know in 102 out of the 146 countries we surveyed from 2019 to 2021.

Lending a Hand

Most likely to help a stranger

Rank	Country	Yes
1	Sierra Leone	80%
2	Liberia	77%
3	Kenya	76%
4	Libya	75%
5	Zambia	74%
	Nigeria	74%
7	Iraq	73%
	Turkmenistan	73%
	Uganda	73%
10	Cameroon	70%
	Gambia	70%
	Jamaica	70%

Least likely to help a stranger

Rank	Country	Yes
146	Japan	17%
145	Belarus	24%
144	Cambodia	26%
143	Belgium	30%
142	Luxembourg	34%
	Azerbaijan	34%
	France	34%
139	Laos	35%
138	Switzerland	36%
137	Italy	38%
136	Latvia	39%
	Netherlands	39%

Have you done any of the following in the past month? How about helped a stranger or someone you didn't know who needed help? Averaged over 2019-2021.

Source: Gallup

People who give back don't just increase others' wellbeing; they increase their own wellbeing too. Research suggests that donating a certain amount of money gives you more of an emotional boost than receiving that same amount of money. Volunteering and helping strangers has a similar effect — the volunteer or helper can get a greater rise in wellbeing than the people they're helping.

Living in a great community matters. Many places such as the Gambia have the potential for great communities, precisely because of the people. Despite being poor, Gambians find a way to donate their money and their time, and they even help their neighbors in need at a higher rate than people in most countries in the world. Yet 47% of Gambians still want to leave their communities.

Gambians report more fear than most countries' residents and report among the lowest satisfaction with basic infrastructure. Until those perceptions improve, their communities will never thrive despite being home to some of the most generous people in the world.

Billions of people are giving back to their communities, but amid rampant fear and poor infrastructure, those communities cannot flourish. Leaders must prioritize making people feel safe and improving infrastructure if they are going to create great communities.

CHAPTER ELEVEN
The Global Hunger Crisis

Food is national security. Food is economy. It is employment, energy, history. Food is everything.

— Chef José Andrés

Fatigue, inability to concentrate, increased blood pressure, weakened immune system, and blurry vision are just some of the immediate consequences of hunger. Kerry Wright from Aberdeen in Scotland was no stranger to any of them.

Kerry, a single mother of three children, was struggling to find work and unable to afford food for her family. Feeding herself was never her priority; feeding her children was. Each night, she found a way to feed her family but not herself. Then the deadly symptoms of hunger set in. Things got so bad that when she came home one day, a glass of milk was on the table. Her son had put it there. He could no longer sit by and watch her waste away day after day. He wanted her to drink the milk in front of him so he would not have to see her suffer.

Kerry didn't want to go to a food bank. She was afraid the authorities would think she was neglecting her children and take them from her. To prevent that from happening, she came up with a plan. Instead of asking for help from a food bank, she would volunteer at one. She could get food while volunteering and bring it back to her children.

Her strategy worked beyond her wildest dreams. Not only did Kerry get food for her children, she also got offered a job at the food bank. Now she had a steady income and could feed her family.

Kerry's story ends happily, but her experience with hunger is becoming far too commonplace. For decades, global hunger was decreasing. But in 2014, the trend reversed and has steadily increased ever since.

According to the U.N. Food and Agriculture Organization (FAO), "The decades-long decline in hunger in the world, as measured using the prevalence of undernourishment (PoU), [has] unfortunately ended." PoU quantifies the number of people who do not get enough calories every day. The U.N. found that 720 million to 811 million people faced hunger in 2020, up by more than 100 million from the year before.

FAO takes the measurement of global hunger so seriously that it uses another metric to support its research — one that looks at a person's access to food. This metric, the Food Insecurity Experience Scale (FIES), is based on an eight-item survey that classifies people's level of food insecurity. Here are the questions:

During the last 12 months, was there a time when, because of lack of money or other resources:

1. You were worried you would not have enough food to eat?

2. You were unable to eat healthy and nutritious food?

3. You ate only a few kinds of foods?

4. You had to skip a meal?

5. You ate less than you thought you should?

6. Your household ran out of food?

7. You were hungry but did not eat?

8. You went without eating for a whole day?

According to the FIES, in 2020, 18.5% of people globally experienced moderate food insecurity, and 11.9% experienced severe food insecurity. Combined, 30.4% of people worldwide experienced food insecurity, which is over 2 billion people. While the absolute figure is a serious problem, the consistent rise in food insecurity since 2014 is even more troubling.

The Rise of Food Insecurity

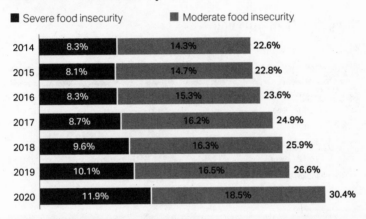

Source: U.N. Food and Agriculture Organization (FAO)

Not surprisingly, the pandemic exacerbated global hunger. According to FAO, "While the global prevalence of moderate or severe food insecurity has been slowly on the rise since 2014, the estimated increase in 2020 was equal to that of the previous five years combined."

But global hunger was rising before the pandemic. In 2019, Gallup found that a majority of people in 52 countries said that there was a time in the past 12 months when they could not afford food for themselves or their families. If we surveyed every country globally, unfortunately the list would be a lot longer.

Gallup cannot conduct surveys in every country in the world because of security and budgetary restraints. For example, we have not surveyed in the Democratic Republic of the Congo (DRC) since 2017. The DRC seriously suffers from hunger. In 2021, FAO and U.N. World Food Programme (WFP) warned that 27.3 million people in the DRC suffer from high levels of acute food insecurity — the worst kind of hunger imaginable. And nearly 7 million Congolese in the DRC experience *emergency* levels of acute hunger — which means death is imminent.

Struggling to Afford Food

Struggle **most** to afford food

Rank	Country	Yes
1	Rwanda	81%
2	Zimbabwe	80%
3	Zambia	79%
4	Lesotho	78%
5	Sierra Leone	77%
6	Gabon	75%
7	Eswatini	74%
	Nigeria	74%
	Afghanistan	74%
10	Malawi	73%
	Venezuela	73%
	Chad	73%

Struggle **least** to afford food

Rank	Country	Yes
145	Luxembourg	3%
144	Sweden	6%
	Switzerland	6%
	Denmark	6%
141	Netherlands	7%
	Singapore	7%
	Norway	7%
138	Germany	8%
	Finland	8%
	Israel	8%

Have there been times in the past 12 months when you did not have enough money to buy food that you or your family needed? Averaged over 2019-2021.

Source: Gallup

No country in the world is immune from the global hunger crisis. Only 14 countries report less than 10% of people struggling to afford food. The U.S. is no exception: 20% of Americans said they struggled to afford food in the last 12 months. This may not be surprising considering that 38 million Americans receive help from the Supplemental Nutrition Assistance Program.

Hunger is the single greatest threat to humanity's physical wellbeing today. And its impact on the global rise of negative emotions and the widening of wellbeing inequality cannot be overstated. According to research published in *The Journal of Nutrition*, food insecurity affects wellbeing more than income, housing and shelter, and employment status. Hunger not only makes you *see* your life worse, it also makes you angrier, sadder, and more stressed. And it decreases your chances of feeling well-rested, experiencing enjoyment, and laughing and smiling a lot.

According to FAO, the three most significant contributors to the global rise of hunger are climate change, growing conflicts, and slowing economic growth. But whatever its causes, global wellbeing will not improve until people are properly fed.

Obesity — Another Global Challenge

The resurgence of hunger may come as a surprise to some. In the West, hunger is not what is killing people — obesity is. According to the CGIAR Research Program on Climate Change, Agriculture and Food Security (CCAFS), "65% of the world's population lives in countries where overweight and obesity kills more people than do factors related to underweight."

Obesity contributes to roughly 4 million deaths per year from related diseases, such as Type 2 diabetes, heart disease, stroke, and some cancers. And while hunger is rising, so is obesity. According to the WHO, global obesity has nearly tripled since the mid-1970s. Today, 650 million people (13%) are obese, and 1.9 billion people (39%) are overweight. This epidemic is particularly acute in the U.S., where eight in 10 Americans are overweight or obese.

The fundamental cause of obesity is eating too much and not moving enough. And people are surprisingly open about how little they move. For three years, Gallup asked people how much they agree with the following statement: "In the last seven days, you have felt active and productive every day." According to our most recent data, 17% disagree, including 6% who strongly disagree.

This statement and how we worded it was not random. We tested it against similar question items to see how it correlated with questions people answered about how much they weigh, their workout habits, or how much they walk in a day. This item was one of the most predictive of how physically active a person is. And perhaps not surprisingly, people who respond positively to this item also rate their lives better and report more positive experiences and less negative experiences.

But how is the world struggling with rising hunger and obesity at the same time?

This phenomenon is known as the double burden of malnutrition (DBM). According to the WHO, DBM "... is characterized by the coexistence of undernutrition ... [and] overweight and obesity." Obesity and hunger can affect the same country; they can even affect the same household or the same individual. Someone can be overweight and moderately food insecure at the same time. In fact, living in a food-insecure household is a predictor of obesity in school-aged children, adolescents, and adults.

This dual challenge of obesity and hunger will not be resolved unless diets are addressed. Poor diets and malnutrition are two of the biggest risk factors for the global burden of disease and the dual challenge of hunger and obesity. But many countries lack routine and internationally comparable data on what people are eating. Unlike many other public health priorities such as HIV and smoking, there is not a global monitoring system for diets.

Monitoring diets for an entire country is hard. But Harvard University, Gallup, and the Global Alliance for Improved Nutrition (GAIN) are trying to figure out a way to record what people are eating using consumption information from 29 different food groups (both healthy and unhealthy food) worldwide. As of this writing, data are still being collected, but we have early results from two countries in sub-Saharan African — Tanzania and Ghana. And the results show just how prevalent poor diets are in Africa.

Less than half of adults in Tanzania and Ghana consume diets that meet the minimum guidelines established by the WHO — and those are just the first two countries where we have completed surveys. Even if a person consumes some calories, it does not necessarily mean they are getting the right vitamins to help them think or see clearly.

A better understanding of what people are eating will help inform leaders on policy initiatives that can improve nutrition everywhere. And improved nutrition will combat the global obesity epidemic as well as the food insecurity epidemic.

But even if we improve what is in people's food bowls, we also need to make sure those bowls are full. Because as FAO reports, *severe* food insecurity is also on the rise, and those who experience it are in a precarious state because they do not have any food at all. Obesity and poor nutrition are contributing to the rise of negative emotions and widening wellbeing inequality, but not like severe food insecurity.

Not only is severe food insecurity increasing now, it is projected to be even worse in the next few years. According to *The State of Food Security and Nutrition in the World 2020*, "The world is not on track to achieve Zero Hunger by 2030. If recent trends continue, the number of people affected by hunger will surpass 840 million by

2030, or 9.8% of the population. This is an alarming scenario, even considering the potential impacts of the COVID-19 pandemic."

On March 11, 2021, António Guterres, the U.N. secretary-general, warned the world, "If you don't feed people, you feed conflict." People starving is bad enough for the world, but according to Guterres, global hunger can have consequences that extend beyond the harm it causes the individual.

CHAPTER TWELVE
A Lonely Planet

Gallup interviewed a man in Canada about how his life was going. At one point during the interview, the man said it was the only phone call he had received that day. It also happened to be his birthday.

At the end of the call, the interviewer thanked him for his time and said, "Happy birthday."

The man replied, "Thank you. You made me feel less alone today on my birthday."

How many friends do you talk to each week?

If you said one to two friends, you are like 23% of the world. If you said three to four, you are like 20% of the world. If you said five to nine, you are like 23%. And if you are really popular and said 10 or more friends, you are like 28% of people worldwide.

Now imagine if you said *none*.

Six percent of the world does not have to imagine that — they live it. About 330 million people are so lonely that they do not talk to a single friend or family member for two weeks at a time. They are friendless.

But just because someone *has* friends does not mean they are *good* friends. While 6% of people are lonely, 23% do not have friends or relatives they can count on whenever they need them.

The pandemic intensified global loneliness. According to the Survey Center on American Life, 10% of women reported having no close friends in 2021, up from 2% in 1990. Men have it worse: Over the same time span, 15% reported having no close friends, up from 3%.

The Importance of Social Wellbeing

Having high social wellbeing means having strong relationships and love in your life. Social wellbeing is one of the most important aspects of a great life but also the least appreciated. When people hear about global suffering, they often think of poverty. But what about the pain of being lonely?

Social wellbeing gets the least amount of attention because it is "soft." It is not measured using hard economic data such as income; it involves counting a person's friends or evaluating the quality of their relationships. Yet, low social wellbeing is a serious problem — so serious that it is not an exaggeration to say it is killing people.

Brigham Young University researcher Julianne Holt-Lunstad reviewed 148 studies globally and found that people who have adequate social relationships are 50% less likely to die compared with those who have poor or insufficient social connections. This increase in survival rate is comparable to quitting smoking.

And people with good relationships live better, longer lives. Elizabeth Anne Bernstein, who writes the "Bonds: On Relationships" column for *The Wall Street Journal*, says, "Friendship decreases blood pressure and stress, reduces the risk of depression and increases longevity, in large part because someone is watching out for us."

Having at least one friend you talk to a minimum of once every two weeks increases your chance of living a thriving life by over 50%. Having five close friends decreases your chances of living a life of suffering by more than 50%. We find this pattern in every country in the world.

Every hour you spend with your friends makes life a little better. Six hours of social time each day doubles your chances of thriving overall; six hours of social time also decreases your chances of suffering by 50%.

Spending time with your friends not only improves how you *see* your life, it also improves how you *live* your life. People who spend time with at least one friend a week experience less stress, sadness, and worry. And most importantly, people with friends have more fun. They are more likely to experience enjoyment and to laugh and smile a lot.

Friendship Deserts

Loneliness is most prevalent in the Middle East and North Africa. Almost 10% of people throughout the region say they have no friends with whom they regularly interact. East Asia and Latin America follow, at 8% and 7%, respectively. People in North America and Australia-New Zealand are the least likely to report having no interactions with friends, at 2% and 1%, respectively.

Loneliness is not just a product of having no friends; you also need people in your life who you can count on for help. There are three countries in the world where a majority of people do not have someone they can count on to help if they are in trouble.

No One to Count On

If you were in trouble, do you have relatives or friends you can count on to help you whenever you need them, or not?

Rank	Country	No
1	Afghanistan	59%
2	Benin	54%
3	Rwanda	51%
4	Morocco	47%
5	Malawi	45%
6	Togo	43%
7	India	42%
8	Congo Brazzaville	40%
9	Pakistan	39%
	Sierra Leone	39%

Averaged over 2019-2021.

Source: Gallup

The Ministry of Loneliness

Governments are starting to take loneliness seriously. For example, Japan and the U.K. each have ministers of loneliness to tackle this problem.

Loneliness is a critical matter in Japan because of a parallel problem — suicide. The suicide rate peaked in Japan after the 1998 recession. At the turn of the century, Japan was losing nearly 24 out of 100,000 citizens to suicide. But after years of intervention, suicides plummeted — hitting a record low in 2018. Then during the pandemic, the 10-year trend reversed, causing Japan to revive its ministry of loneliness.

Japan's minister of loneliness took two approaches to address the increase in suicides: Find the people most at risk, and develop networks to get them the help they need. "Women especially are feeling more isolated and face increasing suicide rates. I'd like you to examine the issue and put forward a comprehensive strategy," then-Prime Minister Yoshihide Suga reportedly said to his newly appointed minister of loneliness. The country's efforts appear to have worked. Suicide rates were down in the first quarter of 2021.

The U.K. established a similar ministry after a recommendation from the Jo Cox Loneliness Commission. The Commission's namesake is a former member of parliament who was assassinated in 2016. She was passionate about the issue of loneliness.

The Commission put together a report on the state of loneliness in the U.K., finding: "More than 9 million people always or often feel lonely, around 200,000 older people have not had a conversation with a friend or relative in more than a month, [and] up to 85% of young disabled adults … feel lonely."

According to the U.K. government, a ministry of loneliness has four primary responsibilities: measurement, public health campaigns, encouraging practitioners to do more social prescribing (encouraging people to join loneliness groups), and, in the words of former Prime Minister Theresa May, "Create new community spaces, for example by creating new community cafes, gardens, and art spaces."

All the U.K. ministry's goals are laudable, but creating community spaces might need the most attention because one of the biggest barriers to people making friends is the opportunity to meet other people in the first place. About one in six (16%) people worldwide say that they are not satisfied with the opportunity to make friends in their community.

Meeting People and Making Friends

Most satisfied with
opportunities to make friends

Rank	Country	Satisfied
1	Cambodia	91%
	Denmark	91%
3	Indonesia	90%
	Philippines	90%
5	Paraguay	89%
	Slovenia	89%
	Singapore	89%
	Vietnam	89%
9	Bangladesh	88%
	Thailand	88%
	Niger	88%
	New Zealand	88%

Least satisfied with
opportunities to make friends

Rank	Country	Satisfied
146	Algeria	54%
145	Eswatini	56%
	Togo	56%
143	Tunisia	58%
	Lebanon	58%
141	Belarus	59%
140	Benin	60%
	Lithuania	60%
138	Morocco	62%
137	South Korea	63%
	Jordan	63%

In the city or area where you live, are you satisfied or dissatisfied with the opportunities to meet people and make friends? Averaged over 2019-2021.

Source: Gallup

Six of the 12 countries where people are most satisfied with opportunities to meet people and make friends are in Southeast Asia. According to Gallup's Director for Asia-Pacific, Chayanun Saransomrurtai (who goes by "Gap"), the region is an outlier on this item for cultural reasons. He notes that Asians are more collectivistic — they put group and community desires over their own. Southeast Asians place importance on neighbors, friends, families, and communities. They are also known for their hospitality, openness, and smiles.

Social wellbeing is woven into the cultural fabric of Southeast Asia. But there is something structural happening in the region that further explains these scores: their workplaces. Southeast Asia tops the list on another item in Gallup's global database — having a best friend at work.

Gallup asks workers globally how much they agree (on a 5-point scale) with the following statement: I have a best friend at work. In organizations Gallup has studied globally, one in three employees have a best friend at work. This compares with one in two employees for organizations in Southeast Asia. There is an important lesson the world can learn from Southeast Asia about encouraging workplace friendships. But before diving into this topic — how does age affect friendships?

People make more friends when they are young. Only 3% of people aged 15-29 report no interactions with friends. That number is more than three times higher for people 55 and older (10%).

The inverse relationship between a person's age and the number of friends they have is usually explained by "life just getting in the way." The demands of family and a job make friendships harder to maintain. And research suggests that after you get a romantic partner, you lose two friends on average.

But maybe getting older is not the reason for fewer friendships. Maybe it is because places like schools are highly conducive to friendships, and when you leave school and start working, you no longer have as many opportunities to make friends. Maybe workplaces do not foster friendship-friendly environments.

Only 15% of people say they have a "real friend" at work. This is tragically low. According to the Survey Center on American Life, people with close friends are most likely to say they met them at work. As a source of friendships, workplaces topped school, their existing network of friends, their neighborhood, a place of worship, a club or organization they belong to, and through the parents of their children's friends (in that order).

But many organizations believe that friendships do not belong in the workplace. Employers (including managers) should encourage friendships at work — not just because they are good for workers' personal wellbeing, but because they also increase productivity and worker engagement.

Researchers at the University of Pennsylvania and University of Minnesota conducted an experiment and found that friendships at work do, in fact, increase productivity. But more importantly, they found out *why*. "Friends were more committed at the start of a project, showed better communication while doing the activity, and offered teammates positive encouragement every step of the way. They also evaluated ideas more critically and gave one another feedback when they were off course," the study found.

Workplace relationships are also critical to job satisfaction. According to the International Social Survey Programme, these relationships are even more important than pay. The authors of "Work and Well-being: A Global Perspective" stated, "Interpersonal relationships have a sizable and significant positive effect on the job satisfaction of the average employee. [Relationships] rank first out of our 12 domains of workplace quality in terms of power to explain variation in job satisfaction."

Maintaining friendships can be difficult, especially as people age. But while career, children, and hobbies can conflict with maintaining relationships, *not* integrating friendships creates a wellbeing deficit.

To curb the rise of negative emotions and to close the wellbeing inequality gap, leaders must consider the aspects of a great life that do not include work or money. Social wellbeing embodies just how multidimensional a great life is.

CHAPTER THIRTEEN
The Serious Outcomes of Unhappiness

Openly telling a pollster that you have the worst life imaginable reveals an awful state of mind, and roughly 8% of the world tells Gallup exactly that. But that is only the percentage of people who rate their lives a zero — 24% of the world rates their lives a 3 or lower on a scale of zero to 10.

People who rate their lives this low are usually hungry, live in broken communities, struggle on their current income, do not have social networks they can count on, and have no hope for a great job. But the people who are living this kind of life are feeling even worse about it today.

Negative emotions for this group, the lowest quintile for life ratings, are skyrocketing. In 2007, 29% reported a lot of sadness, 39% reported a lot of stress, and 42% reported a lot of worry; in 2021, those figures were 49%, 49%, and 59%, respectively.

But now add to those feelings a sense that the system is rigged against you. In 2021, among the 20% of the world rating their lives the lowest, 71% thought corruption was widespread in business, and 69% believed corruption was widespread in government.

This widespread distrust, coupled with wellbeing inequality, may be causing misery to turn to anger. The anger in this group has increased 50% over the past 15 years (from 24% in 2007 to 36% in 2021).

But should individuals or countries be concerned that people will act on this anger? According to the Global Peace Index, riots, strikes, and anti-government demonstrations increased 244% from 2011 to 2019. And this rise in civil unrest happened before the global pandemic.

In 2020, civil unrest increased exponentially. According to the founder of the Institute for Economics and Peace, Steve Killelea, there were "nearly 15,000 demonstrations globally in 2020, with 5,000 COVID-related incidences."

Civil Unrest

Number of unrest events

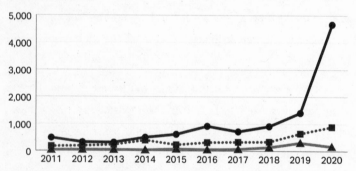

Source: Institute for Economics and Peace

If the increase in negative emotions is causing people to express their frustration in the streets, are they also expressing it at the ballot box?

Behavioral scientist George Ward thinks so. In an unpublished paper, he reviewed Gallup's negative emotions data from Europe to see if they had any relationship to populist attitudes and the success of populist parties. He defined "populist attitudes" by looking at people's opinions toward their government, the media, immigrants, and leaving the European Union (EU).

Ward found that "Negative [emotions] — both in the form of general sentiment and discrete emotions — [are] predictive of populist beliefs and voting."

How people feel affects how they act. If there is a relationship between negative emotions and civil unrest or populist attitudes, it should capture the attention of leaders everywhere.

A Separate Concern — The Rise of Physical Pain

While the rise of any negative emotion is concerning, one might be slightly more concerning than the rest — daily physical pain.

Pain is not uncommon, but imagine living with physical pain every single day. For 30% of people, that is a reality. The 31% we recorded in 2017, 2018, and 2019 was the highest in our tracking, up from 23% in 2008. And, as I previously mentioned, for the people who rate their lives the worst in the world, 45% of them say they live with daily pain (up from 30% 15 years ago).

It is easy to conclude that the rise in physical pain is attributable to the world's aging population. Indeed, the world is getting older. The population replacement rate is declining, and people are living longer. In fact, 2018 marked the first year that there were more people who were 65 and older than there were children 5 and younger.

As people get older, they often have more health problems. But age does not appear to be driving the increase in physical pain. Before the pandemic, *every* age group was feeling more physical pain. From 2006 to 2019, we saw a six-point increase for people aged 15-29, a nine-point increase for people 30-49, and an 11-point increase for those 50+.

Rising physical pain does not appear to be directly attributable to a fundamental breakdown of healthcare either. People have more confidence in the quality of their healthcare than ever before. In 2021, 67% of people were satisfied with their local healthcare, up from 54% in 2006. How people perceive their healthcare is a good gauge of the quality of that healthcare. This metric highly correlates with life expectancy and health expenditure per capita.

So while we are not entirely sure about the causes of the global increase in physical pain, the outcomes can be deadly.

Princeton professors Anne Case and Angus Deaton discovered that life expectancy among non-college-educated white males in the U.S. is declining because of a recent phenomenon known as "deaths of despair," which is also the title of their book. Deaths of despair include opioid overdoses, alcohol poisoning, and suicide. These types of deaths among this population have increased dramatically since the mid-1990s, from about 65,000 in 1995 to 158,000 in 2018. The problem is so severe, it is bringing down the average life expectancy among all Americans.

Case and Deaton found that one variable that highly correlates with deaths of despair is self-reported physical pain — the same indicator that is increasing globally.

People who are struggling with daily pain need an escape from it. Unfortunately for too many, drugs and alcohol help alleviate that pain. If deaths of despair and the feeling of physical pain are linked beyond a simple correlation, the trend of increasing physical pain does not bode well for the world.

PART IV
Four Unanswered
Questions

So far in this book, I have discussed the global rise of unhappiness, how Gallup measures happiness and wellbeing, and where the world is falling short on the five elements of a great life. But our research has also produced discoveries that we cannot fully explain.

The first is related to a surprising gender parity. Without question, women face more hardships in life than men, yet they rate their lives similarly to men. Why is this?

The second involves Singapore. A Gallup report caused the media to brand Singapore as the "emotionless society." The data in that report remain true, but why did one of the most well-run societies in the world report such low positive *and* negative emotions?

The third involves the "Singapore of Africa," Rwanda. When looking at the list of the world's happiest countries, Rwanda ranks unusually low. How is that possible considering how successful Rwanda has been on virtually every development metric?

The fourth looks at 2020. The COVID-19 pandemic was devastating — pushing already high levels of stress, sadness, anger, and worry higher than ever — but how did people *see* their lives? People rated their lives in a way you wouldn't have expected.

The following chapters describe what we found.

CHAPTER FOURTEEN
How Are Women's Lives Going?

"I did it. There was no one else. I closed the latch and did it. The body is in the room," Sarvesh Kumar said as he walked toward a local police station in Uttar Pradesh, India.

Sarvesh was there to confess a heinous crime. Hours before, he had murdered his 17-year-old daughter, Neelam. Her crime? Dating a man he did not like.

Two bystanders pulled out their phones as he walked toward the police station because they wanted to capture the gruesome moment on video. While confessing the murder, Sarvesh was holding his daughter's severed head.

He was unfazed by what was happening. One person claimed that the father was holding a victory sign to the people recording the incident. More disturbingly, all of this took place in 2021, five days before International Women's Day.

If you search the internet for this incident, do not confuse it with the time this *exact* same thing happened in 2012, only in Rajasthan. The only difference is that the father in Rajasthan carried his daughter's severed head in one hand and a sword in the other.

The Global State of Women's Safety, Economic Opportunities, and Health

Neelam's death was unusually horrific, yet women face varying degrees of violence everywhere. According to the World Health Organization (WHO), one-third of women experience violence in their lifetime. In most cases, it is their partner harming them. In fact, two in three women say that domestic violence is a widespread problem in their country (nearly six in 10 men agree), according to the Hologic Global Women's Health Index. In some countries, such as Peru and Turkey, almost all women (94%) believe domestic violence is widespread.

Even the most extreme forms of violence against women are far too commonplace. For example, 3 million girls are at risk for genital mutilation each year. Modern slavery also disproportionately affects women. Seven in 10 of the more than 40 million people living in slavery are women and girls, according to the Walk Free Global Slavery Index. Additionally, 99% of the victims of forced labor in the commercial sex industry are women and girls.

The global figures are staggering, but the individual stories are even more tragic. Here is one example from 15-year-old Anita from Kenya — one of the thousands of women we interviewed about modern slavery:

> I was out grazing the cows when my father said it was time to get married. I was woken up early and circumcised. The elders said the man was to be my only husband. He was 55. I was very confused. I was only 10. Nine months later, because I had not given him a baby, he began tasking me with the difficult jobs. I decided I had to escape — he beat me so hard my leg wouldn't stop bleeding. I was taken in by the Catholic Sisters and started school in 2013. I hope to be a doctor.

In many countries, men are not even ashamed to admit to their complicity in gender violence. In dozens of countries, including India (35%) and Afghanistan (71%), more than one-third of men believe it is justified for men to beat their wives. Two reasons men give for spousal abuse are refusing sex with the husband or burning the food.

Many women live in constant fear of this violence. One-third of women worldwide — and a majority of women in 52 countries — are very worried that violent crime will cause them serious harm, according to the Lloyd's Register Foundation World Risk Poll.

Women not only fear domestic violence; they also worry about violence in the streets. Nearly one in three women say they do not feel safe walking alone at night in their community, compared with about one in five men. And, according to Gallup, there is no place in the world where women are more likely than men to say they feel safe walking alone at night.

Women also face unique economic challenges. Less than half of women participate in the global workforce, compared with roughly three-quarters of men. The workplace challenges for women are extensive, including some that are embedded deeply within countries' cultures. One of the most significant disparities is in India, where more than three-quarters of men participate in the workforce, compared with only one-fifth of women.

Unequal pay also remains a critical concern. In fact, people in the U.S. and in some of the Western world consider it the most significant issue facing women who work at paid jobs. Understandably so: Women receive 12.5% less pay than men in wealthy OECD countries.

In the informal sector in poorer countries, women earn almost half the pay that men earn. This is a considerable concern, but not the No. 1 concern for women in these countries. For them, the top issue is "abuse, harassment, discrimination, and generally unfair treatment at work," according to the report *Towards a better future for women and work: Voices of women and men* by the ILO and Gallup. Women in these countries also want equal pay, but first they want to feel safe.

Women's physical health is also a global concern. While over 30% of the world suffers from moderate or severe food insecurity, women are disproportionately affected. According to FAO, this has been true since they began tracking food insecurity.

More generally, 20% of women say they have health problems that prevent them from doing things people their age can normally do. The problem is so severe that the Hologic Global Women's Health Index finds that not a single country scores high enough on its index to receive a passing grade for women's physical health — stating in its 2020 report, "Every country or territory has room to improve."

How Women's Lives Are Going, According to Women

The global data on women's safety, economic opportunities, and physical health demonstrate the ongoing and unique difficulties for women everywhere. Considering these hardships, how do women rate their lives? And how do their ratings compare with men's ratings?

Surprisingly, women rate their lives *almost exactly the same as men*. This is not only true at the global level, it is true in every individual country since Gallup began tracking it. (Women even rate their lives *slightly higher* than men in some places.)

For example, in 2020, women in Switzerland rated their lives a 7.5 on average; men rated their lives exactly the same. In Afghanistan, women in 2019 rated their lives only a 2.2, which is also comparable to how men in Afghanistan rated their lives (2.6). This similarity is true *everywhere*. In fact, the statistical correlation between how women rate their lives and how men rate their lives is 0.96 (the highest value is 1).

Global Life Ratings by Gender

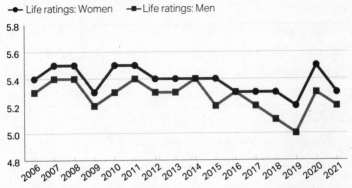

Respondents' perceptions of where they stand "at this time." Life ratings range from 0-10.
Source: Gallup

When people see these data, they often reject the results — and understandably so. Given the overwhelming information about the hardships women face globally, it is surprising that women and men would rate their lives so similarly everywhere.

I shared these trends with an official at the U.S. State Department. More specifically, she saw this chart, which shows how women and men rate their lives in Saudi Arabia:

Saudi Arabia: Life Ratings by Gender

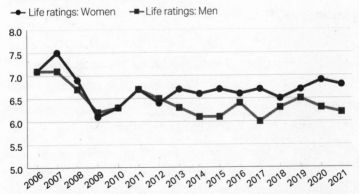

Respondents' perceptions of where they stand "at this time." Life ratings range from 0-10.
Source: Gallup

After seeing the chart, she said, "These data are wrong. Women have horrible lives in Saudi Arabia — everyone knows that."

She is right that women's lives in Saudi Arabia are far from perfect. Saudi women not only face the same challenges that women face globally, they also face challenges unique to women in Saudi Arabia. For example, women in Saudi Arabia could not drive until 2018.

But are the data wrong?

Just because women rate their lives the same as men does not mean women give their lives a *high* rating. Globally, women rate their lives only a 5.3. Additionally, only 28% of women — roughly 750 million — are thriving globally. This means that 72% of women (nearly 2 billion) are either struggling or suffering.

But again, why do women and men rate their lives so similarly?

To help answer this question, I turned to Brookings Senior Fellow and University of Maryland Professor Carol Graham, who is a foremost expert on wellbeing and one of the most cited female economists globally. In her influential paper *Gender and Well-Being around the World*, she says, "Women around the world have higher levels of well-being than men, regardless of which well-being question is used."

Summarizing the paper's findings, Graham told me, "We found that women were happier than men except in places where gender rights are super compromised. We also found that women's happiness dropped temporarily when gender rights improved." Graham's first statement seems intuitive, but her second statement is surprising.

Graham believes that this temporary decline in women's happiness might be because people who previously had the power (men) didn't like it changing. She states that the very act of challenging gender norms can temporarily make things more difficult for women, as the men in their lives may not want the gender roles to change, thus creating tension in the workplace and at home.

Another explanation for this temporary decline has to do with expectations. According to Graham, when women expect greater gender rights — and then receive those rights — they do not necessarily see an immediate increase in their wellbeing precisely because they already expected to have those rights in the first place.

To elucidate her point, Graham cites a study from Switzerland that looked at the wellbeing of women following an equal rights referendum in 1981. The researchers wanted to know how women's wellbeing was affected after the resolution passed — more specifically, they compared the wellbeing of working women in the cantons that voted for the referendum with the wellbeing of working women in the cantons that voted against it.

Of the 26 cantons in Switzerland, 17 voted in favor of the referendum, and nine voted against it. The researchers found that in the cantons that voted *for* the referendum, working women and men rated their lives the same; but in the cantons that voted *against* the referendum, working women rated their lives *higher* than men did.

Graham and coauthor Soumya Chattopadhyay concluded that the "… higher expectations in the more liberal Swiss cantons likely affected the life and job satisfaction of women, at least in the short term." Graham's research shows that gender rights are critical to improving women's wellbeing everywhere, but implementing them may come with temporary declines in wellbeing.

Maybe comparing women's wellbeing to men's is the wrong analysis. Maybe women rating their lives similarly to men is exactly what we should have expected.

I interviewed former Ambassador Robin Renee Sanders, who served as the U.S. ambassador to the Republic of Congo and Nigeria, about why women and men rate their lives so similarly. "Rarely do women compare themselves to how men *feel*. But how they feel and how the world *treats* women are different issues," Sanders told me.

She further said, "The only one who underestimates women are men, and it is mostly men that say, 'This is not for a woman.' Women may lack financial resources, education, and opportunity, and may even face incredible life hardships, but women always believe they can achieve something."

While Sanders' experience spans the globe, she is widely known for her work with the Uli women of Nigeria, about whom she authored a book. She is also known for her leadership during the reconstruction efforts in the Republic of Congo, where she worked with UNDP to build the country's first post-civil-war internet centers:

> From my time in Congo-Brazzaville, which was destroyed by civil war seven years prior to me arriving and nothing had been rebuilt, it was the women to whom my embassy team and I gave small loans in order to create income-generating projects, which was the precursor to small- to medium-sized businesses in developing regions like Africa. It was the women that always did the most with the loans and turned them into something sustainable for their families. The majority were not formally educated and alphabeted, and they were victims of the civil war or other violence.

She goes on to say, "The resilience I have seen from women around the world, after having experienced or gone through all the difficult challenges I noted earlier, has always been incredible not only to see, but also to respect."

Her analysis makes clear that women are probably not taking their cues from men in terms of how their lives are going. And her mention of "resilience" is worth further exploration.

"The setbacks women have faced globally is what make them more resilient," Shauna Olney, former chief of the Gender, Equality and Diversity branch at the ILO, told me. Olney's extensive experience positioned her to lead the ILO's women at work centenary initiative, and more recently she became a member of the International Civil Service Commission. She was also named as one of the 100 most influential people in gender policy by Apolitical.

Citing research by Graham, which reviewed a study of young women in Latin America, Olney told me, "Those with the highest aspirations are the ones with the most negative shocks in their life. It is harder to be resilient to shocks if you've never faced them." Although experiencing shocks in life may lead to more resilience, there is probably a threshold. Olney further said, "Like how there is a limit to how income can impact your life, there might also be a limit to how many setbacks you can take when it comes to resilience."

Olney also emphasizes the link between a woman's wellbeing and her family, saying, "Women undertake over 75% of unpaid care work. The connection with the family is statistically strong. You've got that investment in the family; the investment in the future." According to previous research, she finds that, "When you support women, when you give them money, they will use it for their family, and they will use it for education. It was the women that deprive themselves before their families."

Olney stresses that Gallup's wellbeing data may be uncovering a resiliency shared by women globally. And investments in women are not only good for women, they are also good for all of society.

Julie Ray, the managing editor of Gallup's World News, shared a similar perspective: "There's a reason why there's such a strong relationship between how women rate their lives and the U.N.'s Human Development Index. What's good for women is good for everyone."

Ray has analyzed all of Gallup's global data and, more specifically, all of Gallup's gender-related wellbeing data. She also finds that what is *bad* for women is bad for everyone. "Countries where women rate their lives the worst tend to be experiencing instability, such as Afghanistan, where just 1% of women rated their lives positively enough in 2019 to be considered thriving. Numbers were also in the single digits in Lebanon and Zimbabwe that same year — both countries saw massive protests and unrest."

Where Women Are Thriving and Suffering

Most likely to be **thriving**

Rank	Country	Thriving
1	Finland	75%
	Iceland	75%
3	Denmark	71%
4	Sweden	64%
5	Netherlands	63%
6	Switzerland	62%
7	Israel	60%
	Norway	60%
9	Canada	59%
	Luxembourg	59%
11	New Zealand	58%
	United Arab Emirates	58%

Most likely to be **suffering**

Rank	Country	Suffering
1	Afghanistan	94%
2	Lebanon	51%
3	Rwanda	39%
4	India	35%
5	Zimbabwe	34%
6	Chad	33%
7	Mauritania	28%
8	Lesotho	26%
9	Tanzania	25%
10	Pakistan	24%
11	Zambia	23%

Averaged over 2019-2021.

Source: Gallup

These rankings closely align with the U.N.'s Gender Inequality Index, which quantifies the loss of achievement in a country due to gender inequality. It uses reproductive health, empowerment, and labor market participation as its inputs.

"The countries where women are most likely to be thriving are developed countries with low gender inequality," Ray found. "In Finland, Iceland, and Denmark — all countries at the top of the U.N. Gender Inequality Index — more than seven in 10 women are thriving."

Overall development and gender equality might help explain why women rate their lives so similarly to men. But how do women *experience* life compared with men?

In 2021, women experienced more physical pain, sadness, worry, anger, and stress than men. The gaps have widened over time. In 2006, the average gender gap across all these measures was two points. Now, it is four points — which is mostly driven by physical pain and sadness.

The global gender gap would be wider if not for China, which represents more than one-seventh of the world's population. Reported negative emotions are nearly the same for women and men in China, which has been true throughout the history of our tracking. On the other hand, India, which represents another one-seventh of the world, has a wider gender gap. From 2019-2021, the Negative Experience Index for women in India was nine points higher compared with men.

Where Women Are Most and Least Likely to Experience Negative Emotions

Most likely to experience negative emotions

Rank	Country	Score
1	Afghanistan	61
2	Iraq	57
3	Lebanon	55
4	Rwanda	53
5	Jordan	51
6	Sierra Leone	50
	Peru	50
	Chad	50
9	Libya	48
10	Ecuador	47
	Iran	47
	Bolivia	47

Least likely to experience negative emotions

Rank	Country	Score
146	Azerbaijan	14
	Taiwan, Province of China	14
	Kazakhstan	14
143	Turkmenistan	18
142	Singapore	19
	Mauritius	19
140	Estonia	21
139	Mongolia	22
	Belarus	22
	Kosovo	22

The Negative Experience Index is a composite measure of the five negative experiences (anger, stress, sadness, physical pain, and worry). Index scores range from zero to 100. Averaged over 2019-2021.

Source: Gallup

For the most part, this list corresponds with the global ranking for men. But it is important to note that women are more likely than men to experience negative emotions in almost all countries we measure. The two regions where women are significantly more likely to experience negative emotions are the Middle East and North Africa (MENA) and Latin America.

There is more than a 10-point gender gap in the Negative Experience Index in countries such as Libya, Peru, and Guatemala. Cultural norms that are extremely harmful to women explain some of these gaps. In Libya, for example, 53% of women experience physical pain on a daily basis, compared with 38% of men.

Latin America presents its own unique hardships for women. As one example, Ecuador gave women the right to vote in 1929 — 10 years after the U.S. But in Ecuador, voting was limited to literate women. It was not until 1979 that Ecuador dropped the literacy requirement.

More recent increases in women's negative emotions may be attributable to COVID-19, but the tendency for women to experience more negative emotions than men predates the pandemic. According to previous research, crises such as financial downturns, war, and disease outbreaks may place a disproportionate burden on women. As we will explore later, the pandemic was harder on women everywhere — particularly women with children.

A Better World for Women

How women see and experience life varies considerably by the wealth, development, and stability of the countries where they live. But three of the most significant opportunities for improving women's lives everywhere are personal safety, economic opportunities, and helping with child care.

As I previously mentioned, the largest gender gaps in Gallup's entire database outside of economic opportunities have to do with personal safety. Building safer communities for women is especially important to improve their wellbeing. Safety and security are the foundation of a great society — and improvement would pay wellbeing dividends not just for women but for society as a whole.

In terms of economic opportunities, a great job — steady work, a paycheck, and being engaged and thriving in their work — improves women's wellbeing significantly. Women with great jobs are more likely to be thriving in life and much less likely to be suffering compared with women in all other employment categories, including those who are out of the workforce or unemployed.

Increasing women's participation in the workplace, particularly in emerging markets where gender gaps are the widest, would improve women's wellbeing and fuel economic growth in their countries.

Women also need help with child care. According to Gallup's global data, the more children women have, the less likely they are to have a good job, because the burden of child care falls disproportionately on them. (See References for table: Percentage of Women and Men in the Workplace by Number of Children in Household.)

The Positive

Despite the adversities women face, most still find a way to experience the positive side of life, and in some cases, more often than men.

In 2020, 74% of women worldwide said they smiled and laughed a lot, compared with 71% of men. The difference between those two figures may not seem like a lot, but that three-point difference accounts for more than 75 million women. And Gallup has always found that women are more likely than men to report smiling and laughing a lot.

Women are also more likely than men to say that they are treated with respect. In 2020, 87% of women said they were treated with respect, compared with 84% of men. Seventy-two percent of women expressed feeling a lot of enjoyment, and that same number said they felt well-rested.

One reason women have more positive experiences might be because they have more and better relationships with family and friends. Gallup finds that people who have high social wellbeing also experience more positive emotions. Having several close friends also probably means you have a lot more fun.

A few years ago, a Gallup interviewer in Colombia shared a story with us about an interview she conducted with a middle-aged woman in a very poor area of the country:

> When we asked about her positive experiences, she started laughing and couldn't stop. It took us a long time to finish the interview because she was having so much fun sharing her stories. At the end of the interview, she thanked us for listening to her stories and helping her remember good memories. And then she said, "No one has asked me about how I feel and if I laugh. This time with you helped me forget all the hard times I am living now." She smiled and went back to her day-to-day reality.

The woman we interviewed that day had a difficult life, but she still found a way to have fun — even if it was with strangers.

Why women rate their lives the same as men in every country is still something we cannot completely explain. But regardless, too many women globally rate their lives poorly — and that needs to change.

Women everywhere deserve a better world. And to build a better world, leaders need more indicators that give women the primary role in telling the story of how their lives are going.

CHAPTER FIFTEEN
The Emotionless Society

"All work and no play" may have indeed made us a dull society.

— CheeTung Leong, CEO and Co-Founder,
EngageRocket, Singapore

Singapore is one of the most admired countries in the world — so admired, some countries aspire to be just like it. Global leaders admit to using Singapore's journey as the blueprint for their own countries, including Kazakhstan's first president, Nursultan Nazarbayev.

The admiration for Singapore might be because its success is so easy to quantify. And a great deal of that success is just economics. When it comes to money, Singapore is rich — ranking in the top 10 of GDP per capita, regardless of whether you look at purchasing power parity or nominal GDP.

But wealth is not the only reason Singapore is so revered.

Singapore is fourth in the world for life expectancy (83.6 years) and tied for 11th for human development, according to the HDI 2019 ranking. It also has an unusually strong jobs market, according to traditional employment metrics. Unemployment has not exceeded 6% in over 20 years of tracking. This is remarkable considering 5% is what many economists consider the natural rate of unemployment (or "full employment").

Singapore is also one of the safest places in the world. If you have ever walked down the city's streets late at night, you can feel it. And the data substantiate that feeling.

In 2021, nearly all Singaporeans (95%) said they feel safe walking alone at night. While that number is high, it is not unusual for Singapore. Gallup has been asking this question since 2006, and every year, over 85% of Singaporeans say they feel safe walking alone at night. Singapore has ranked No. 1 globally on this metric 11 times in the history of our tracking.

The country is not only rich, healthy, well-educated, and safe — the city even sparkles. First-time visitors are struck by the city's cleanliness. Driving from the Changi Singapore Airport to the city, you cannot help but notice how clean the streets are and how perfectly manicured the trees and bushes are. It feels like everything is perfect in Singapore.

But is it?

In early 2012, I flew to Singapore to join my colleagues for a presentation to a large group of government officials. The government wanted to learn more about what Gallup knows about happiness in the country.

Before the meeting, I looked at our 2011 data for Singapore. Almost all our data corroborated the conventional wisdom — everything was perfect.

We asked Singaporeans whether children had the opportunity to learn and grow and if they felt like children were treated with respect. Almost everyone in the country agreed, and Singapore ranked among the highest in the world on both metrics.

Singaporeans also trust their government. In fact, the Singapore government received some of the highest confidence ratings globally. And less than 10% of Singaporeans felt like corruption was widespread in the government.

Even when we ask questions on basic numeracy, Singaporeans show how smart they are compared with the rest of the world. We once asked, "Do you think 10% is bigger than one out of 10, the same as one in 10, or smaller than one in 10?" (The correct answer is, of course, they are the same.) Only 40% of people globally get it right. In Singapore, 76% get it right, ranking it ninth out of the 141 countries we tested.

But while almost everything looked perfect in Singapore, one thing did not — the way Singaporeans responded to Gallup's life experience questions.

Before we look at how Singaporeans *live* life, let's look at how they *see* life. About one-third (34%) of Singaporeans rated their lives high enough to be considered thriving in 2011. The global average that year was 24%. Considering Singapore outperforms the world in almost everything, it is no surprise that it also exceeded the global average for thriving.

But now, look at how Singaporeans *live* life. Here is the Positive Experience Index trend in Singapore from 2006-2011.

Singapore: Positive Experience Index

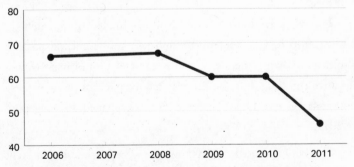

The Positive Experience Index is a composite measure of the five positive experiences (enjoyment, learning or doing something interesting, feeling well-rested, smiling and laughing, and feeling treated with respect). Index scores range from zero to 100.

Source: Gallup

The dramatic drop is not the only surprise. Globally, out of the 148 countries we measured in 2011, Singapore ranked *dead last*.

This decline made me wonder: If positive emotions are plummeting, then negative emotions must be skyrocketing. If people are not having fun, then they must be angry, sad, worried, or at least stressed? Right?

Apparently not. Here is the Negative Experience Index trend in Singapore from 2006-2011.

Singapore: Negative Experience Index

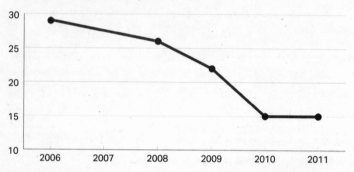

The Negative Experience Index is a composite measure of the five negative experiences (anger, stress, sadness, physical pain, and worry). Index scores range from zero to 100.

Source: Gallup

I should have known better. Norman Bradburn's research (as I mentioned in Chapter Four) found just how unrelated positive and negative experiences can be. You can feel a lot of positive *and* negative emotions, but you can also feel very little of any of these emotions — which is apparently what happened in Singapore in 2011.

This finding caused us to rethink how we report our data entirely. We typically report two rankings: one that ranks the countries with the highest positive emotions and one that ranks the countries with the highest negative emotions. But what if we combined them? This would allow us to see which countries are most likely to report a lot of emotions, regardless of whether those emotions are positive or negative.

The country that expressed the most emotions that year was the Philippines. People in the Philippines were the most likely to tell us that they felt a lot of enjoyment, laughed and smiled a lot, felt rested, *and* felt a lot of anger, stress, and sadness. Latin America dominated the rest of the list, which also included the U.S. and Canada.

But the country that was least likely to express *any* emotions? Singapore.

Most and Least Reported Emotions Globally

Most reported emotions

Rank	Country	Yes
1	Philippines	60%
2	El Salvador	57%
3	Bahrain	56%
4	Oman	55%
	Colombia	55%
6	Chile	54%
	Costa Rica	54%
	Canada	54%
	Guatemala	54%
	Bolivia	54%
	Ecuador	54%
	Dominican Republic	54%
	Peru	54%
	Nicaragua	54%
	United States	54%

Least reported emotions

Rank	Country	Yes
151	Singapore*	36%
150	Georgia	37%
	Lithuania	37%
148	Russia	38%
	Madagascar	38%
	Ukraine	38%
	Belarus	38%
	Kazakhstan	38%
	Nepal	38%
	Kyrgyzstan	38%

*Singapore's 2011 measure was 30%.

Did you feel well-rested yesterday? Were you treated with respect all day yesterday? Did you smile and laugh a lot yesterday? Did you learn or do something interesting yesterday? Did you experience the following feelings during a lot of the day yesterday? How about (enjoyment, physical pain, worry, sadness, stress, anger)? Averaged over 2009-2011.

Source: Gallup

When we first launched these results in 2012, they went viral. The findings were covered on the front page of *The Straits Times* for three days in a row, including a scathing dissent written by former Senior Minister of State for Law and Education Indranee Rajah.

Social media also erupted. "That [poll] is a lie," commented one person. Another posted several videos on YouTube of a day in the life of an "Emotionless Singaporean," which simply followed a Singaporean with an expressionless look on his face around Singapore.

Critics of the findings said the underlying methodology was flawed. Maybe they're right. When someone conducts a survey and says in the fine print, "The margin of error is plus or minus three percentage points with a confidence interval of 95%," that means that one out of 20 times, the data point may fall outside that range.

But were the results also wrong the year before that? And how about the year before that? In 2010, Singapore ranked 93rd out of 120 countries for positive emotions, and in 2009, 87th out of 115 countries. 2011 was not an outlier — the scores were low for three straight years.

If the data are accurate, why did Singapore have such an emotions deficit? Here are three possible explanations:

First, a society that relentlessly pursues money does so at the expense of everything that makes life worth living.

Singapore was under British control for over a century and then, in the 1960s, was briefly part of Malaysia. That ended on August 9, 1965, and Singapore became independent.

Although independent, the country was struggling by every objective indicator. Most Singaporeans were unemployed, and GDP per capita was low. Singapore had limited natural resources, and the international community had no interest in helping the country.

Under the leadership of Lee Kuan Yew, the country turned to its most valuable resource — its people. Lee's original strategy focused on manufacturing and bringing in foreign investment. It worked. From 1966-1973, the country experienced double-digit economic growth annually. Singapore continued to invest in its people, and the country went from poor to rich in a matter of decades. Nominal GDP per capita increased from $320 in 1960 to almost $60,000 in 2019 — PPP GDP per capita was $100,000.

Some believe that the country's work ethic to escape poverty may have become too deeply engrained in the culture. For example, Singaporeans openly talk about the "Five Cs" culture, which stands for your cash, car, credit card, condominium, and country club membership. The concept is so well-known, it even has its own Wikipedia page.

Did "All work and no play," in the words of Singapore native CheeTung Leong, cause Singapore to be a dull society?

Bobby Kennedy and Bhutan's Fourth Dragon King would have thought so. They believed that the overzealous pursuit of money causes people to lose sight of what really matters in life. There is merit to this famous observation, but it does not appear to apply to Singapore. Singaporeans work hard, but working hard does not necessarily make people miserable. *Miserable work* makes people miserable. This leads to the second potential reason for the 2011 emotions deficit.

Singapore was unrivaled when it comes to misery in the workplace.

Singapore's work ethic is famous. In 2015, Singaporeans worked more hours per week (45.6 hours) than any other developed city in the world except for Hong Kong (50.1 hours). Millennials work even longer. Singaporean millennials worked more hours than millennials in every other country except India (and they were tied with Chinese and Mexican millennials), according to a 2016 report by ManpowerGroup.

Singapore's Ministry of Manpower has actively worked to address this issue and is making progress. But is the number of hours that Singaporeans work what is taking the life out of Singapore? Or is it what happens *during* those working hours?

In 2011, there was no workplace more emotionally detached than Singapore. Only 2% of Singaporean workers were engaged and thriving in their jobs — the lowest in the world.

Singaporeans not only worked among the most hours in the world, they also had among the highest workforce participation rates. So, everyone worked, everyone worked a lot, and everyone hated their work. *That* could make any society numb.

But here is a problem. Hating your job decreases your positive emotions, but it *increases* your negative emotions. Positive emotions were extremely low in Singapore, but so were negative emotions. If workplace misery was a contributing factor, it was only contributing to lower positive experiences.

This brings us to the third potential reason for the emotions deficit: Singaporeans excel in something else globally — modesty.

According to Singaporean psychiatrist Adrian Wang, "We're less inclined to make a big show of how we feel. It may be because we're a bit more conservative and tend to keep things to ourselves. But when we're warmed up, we can be quite expressive — take a look at our National Day celebrations."

People in many rich Asian societies rate their lives lower than you might think, considering their countries' wealth. Take Japan, for example. In the 2020 *World Happiness Report*, Japan ranked 58th out of 158 countries. That put Japan below Costa Rica, Mexico, and Guatemala. Japan's GDP per capita is roughly 10 times larger than Guatemala's. Yet, Guatemalans rate their lives higher than the Japanese.

Researchers have established that, for cultural reasons, Latin Americans are more expressive in reporting how their lives are going. On the other hand, Asians appear to exhibit more modesty when rating many things, especially their lives.

This modesty is often attributed to many Asian societies' embrace of collectivism, which stresses the importance of the community. As a result, self-ratings are humble because collectivist cultures focus less on the individual and more on society. This may explain why Singaporeans and people in other Asian societies give higher ratings on societal matters, such as how children are treated or how institutions are performing.

By the way, we cannot minimize the positive ratings of Latin Americans. Latin Americans find a way to experience more fun in life than the rest of the world despite having less money. We should celebrate this and try to understand it more deeply because the world has a lot to gain from whatever they have figured out.

To better understand these cultural differences, Gallup began a project with the Japan-based Well-being for Planet Earth Foundation. The project's objective is to develop a more all-encompassing metric for happiness for the entire world. As of this writing, we are in the field testing to see if we can build statistics for concepts such as balance and harmony. Our research is still in the early stages.

But Is it Cultural?

If the results in Singapore were strictly cultural, how did Singapore reverse the trend on positive emotions?

Singapore went from ranking dead last on the Positive Experience Index in 2011 to 67th in 2012. In 2014, it climbed to 14th, and ever since, Singapore has remained in the top quartile for the world.

Positive Emotions in Singapore

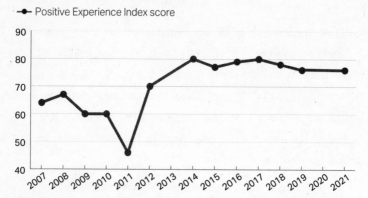

The Positive Experience Index is a composite measure of the five positive experiences (enjoyment, learning or doing something interesting, feeling well-rested, smiling and laughing, and feeling treated with respect). Index scores range from zero to 100.

Source: Gallup

So What Happened?

Curiously, the only other indicator that improved during this time was worker engagement. From 2011 to 2012, engagement improved seven points (to 9%); in 2015, it increased to 16%, putting Singapore 100 spots higher in the global rankings. The sudden increase might make you wonder if something happened nationally. We know that managers are consistently the most significant influence in worker engagement, but the sudden increase in Singapore may have resulted from government action.

The Singapore government has recently enacted legislation to curb abusive workplace practices. For example, workers covered by the Employment Act can work a maximum of 44 hours a week. They also cannot work more than 12 hours per day or more than 72 hours of overtime per month. Prime Minister Lee Hsien Loong also reduced the country's workweek from five-and-a-half days to five days. Working hours have indeed declined consistently since 2010, according to Singapore's Ministry of Manpower.

But national policy alone will not fix Singapore's workplace woes. Gallup knows that the adage "People join companies but leave managers" is true and is supported by data. Seventy percent of a person's emotional attachment to work is determined by who their manager is. Pick a bad manager, and no matter how good national policy is, workers will still be miserable.

Singapore's workforce development strategies have been shifting toward improving engagement since 2011 — including moving away from tenure-based progression to performance-based development. This alone could account for rising engagement because it implies that managers are more effectively supporting Singapore's workers. For example, in 2015, Singaporeans were significantly more likely to say that they have opportunities to do what they do best at work and that there is someone at work who encourages their development.

Better workplaces may not be the only reason Singapore's positive emotions increased. When Gallup first reported Singapore's 2011 emotions data, it went so viral that *everyone* heard about it. Its ubiquity may have even influenced the survey results. When we conducted interviews the following year, Singaporean respondents told us during the survey, "I know what this survey is about."

Private sector organizations even ran campaigns featuring the findings — promoting how great and how happy Singapore is. Advertisements ran in newspapers, on billboards, and in movie theaters. Since those campaigns, Singapore's scores have remained unusually high for positive emotions and very low for negative emotions.

So, did Singaporeans' emotions truly improve, or was everyone simply trying to boost Singapore's score on the index?

Singapore has figured out the secret to success for almost everything. If the country indeed meaningfully improved positive emotions, the world would benefit greatly from knowing what Singapore did.

CHAPTER SIXTEEN
A Letter to Rwandan President Paul Kagame

Mr. President,

You recently took issue with the *World Happiness Report* and Gallup's global project to understand how people's lives are going. Here is what you said during a speech at Columbia University on September 26, 2019:

> But today, I would like to say a bit more about the intangibles of the development process. Numbers tell us a lot. But behind the data, you find real people.

> The progress we have seen over time in Rwanda is the result of a deliberate effort to nurture our unity. It is not just because we have capable women and men formulating and carrying out policy. Of course we do, and that is very important.

> However, it is really about citizens themselves being part of the whole process. Each one of them, in some way, is in the driver's seat, making sure that things happen which benefit them, their families, and the wider community.

> You see, well-being has both objective and subjective dimensions. You cannot dictate how people should feel. People who feel hopeful about their lives are not going to change their minds because you tell them the data show they should actually be unhappy.

Africans are constantly subject to this kind of gas-lighting. It is as if the reality we know and live and see requires external validation. You begin to doubt your own perception, which is, of course, the whole point. ...

[For example, there] is an annual survey known as the *World Happiness Report*. The goal is laudable. Gross Domestic Product is not the only measure of development. And yet Rwanda always ranks near the bottom, alongside countries mired in conflict.

How could the citizens of the most improved country in the history of the United Nations *Human Development Report* also be amongst the world's most miserable? There is a contradiction here.

We looked into it. It turns out that the *World Happiness Report* is based on a single question from the Gallup World Poll. The way that question is phrased leads Rwandans to answer very pessimistically, for cultural reasons.

In the same survey, Rwandans report high rates of positive and happy experiences every day. Ironically, the question on happiness is not used in the *World Happiness Report*. The organisers agree the ranking makes no sense. And yet, year after year, the same absurd conclusion is published.

It takes real determination to stay committed to the reality in front of our eyes.

I think it is time to have better conversations. Partnership has been a very significant part of Rwanda's story. We have benefited greatly by being open to the ideas and experiences of others and applying them to our situation.

As Gallup's CEO, I feel compelled to respond.

First, let me be clear. You are right. Rwanda's ranking in the *World Happiness Report* (*WHR*) is shocking — so shocking that I too have wondered if the data are wrong.

People in the survey research community often say, "I can tell you with 95% confidence that these data are accurate within a margin of error of plus or minus three percentage points" — meaning there is a 5% chance that the data are wrong. Rwanda's ranking toward the bottom of the *WHR* actually made me wonder if that might be the case here.

But what if the data are not wrong?

Gallup has conducted this study in Rwanda since 2006. Every time, the results are the same. Rwandans rate their lives very poorly every time we interview them, and the country always ends up near the bottom of our international rankings.

Here is the trend since we began conducting this survey in Rwanda.

Rwanda: Life Ratings

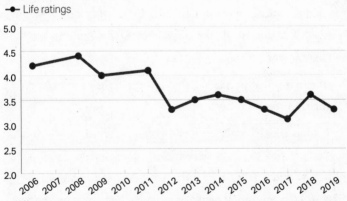

Respondents' perceptions of where they stand "at this time." Life ratings range from 0-10.

Source: Gallup

Rwandans rated their lives the highest in 2008 (an average of 4.4). That year, Rwanda tied for 94th out of 115 countries, which was Rwanda's highest global ranking ever. In 2019, Rwandans rated their lives an average of 3.3, which ranked Rwanda 142nd out of 145 countries.

Rwanda does not belong near the bottom of these rankings precisely because the country has been exceptional with respect to development. Every objective indicator shows just how successful Rwanda has been over the past two and a half decades. Indicators like GDP growth, child mortality, school enrollment, and life expectancy all show that Rwanda has not just made improvements, but excelled. The country's success is so well-known globally that some refer to Rwanda as "the Singapore of Africa."

So if Rwanda has excelled on virtually every objective measure, then why do people continue to rate their lives so bad?

Whatever the disconnect is, it is a problem. Either there is a methodological challenge, or people's lives are not going as well as we think they are. Maybe this is a case study for why chasing GDP growth too quickly hurts livelihoods. Or maybe it is something entirely different. Here are three hypotheses for why Rwandans rank their lives so low.

The first is that people are afraid to speak their minds, and they rate their lives worse because of it.

Gallup asks Rwandans — and people everywhere — whether they are confident in their national government, local police, military, and judicial system and courts. And the responses we get to these questions in Rwanda are astonishing. Almost everyone expresses confidence in those institutions.

You and your government receive some of the highest approval ratings in the world — and it has been this way throughout the entire history of our tracking. Look at how Rwanda's institutions performed compared with the global averages:

Confidence in Governmental Institutions

	Global median	Rwanda	Rwanda's 2019 global rank
National government	48%	99%	No. 1
Local police force	66%	94%	No. 1
The military	72%	98%	No. 1
Judicial system and courts	51%	91%	No. 1

Do you have confidence in each of the following, or not? How about …? Percentage responding yes. 2019.

Source: Gallup

Rwanda is No. 1 in *every category*. There appears to be universal agreement that each aspect of the government is functioning well. And this is what Rwandans report *every single year*.

We even asked specifically about you, Mr. President: "Do you approve or disapprove of the job performance of President Paul Kagame?" The last time we did the survey, all 1,000 of the people we interviewed said they approved of your job performance. Again, this is highly unusual. This is also the highest approval rating for any leader we have ever recorded.

You are familiar with these trends. When Fareed Zakaria interviewed you on CNN in 2012, you used these figures to defend yourself from his inquiry about whether Rwanda's tremendous progress was "done with the absence of democracy."

> **ZAKARIA:** There is the perception that while you have been able to institute a very good sense of rule of law in Rwanda, economic growth, it has all been done with the absence of

democracy. The way "The Economist", which praises Rwanda in its article puts it, the elections are a sham. Many people feel that your party has extraordinary and unfair advantages over other parties.

KAGAME: Well, it is said like that from the outside. When you come to the country, the situation is entirely different. And in fact even partly from outside, if you look at, say, the Gallup polls that have recently been carried out in Rwanda on everything, they show the confidence that people have in the institutions, people have in the government. They all score above 85 percent. Better than you can witness in any African country or even other countries outside. This is ...

ZAKARIA: But you understand the suspicion people have. You win the elections with 95 percent of the vote. I mean--

KAGAME: Yes.

ZAKARIA: That's the kind of margin that Mubarak used to win with in Egypt.

KAGAME: Right.

ZAKARIA: And so at least people think either you are wildly popular ...

KAGAME: Yes.

ZAKARIA: ... or there's something going on.

KAGAME: You see, but that's where the problem is. Those judging from outside would never accept that there is an issue of popularity in Rwanda or in Africa. Whenever that issue comes up, of popularity, they call it a dictatorship. They think popularity is a preserve of developed countries. But in other situations, leaders can be popular and unpopular.

ZAKARIA: And popular is one thing, but winning 95 percent of the vote is another.

KAGAME: Absolutely. But you see, you have to put all matters in context. If you take it out of context, then you lose the point. One, I have told you about outsiders coming to the country and assessing the feelings of the citizens of our country. Which they have interacted with independently and at all levels, the score is very high. This is a practical thing, this is a fact. Now, the other is in that context, you have to know where Rwanda is coming from. Rwanda the other day, 18 years ago, starting from scratch. In fact, supposed to be a failed state. And it has come out of that. People rallied around the leadership that was there and building on their own effort and a desire to be out of this situation, this is what produces the kind of things you see. (*Transcript from CNN website*)

Your defense is persuasive. We should not impose the West's views or beliefs on Rwanda, but we can ask this question: Are Rwandans telling us the truth?

Maybe they don't feel like they can freely express themselves. And freedom is important. According to the 2019 *WHR*, a sense of freedom matters significantly in the making of a great life.

One way to evaluate the freedom of a country is through the Human Freedom Index produced by the Cato Institute. In 2020, it found that Rwanda ranked 78th out of 162 countries with respect to freedom. Rwanda received this middle-of-the-pack ranking because while the country excels in *economic* freedom (ranking 59th), it performs poorly on *personal* freedom (ranking *102nd*).

The latter evaluates personal freedoms such as religion, movement, and assembly. Seven subindexes are compiled to determine a country's final score for personal freedom. Of the subindexes, Rwanda ranks the worst on the Association, Assembly, and Civil Society subindex, which covers these political freedoms: civil society entry and exit, assembly, freedom to form political parties, autonomy of opposition parties, and civil society repression. Rwanda also receives a score of zero for media freedom in a separate subindex.

The impact of freedom of expression is hard to quantify, but it could be affecting how Rwandans rate their lives.

The second hypothesis for why Rwandans rank their lives so low is that there may be a measurement issue. Our survey questionnaire could be creating confusion with one of the government's most popular benefits schemes.

The *Ubudehe* classification system is the Rwandan government's program to determine which people qualify for education and healthcare benefits. The level of benefits a person receives is determined by where they rate in this classification.

The classifications are straightforward: Every person is categorized using a number system from one to four. A one means that you are part of the lowest income group in Rwanda, and you receive the maximum benefits from the government. If you receive a four, it means that you are among the wealthiest people in Rwanda, and you receive the least benefits. Getting in a lower category gets you more benefits from the government.

Now imagine someone comes to your house, knocks on your door, and says, "Rate your life on a scale of zero to 10." If you thought you were being asked a question that might affect how you are categorized in the Ubudehe classification system, you might want to score it as low as possible to increase your chances of receiving more benefits from the government. If this confusion were happening — it could unintentionally lower scores for the entire country.

However, when we begin each of our interviews, we are clear about the purpose of the survey. This theory would mean that people are getting confused despite interviewers explicitly telling them what the survey is about. Plus, the Ubudehe classification is a 4-point scale, and our life evaluation question is an 11-point scale (zero to 10). This hypothesis is a stretch, but it is possible.

Of course, in December 2021, the government changed the Ubudehe classification categories from numbers to letters (A-E). While we have not conducted a survey in Rwanda since 2019, future surveys may help us understand if people were confusing Gallup's zero to 10 life evaluation scale with the numerical Ubudehe classification system.

The third possible reason why the happiness scores in Rwanda rank low may have to do with how the perpetrators of the 1994 genocide and their families rate their lives — an idea I first heard from a bishop in Rwanda.

I will never forget meeting this bishop. During one of my visits to Rwanda, I drove about two hours outside of Kigali to speak with this well-known and very influential religious figure. He operates out of a small community center, which is where I met with him.

The bishop got down to business before I even sat down. He had his iPad with him, and on the screen was the *World Happiness Report*. He held up his device, showed me the image of the *WHR*, looked at me, and said, "You know this is rubbish, right?"

I knew beforehand that he hated the results of the *WHR* — like so many leaders in Rwanda — so I was not surprised when he said it. "Well, let's start there," I said. "Why do you think that?"

He told me what I had heard from so many other Rwandan leaders before: Rwanda was a shining city on a hill for Africa, and any objective measure will tell you that.

I was not there to persuade him that the data were right; I was there to listen. But most of the meeting failed to produce any new insights. He talked about why Rwanda was having so much success and said that Gallup's data were wrong. He kept talking, and it was starting to get dark out.

So I took a different approach. "What if we assume for the moment that the results of the survey are right? Let's assume that Rwandans actually rate their lives as low as that report says. If it were true — why would they rate their lives like that?" I asked him.

I could tell that the question surprised him. He sat back and really thought about it. Honestly, I was surprised he even entertained the question.

After sitting in silence, he paused, looked at me, and offered one of the most profound insights in wellbeing research I have ever heard.

"As you know, our country went through a devastating genocide in 1994. One out of every 10 people in my country died. Everyone lost someone. But I do not think it is the victims of the genocide that are rating their lives badly. I think the people who might be rating their lives lowly are not the victims, but the perpetrators."

When people from the West see Rwanda's poor rankings in the *World Happiness Report*, they tend to think about the one thing they are most familiar with about Rwanda — the 1994 genocide.

As you know, Rwanda became a colony of Belgium following World War I. And while distinctions based on class existed during prior German rule and perhaps longer, the Belgians made it official. According to the Belgians, the minority of the population — the Tutsis — had physical and cultural characteristics that distinguished them from the Hutus, the majority. The Belgians considered the Tutsis to be taller and more affluent than the Hutus and therefore put them in charge of the country. This caused the Hutus to resent the Tutsis.

In 1962, Rwanda became independent. The Hutus took power not long after a military coup under Juvénal Habyarimana in 1973. His presidency lasted 20 years, with Tutsi-Hutu relations descending into civil war in the early 1990s. Then, with international support, the warring parties signed a truce known as the Arusha Accords. And although the conflict ended, it did not ease tensions.

The climate was best described by what was on the airwaves. Hutu radio shows openly referred to Tutsis as cockroaches and called for their extermination. The country was doused with so much emotional kerosene that one match could put Rwanda in flames.

That match was lit on April 6, 1994. That day, President Habyarimana's plane was shot down, killing him and everyone else on board. That moment kicked off one of the bloodiest periods in world history — a genocide that took the lives of roughly 800,000 Rwandans.

The Hutus claimed that the Tutsis were behind the death of the president. Using widespread communication like radio, Hutu leaders encouraged all Hutus to take up arms — mainly machetes — and kill every Tutsi in their neighborhoods. Next-door neighbors were slaughtering each other.

Almost 1 million people died in a matter of weeks. The world stood by while it happened. The genocide ended only with the successful military campaign by the Rwandan Patriotic Front, led by you, Mr. President.

What people internationally are less familiar with is what Rwanda did after the genocide to come together.

Following the genocide, justice seemed impossible. Killing almost 1 million people in just weeks meant that a large part of the population had to be involved. In the aftermath, roughly 600,000 people confessed to participating in the genocide.

No matter what country you live in, 600,000 murder cases is a lot. But for a country with roughly 8 million people, 600,000 is almost one-tenth of the entire population. For everyone to receive a fair trial, the judicial process would take decades and resources the government did not have. Rwanda also could not put 10% of its country behind bars. It needed to do something different.

To solve this problem, Rwanda set up special community courts known as *gacaca* courts. They were established to promote healing between the victims and the perpetrators. If the accused admitted to their crimes and apologized to the victims' families, they would have reduced prison sentences and be allowed to be reacclimated into society.

But reacclimating meant that the people who committed those atrocities against their neighbors would continue to live alongside them. The bishop's theory is that the perpetrators continue to carry the pain from their crimes from 1994 *every day* — and so do their families.

Researchers from the University of Konstanz and the University of Butare attempted to test this theory. According to them, "… no study has yet investigated the mental health of Rwandan genocide perpetrators."

The researchers recruited victims and perpetrators of the genocide to participate in the study. They looked to the prisons of Butare and Kigali to find perpetrators who would be willing to take part in such a study.

The study revealed how much pain the victims continue to carry with them. Almost half experienced PTSD and depression, 59% had anxiety, and 19% were suicidal during the time of the study. The results from the interviews with the victims may very well explain a large part of why people overall rate their lives so poorly in Rwanda.

The researchers also examined the findings from interviews with the perpetrators. While the perpetrators did not experience PTSD (14%) and anxiety (36%) at the same rate as the victims, they *did* experience depression (41%) and were at risk of suicide (19%) at the same rate as the victims. However, the high rates of depression and suicide among the perpetrators may have been caused by the fact that they were in prison.

Another study replicated this research but with genocide perpetrators who had left prison. It found that the perpetrators had similar rates of PTSD, anxiety, and depression as the victims. So imprisonment may not have been the most likely factor for why perpetrators were experiencing these mental health issues.

So, was the bishop right? Understandably, the pain from the genocide has not subsided. Additional research finds that even the children of genocide victims and perpetrators carry this pain.

The enduring emotional effects of the 1994 genocide, not just for the victims but also for the perpetrators and their children, may be what's causing Rwandans to rate their lives so low.

But the truth is, we cannot say definitively why Rwandans rate their lives so low. Yet despite these ratings, Rwanda remarkably remains an economic and development star. And Rwanda's success in development is not the only thing that inspires people everywhere.

In 2019, *Voice of America* ran a story about a woman named Louise Uwamungu. She lost eight family members during the genocide. She even knew the name of the man who killed her cousin — Cyprien Matabaro. He went to jail for his crime, and Louise knew where he went to prison.

Louise wanted revenge. Her brother was one of the prison guards, and she drew up a plan for how he could kill Cyprien — but her brother refused to do it.

Cyprien sat in prison for years after the genocide. When he was released, things got worse for Louise because after Cyprien left prison, he moved in next door to her.

Cyprien tried to make things better. He begged Louise for forgiveness. They went through the process of truth and reconciliation, during which he admitted to his crimes and told her what happened. The process helped Louise and the rest of her family members continue their healing.

The tragedy in Rwanda can never be made right, but inspiring stories — like the story of Louise and Cyprien — can make things a little better. Because today, they are friends. They even farm and socialize together.

People like Louise and Cyprien made Rwanda the shining city on a hill that the world knows it for today. But why people continue to rate their lives so poorly remains a mystery. It might be a lack of personal freedom, confusion with government services, or the emotional trauma from the genocide. The answer may even be a combination of those factors or something entirely different.

I remain equally as surprised as you at the results of the *World Happiness Report*. My hope is that we can arrive at a more definitive answer for why Rwanda ranks so low in happiness despite experiencing so much economic and development success. If we do, it will benefit the entire world.

Very respectfully,

Jon Clifton

CHAPTER SEVENTEEN
How the Global Pandemic Shaped Happiness

*No one has enough food to eat, and the food prices
are soaring. Most are quarantined in their homes.
Until now, no one has asked about the disease that is
ravaging my country and killing my friends and family.*

— Liberian responses to Gallup interviews
during the 2014 Ebola outbreak

COVID-19 has infected over 431 million people and has killed 6 million people as of this writing. But the real death toll might be even higher. According to advanced modeling by *The Economist* using "excess deaths," the actual figure could be as high as 23 million deaths.

The pandemic also wrecked the global economy, which shrank by 3.5% in 2020 — the largest global contraction in 60 years, according to the IMF. That same year, nearly a third (32%) of workers globally told Gallup they lost their job, and 50% said they earned less money.

So how were people's lives going during the pandemic? Most of what we learned will not surprise you, but one thing will.

The COVID-19 pandemic impacted almost everyone: 80% of people worldwide told Gallup in 2020 that the pandemic affected their lives, including 45% who said it affected their lives *a lot* (the most extreme response). The poor, women with children, and the middle-aged were affected most.

And the impact on women with children was particularly acute. Nearly half of women with children younger than 15 (49%) said their lives were affected a lot by the pandemic. They also experienced more stress, sadness, worry, physical pain, and anger compared with all other adults.

These findings confirm conventional wisdom. But here is the surprise. Although people experienced their lives worse in 2020, they rated their lives better. The number of people who rated their lives high enough to be considered thriving increased.

Global Life Evaluation Index

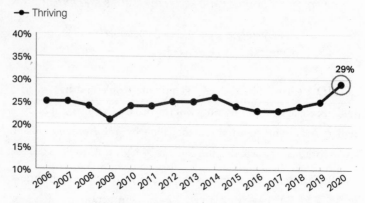

The Life Evaluation Index measures respondents' perceptions of where they stand now and in the future.

Source: Gallup

Did people's views of their lives really improve during the pandemic? If so, it would be a massive finding. But it's hard to believe that people rated their lives better during one of the worst years in recent history. There must be another explanation.

Here are two possible reasons for such a shift: a change in Gallup's methodology and the timing of our surveys.

A World Poll During a Pandemic

Gallup conducts the majority of our global surveys face to face. But in-person interviewing during a pandemic is just not possible. However, we still need to ask people how their lives are going, especially at such a critical time.

Gallup has faced something like this before.

In December 2013, an 18-month-old boy came down with a mysterious illness in a Guinean village. Scientists believe bats infected him. Soon after, five more people died from similar symptoms. The government issued a health warning on January 24, 2014.

Seven weeks later, the illness reached Guinea's capital, Conakry. By mid-March, there were 49 infections and 29 deaths. That same month, the Pasteur Institute in France confirmed what the illness was — the Ebola virus.

Over the next three years, the virus spread to nine more countries — infecting 28,652 people and killing 11,325. One of the most affected countries was Liberia. To better inform its decision-making as the crisis was unfolding, the Liberian government wanted near real-time economic data. But how do you conduct surveys when a virus is raging?

The preferred methodology — face-to-face interviewing — was off the table. To reach Liberians, we had to do something different. So, the World Bank, Gallup, and the Liberia Institute of Statistics and Geo-Information Services (LISGIS) came up with a solution.

LISGIS had access to Liberians' phone numbers, and the national language in Liberia is English. So English-speaking Gallup interviewers could call Liberians from the U.S.

The project worked. We conducted five studies that helped gauge the economic environment throughout the outbreak. While the economic insights informed policy, people's stories from the field, such as the one at the beginning of this chapter, had a profound impact on those conducting the research. Sadly, comments like these were common:

> Please just stay on the phone with me; I need someone to keep me company.

> My family and I are just waiting to die.

> I would rather experience war.

Conducting a global survey in 2020 was a lot like our experience in Liberia in 2014. We had to change the way we did *everything*. 2020 was harder because instead of pivoting our methodology in one country, we had to do it for the entire world.

At a moment's notice, we changed our global methodology from 30% phone and 70% in-person to nearly 100% phone. This shift in methodology may have contributed to the changes in how people see their lives.

For example, in Egypt and Ethiopia, we moved interviewing from face to face to phone in 2020. And thriving unexpectedly increased in both countries in 2020. What changed in Egypt from 2019 to 2020 that would have caused people to see their lives better? Ethiopia is even more perplexing. Thriving reached its highest point in our nine years of tracking despite the country descending into a civil war with the Tigray region.

Thriving in Egypt and Ethiopia

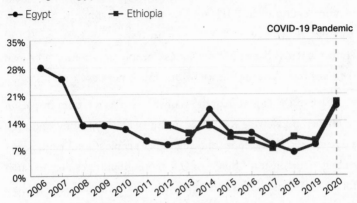

The Life Evaluation Index measures respondents' perceptions of where they stand now and in the future.

Source: Gallup

Egypt and Ethiopia were not the only developing countries that saw an increase. Thriving rates rose an average of five points in developing countries between 2019 and 2020.

In wealthier countries, it was different. There, Gallup saw little change in life ratings, and the European Commission (EC) found similar results. Using the Eurobarometer, the EC looked at life ratings in 30 European countries and found that Europeans rated their lives the same from 2019 to 2020 — exactly what Gallup found in Europe.

So, from 2019 to 2020, life ratings remained the same in many rich countries but *improved* in many developing countries. Why?

The only places where we switched from face-to-face to phone interviewing were developing countries; in wealthy countries, we continued to conduct interviews over the phone.

Further, when we switched back to face-to-face interviewing in some countries in 2021, we saw thriving decline. In Egypt, for example, thriving went back down to 8% (from 18% in 2020).[4] Unfortunately, changing *how* you ask people questions can change their answers. And the science behind this is not new.

One of the largest migrations of survey research from in-person to phone interviewing took place in the 1950s. In wealthy countries, survey researchers stopped showing up at people's homes and began calling them instead. Some of the most groundbreaking research focused on these differences known as "mode effects." Georgetown professor and former head of the U.S. Census Bureau, Robert Groves, even co-wrote one of the initial texts about the differences between the two methodologies in the 1979 book *Surveys by Telephone: A National Comparison with Personal Interviews*.

Switching from in-person to phone interviews can change the outcome of your surveys. According to academics Allyson Holbrook, Melanie Green, and Jon Krosnick, "[Phone] respondents were more likely to satisfice, to be less cooperative and engaged in the interview, and were more likely to express dissatisfaction with the length of the interview. ... Telephone respondents were also more suspicious about the interview process and more likely to present themselves in socially desirable ways than were face-to-face respondents."

The Pew Research Center found similar mode effects for phone surveys compared with web surveys. They found that people rate their lives higher on the phone (compared with web) but report

---

4   We were unable to conduct a survey in Ethiopia in 2021.

experiencing life (for example, positive emotions) the same. Mode adjustments might disproportionately affect the way people report how they *see* life compared with how they *live* life.

Other studies suggest that mode switches do not dramatically affect life ratings. The U.K. government tested this idea by simultaneously conducting in-person and phone surveys using the same questions. If mode effects were present, the impact on how people rate their lives was negligible. People rated their lives 0.04 points higher on the phone compared with in-person surveys.

Just because mode changes did not affect results in the U.K. does not mean they will not influence results somewhere else in the world. For example, following COVID-19 protocols, Gallup conducted some interviews in India using face-to-face methodology. Although we saw an increase in life ratings from 2019 to 2020 in the phone and face-to-face interviews, Indians tended to rate their lives higher on the phone.

But if the methodology change is what caused people to rate their lives differently, then why was everything else in the results of our survey so accurate? Not only did the rest of our data highly corroborate what other surveys were finding, our resulting data also perfectly aligned with conventional wisdom: Almost everyone was affected by the pandemic, especially the poor, the middle-aged, and women with children.

While the change in methodology might have affected our results in developing countries, there may have been another reason people rated their lives better — the timing of our surveys.

The Timing of a Survey

In 2006, only 12% of people in China were thriving. In 2019, before COVID-19 started to spread, that figure was 19%. In our 2020 survey, we found a massive increase. Almost one-third (31%) of people in China were thriving — the most in the history of our tracking there.

Thriving in China

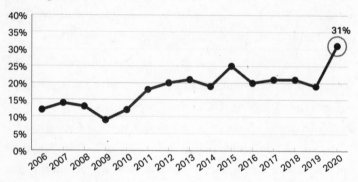

The Life Evaluation Index measures respondents' perceptions of where they stand now and in the future.

Source: Gallup

Like in most countries, we changed our methodology in 2020 from face to face to phone. The survey began in mid-September and lasted for about six weeks — a few months after Wuhan emerged from its lockdown in early April. That fall, it looked like most of China was back to life as usual. Citizens of other countries, who were still in lockdown, saw images of Chinese citizens participating in large events such as concerts. In August of 2020, the BBC ran an article titled "Wuhan coronavirus: From silent streets to packed pools."

While livelihoods appeared to be improving, so was China's economy, which grew 2.3% in 2020 despite the pandemic. So, people may truly have been rating their lives higher at that time.

In terms of how people *lived* life in China, there were also stark differences from 2019 to 2020. Negative emotions increased 10 points — a highly unusual increase for any country. Positive emotions were also affected, dropping nine points. In fact, the decline in laughing and smiling in China was one of the steepest worldwide.

Negative and positive emotions moved predictably in China, but why didn't life ratings?

To further explore how perplexing these shifts are, let's look at another country that was in the news frequently in 2020 — Sweden.

Sweden gained international attention for being one of the few countries in the world that did not immediately go into a lockdown. The country's strategy at the onset of the pandemic was to adopt herd immunity. The government eventually implemented a lockdown of its own, but there was no statistical change in how people rated their lives in 2020 compared with 2019.

Again, the timing of the survey matters. The 2020 survey took place during April, which was one of the months when COVID reached a peak for deaths in Sweden.

The results in Sweden are among the most difficult to explain. The survey modes were the same from 2019 to 2020, and many Europeans rated their lives the same year over year (as was true in the EC's data). One of the reasons the numbers did not decline might be because we did not conduct surveys frequently enough.

Looking at how people rate their lives once per year is like capturing GDP during only one quarter of the year. Imagine measuring GDP during the second quarter of 2020 and considering *that* the measurement for the entire year. The drop in the official statistics would have been spectacular. But that drop would not have accurately described the economic reality for the whole year. Yet, in most countries, that is what we did to measure how people's lives were going.

Ideally, we would track wellbeing in every country at least quarterly, especially during a time of monumental change like that brought on by a pandemic. We have tested a greater frequency of tracking in the U.S. since 2008 and have seen meaningful shifts at key moments. Here is the complete trend:

Thriving in the U.S.

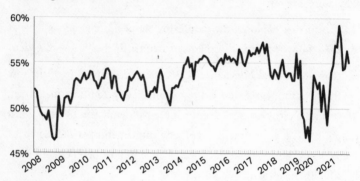

The Life Evaluation Index measures respondents' perceptions of where they stand now and in the future.

Source: Gallup

Notice the volatility when you increase the frequency of measurement. More than half (52%) of people in the U.S. were thriving in early 2008, immediately before the global economic crisis. When America's economy collapsed, so did thriving — dropping almost six points. When the U.S. emerged from the financial crisis, thriving not only rebounded, it exceeded the 52% recorded before the 2008 economic crisis, reaching 57% in late 2017.

When COVID-19 spread to the U.S., thriving collapsed, just like it did during the 2008 financial crisis, hitting the identical low point of 46%. As the economy rebounded, so did thriving, climbing to 54%. As COVID persisted, thriving dropped again to 48%. But when people started getting vaccinated and some lockdowns were lifted, U.S. thriving reached a high never before seen in our tracking (59%).

Would more data points globally have better explained why people rated their lives better? Did an abrupt methodological switch because of the pandemic cause a change in how people see their lives? Or did the pandemic cause people, especially in developing countries, to reflect better on their lives than they had previously?

We do not know for sure. But when we do know more definitively, this knowledge will help advance wellbeing research tremendously.

During the 2014 Ebola crisis, a Gallup interviewer said to us:

> We have received multiple affirmations from Liberians that they are so grateful we have called. Until now, no one has asked them how they feel about the disease that is ravaging their country. So, the importance and significance of this work has been confirmed by the very people we are calling ... Even though it is hard ... we will continue this work to give a voice to the Liberian people. My hope is that voice will be heard loud and clear around the world.

We approached 2020 with this same aspiration.

PART V
What Leaders Can Do to Improve How People's Lives Are Going

CHAPTER EIGHTEEN
What Public Sector Leaders Can Do

Police in Tunisia say they have arrested more than 600 people as a fourth night of violent protests saw protesters return to the streets.

— BBC News, January 19, 2021

These words could have been written about Tunisia in 2010; sadly, they were written in 2021. According to *The New York Times*, some wondered "if the [2010] revolution was worth it." The protesters even used the same words they chanted during the Arab uprisings: "Bread, freedom, national dignity."

In September 2020, four months before these protests, Gallup conducted our annual survey in Tunisia. We found that Tunisians still did not see their lives better than they did before the Arab uprisings: 24% of Tunisians were thriving in 2008; only 19% were in 2020. But the biggest concern wasn't how Tunisians *saw* life — it was how they were *experiencing* life.

Negative emotions had reached record highs in Tunisia that year. Tunisians felt more worry (59%), stress (56%), and sadness (31%) than at any point in the past decade. These increases contributed to Tunisia's fifth-place ranking worldwide for negative emotions in 2020 — behind Iraq, Lebanon, Egypt, and Peru — after ranking eighth in 2019.

Negative Emotions in Tunisia

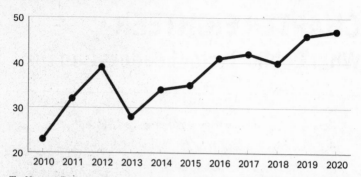

The Negative Experience Index is a composite measure of the five negative experiences (anger, stress, sadness, physical pain, and worry). Index scores range from zero to 100.

Source: Gallup

According to Tunisians, life was becoming unbearable. In that same survey, Gallup found that four in 10 Tunisians were struggling to pay for food, up from 13% in 2010. Forty-four percent were afraid to walk alone at night, which was the second-highest rating of fear we had recorded in Tunisia and the 28th highest rating of the 115 countries we measured that year.

The employment picture was also a mess — 80% of Tunisians believed it was a bad time to find a job. Even among Tunisians with good jobs, almost no one had a great job. The percentage of workers in Tunisia who were miserable at work was tied for the eighth highest in the world.

Hunger, fear, and no hope for a great job is enough to make anyone's life miserable. Now combine that with a constant frustration with the government. Seventy-two percent of Tunisians thought corruption was widespread in the government, up from 53% in 2010.

The unhappiness in Tunisia was understandable. But did the government know how pervasive it was and how quickly it was rising?

This raises a larger question: What can public sector leaders do to make sure these kinds of trends never go unseen again in Tunisia or anywhere else? Here are five actions leaders can take.

1. Include Happiness and Wellbeing Statistics in the SDGs

The U.N.'s Sustainable Development Goals (SDGs) are one of the most significant collaborations by the global community to improve life on Earth. Yet progress toward the goals is predominantly measured using objective indicators, such as income, literacy rates, and unemployment. These measures need to be expanded to include subjective wellbeing indicators, which are the only metrics that give people the primary role in telling the story of how their lives are going.

"Good health and well-being" is actually one of the goals — SDG 3. Even though it purports to measure wellbeing, SDG 3's underlying measures of progress are objective (such as maternal mortality, number of new HIV infections, and suicide rates). This is where subjective wellbeing indicators (life evaluation, negative experiences, and positive experiences) could be included. If this happened, it would put wellbeing and happiness at the forefront of the development agenda.

Including wellbeing indicators may also help create globally comparable data. When governments develop their own subjective wellbeing standards, it may inform their own policies, but they deprive the international community of global comparisons. Is one country doing something better to improve people's wellbeing that everyone else could learn from?

2. Report Wellbeing Statistics More Frequently, and Use Larger Surveys

Many countries measure objective indicators like GDP quarterly. Unemployment is measured even more frequently in some countries. For example, the U.S. reports unemployment monthly and announces the official figure on the first Friday of the following month. Wellbeing statistics need to be reported with this kind of frequency. If they were, leaders would pay attention to them far more closely.

Wellbeing surveys also need larger samples. The U.K.'s Office of National Statistics (ONS) conducts over 300,000 wellbeing interviews per year, which allows for more in-depth analysis. Large samples like that in the U.S. would empower leaders to know how elderly Black women in New York City are doing or how young Asian men in Florida are doing. This information would help leaders create more targeted policies to improve people's lives.

Larger sample sizes could also change how the *World Happiness Report* conducts its rankings. Instead of ranking countries, the *WHR* could rank every city, state, and community in the world and more definitively answer where the happiest and least happy people live.

The U.S. usually ranks in the middle teens in the *WHR*. But why treat a country as large as the U.S. as a monolith? Instead, why not rank each of the states separately and compare them to the world? Utah, Alaska, North Dakota, and Hawaii would join the top 10 list, besting countries like New Zealand.

The New World Happiness Report

If U.S. States Were Countries

Rank	Geography	Thriving	Rank	Geography	Thriving
1	Finland	71%		Nevada	55%
2	Denmark	70%		North Carolina	55%
3	Iceland	68%		Alabama	55%
4	Norway	65%		Indiana	55%
5	Netherlands	64%		Illinois	55%
6	Switzerland	63%		Iowa	55%
7	Utah	62%	43	Florida	54%
	Alaska	62%		South Carolina	54%
9	Canada	61%		Missouri	54%
	North Dakota	61%		Michigan	54%
	Hawaii	61%		New Mexico	54%
12	Sweden	60%		Kansas	54%
13	Israel	59%		Tennessee	54%
	New Zealand	59%		Rhode Island	54%
15	Costa Rica	58%		New York	54%
	New Hampshire	58%	52	Vermont	53%
	Colorado	58%		Oregon	53%
	Montana	58%		Pennsylvania	53%
	Arizona	58%		Wisconsin	53%
	Virginia	58%		Ohio	53%
21	Texas	57%		Maine	53%
	South Dakota	57%		Oklahoma	53%
	Georgia	57%		Louisiana	53%
	Minnesota	57%	60	Ireland	52%
	Australia	57%	61	Mississippi	51%
	Idaho	57%		United Arab Emirates	51%
	Maryland	57%		Kentucky	51%
	Wyoming	57%		Arkansas	51%
	California	57%	65	Belgium	49%
30	Austria	56%	66	Mexico	48%
	Massachusetts	56%		United Kingdom	48%
	Washington	56%		West Virginia	48%
	Nebraska	56%	69	Germany	47%
34	Delaware	55%	70	Brazil	45%
	Connecticut	55%		Luxembourg	45%
	New Jersey	55%		Malta	45%

Averaged over 2016-2018.
Source: Gallup

All 50 states rank higher than all but 18 countries in the world. But there is variation — North Dakota, Hawaii, and Canada rank high (tied for 9th); Mexico, the U.K., and West Virginia rank low (tied for 66th). Imagine if we had every region of the world broken out like this. Are there places where people rate their lives even higher than people in Nordic countries? If they did — who are they, and what can we learn from them?

3. Keep Measurement Honest

One year when the *WHR* was published, the results went viral. And one government in particular did not like the results.

The following year, we approached that government to begin our work again. They wanted to get involved in the data collection by picking the homes where we conduct our interviews. We told the government that we have to use the same standards in their country that we use worldwide. But they wanted to use their own standards.

This disagreement created an impasse that we have not been able to overcome, and the country has not been included in the Gallup World Poll ever since — and thus has not been included in the *WHR*.

The more wellbeing and happiness statistics gain attention, the more governments will want to intervene to get results that favor their administrations or policies. This cannot happen if we are going to get to the truth — third-party organizations need to be able to collect statistics independently, objectively, and neutrally.

4. Build Official Statistics for Great Jobs

Every leader is looking for a silver bullet to improve people's lives. The fastest way to do this is by creating great jobs. Leaders should no longer prioritize unemployment metrics and instead should begin reporting official great jobs statistics.

The world needs to measure the *subjective* part of a job. What is great work to a young woman in Spain may not be great work to an elderly man in Vietnam. Assessing a job's quality solely on income is imperfect, precisely because we know that people take pay cuts to do what they love.

A new metric that quantifies the number of great jobs will inspire world leaders to work relentlessly to improve that number authentically. If leaders move to the official statistics for great jobs, the results will look bad at first because there are so few great jobs in the world today. But as private and public sector leaders continue to create these kinds of jobs, the great jobs rate will improve — and we will never look back.

5. Build Statistics That Reflect the Many Dimensions of a Great Life

The escape from a bad life is not just an economic issue. Economic growth has lifted millions out of poverty, but that alone will not lift billions of people out of extreme anger, sadness, worry, stress, and physical pain. Future indicators still need to include money and economic growth, but the indicators of tomorrow must look more holistically at what makes a great life — including measures of the quality of our communities, our physical health, and our social wellbeing.

CHAPTER NINETEEN
What Private Sector Leaders Can Do

100% of customers are people. 100% of employees are people. If you don't understand people, you don't understand business.

— Simon Sinek, bestselling author

Corporations impact billions of lives. The Fortune Global 500 employs nearly 70 million people — only 19 countries in the world have bigger populations. The largest 7,500 U.S. companies employ over 45 million people. And that is only how many people these companies employ. They affect billions more lives through their interactions with their customers, suppliers, investors, and communities.

The sheer magnitude of this influence is why private sector leaders have a significant opportunity to improve people's wellbeing. Organizations know this and are publicly working to improve wellbeing by redefining the very purpose of a corporation. Often at the behest of investors, companies are building measurement standards to track the difference they are making for their stakeholders, the environment, and the world.

But while they are tracking everything from the diversity of their boards to their environmental footprint, how well are they listening to the voices of their employees, customers, suppliers, and communities?

The Purpose of a Company

Why do companies exist?

Is the purpose of a company just to make money — or something more? According to Microsoft CEO Satya Nadella, "The corporation's purpose is to find profitable solutions to the problems of people and planet."[5]

His sentiment aligns with the philosophy that many CEOs are currently adopting, which is called stakeholder capitalism. The most public example of this came from the Business Roundtable in August 2019 when 184 CEOs of the largest U.S. companies issued a joint statement announcing they were redefining the purpose of a corporation to "promote 'an economy that serves all Americans.'" (Nadella was a signatory.) These companies would no longer serve *just* their shareholders. Now they would serve their shareholders and their customers, suppliers, employees, and communities.

For some, this announcement marked a stunning departure from the previous purpose of a corporation — to increase shareholder value — or shareholder capitalism. Many believe this purpose was established in 1970 when Nobel laureate Milton Friedman published "A Friedman doctrine — The Social Responsibility Of Business Is to Increase Its Profits."

Friedman concluded his nearly 3,000-word *New York Times* article by saying: "There is one and only one social responsibility of business — to use its resources and engage in activities designed to increase its profits so long as it stays within the rules of the game, which is to say, engages in open and free competition without deception [or] fraud." His point: Business exists to make money — any alternative is "unadulterated socialism."

---

5   Nadella credits University of Oxford professor Colin Mayer for this idea. Mayer wrote about it in his book *Prosperity: Better Business Makes the Greater Good.*

Shareholder capitalism flourished after Friedman's essay, and shareholder primacy influenced everything from the boardroom to government policy. That was until the 2008 global economic crisis, when people began wondering if the pursuit of profit had gone too far. Even today, many social ills are blamed on shareholder capitalism's corporate greed, such as the loss of jobs to offshoring, widening income inequality, and the opioid crisis.

The American public isn't happy with large corporations either. In 2022, Gallup found that 74% of Americans were dissatisfied with the size and influence of major U.S. corporations, which is up from 48% in 2001. Further, 64% think corruption is widespread in U.S. businesses today, and a majority have felt this way since 2006. They may have felt this way longer; this just happens to be when we began tracking it.

The negative sentiment toward corporations is so serious that it may be eroding the perception of capitalism itself. In fact, there is a rising interest in socialism in America. In 1942, 25% of Americans thought some form of socialism was a good thing for the country; in 2019, that number was 43%.

And widespread distrust of business is not just an American problem. In 2021, 70% of people worldwide believed corruption was widespread in business — and no less than two-thirds have felt that way for at least 15 years. This sentiment is so pervasive that a majority of people in 113 out of 140 countries we measured between 2019 and 2021 said business is corrupt.

This might be why so many business leaders are looking to move to a different form of capitalism. In the words of Salesforce CEO Marc Benioff, "It's time for a new capitalism — a more fair, equal, and sustainable capitalism that actually works for everyone." (Benioff also signed the 2019 Business Roundtable Statement.)

But is stakeholder capitalism new? According to Steve Denning of *Forbes*, stakeholder capitalism was launched in the 1932 book *The Modern Corporation and Private Property* by Adolf Berle and Gardiner Means. The book conceptualized the idea that "public firms should have professional managers who would balance the claims of different stakeholders, taking into account public policy," said Denning.

Stakeholder capitalism may have even originated much earlier. The new 10,000-yen bill in Japan features Shibusawa Eiichi (1840-1931), the father of Japanese capitalism. He founded 500 companies throughout his life, and his business philosophy was "buyers, sellers, and society," which many Japanese believe perfectly articulates stakeholder capitalism.

Regardless of where it came from, stakeholder capitalism has its detractors. Denning is one of them. He believes that shareholder and stakeholder capitalism are not so different; both exist to extract value from the economy. Where they differ is how the extracted value is distributed (either to shareholders or stakeholders). The alternative to the value-extraction approach is value *creation* (or "customer capitalism"), which stems from the philosophy of the late Peter Drucker. Drucker's best articulation of customer capitalism was: "There is only one valid definition of business purpose: to create a customer."

So, does business exist for the shareholder, the stakeholder, the customer ... or the state?

In 2012, the cover of *The Economist* featured "The rise of state capitalism," which emphasized "a new kind of hybrid corporation, backed by the state but behaving like a private-sector multinational." At the time, the newspaper said the philosophy claimed 13 of the world's largest oil firms and the world's second-largest economy — China.

The architect of China's modern economy, Chairman Deng Xiaoping, is widely credited for the market reforms he introduced in the 1980s that caused China's rapid economic development. According to Deng, China was still practicing socialism, but "socialism with Chinese characteristics." The very idea of state capitalism is probably oxymoronic to free enterprisers, but, as *The Economist* notes, state-controlled capitalism has been around for a long time (their example: the East India Company).

But "the force we have seen at work in the past few decades" is stakeholder capitalism, according to the World Economic Forum (WEF). If this is the prevailing trend, are companies taking stakeholder capitalism seriously?

Not according to Lucian Bebchuk and Roberto Tallarita of Harvard, who authored the *Wall Street Journal* article "'Stakeholder' Capitalism Seems Mostly for Show." They contacted 173 of the 184 companies that signed the Business Roundtable Statement and asked them if their CEOs got board approval to sign the statement.

Bebchuk and Tallarita believe that getting board approval meant companies were not just signing the statement for good publicity — they were taking it seriously. Of the 173 companies that the Harvard academics reached out to, they heard back from 48 and found that only one got board approval. Their conclusion: It was all for show.

But the absence of board approval should not solely determine the sincerity of these CEOs. They might have had tacit approval from the board before signing. Or they may have believed their company already embraced stakeholder capitalism — and signing the statement was just their way of communicating it to the world. But whether or not the Harvard study's conclusion is right, it raises an important question: How do we know if these companies are delivering on what they signed?

A New Kind of Audit

"We are a disclosure economy," Nasdaq's CEO Adena Friedman told CNBC's *Squawk Box* in 2022. "If you really think about the public market and what the SEC requires, it requires disclosure for investors to make an informed choice." That day, Friedman was being interviewed not about the financial disclosures companies regularly make, but about a new kind of disclosure that looked at companies' commitment to the environment and society.

Today, many investors want more from companies. They still want high profits and returns, but they also want to see companies make a positive impact on the environment and society. This is why more investors are adopting investment philosophies such as socially responsible investing (SRI) and environmental, social, and governance (ESG) investing. And these kinds of investments are booming. "Since 2016 the value of investments in financial products that claim to abide by environmental, social and governance (ESG) rules has grown from $23trn to $35trn … [and] could exceed $50trn by 2025," according to *The Economist*.

ESG disclosures allow investors to track a company's progress on its environmental and societal impact. WEF produced a standardized approach for ESG in 2020 using 55 core and expanded metrics, including greenhouse gas emissions, diversity and inclusion metrics, wage levels, number of work-related injuries, and average hours of training per person.

Governments even want in on the action. The European Union is mandating ESG compliance. In 2021, a new EU regulation went into effect — the Sustainable Finance Disclosure Regulation (SFDR). But does forcing companies to comply with ESG tracking make them better?

The Indian government recently tried to intervene with respect to corporate social responsibility (CSR), which some consider a precursor to stakeholder capitalism and the ESG movement. The reason for the intervention had to do with how little trust the public had in businesses throughout the country. In 2021, Gallup found that 73% of Indians thought corruption was widespread in the country's businesses. To fix the Indian business community's image, the government mandated that Indian companies give 2% of their profits to CSR activities each year.

The law did, in fact, cause Indian companies to give more to charity overall. The companies that gave almost nothing before started giving something. But here is the catch. While the least charitable companies gave a little more, the most charitable companies started giving a lot less. Those once-charitable companies felt that all they had to do now was hit government targets, which they were previously exceeding.

Too heavy a hand by governments or investors could have similar effects. So far, it appears that most interventions are mandating metrics — not necessarily targets to achieve.

But while these new metrics include almost everything, how are companies incorporating the voice of the worker, customer, supplier, and community?

Helping Stakeholders Be Heard

I was reviewing a major company's ESG report that featured a comprehensive section called "Supplier Engagement." The company made many of the disclosures that WEF recommends: the diversity of its suppliers, the amount of money it spent with each of them — and the company even lists the audits its suppliers are asked to comply with.

But something was missing. Not once did the company ask its suppliers how the relationship itself was going.

Think of it this way: Company X is a large retailer that has a reputation for being disrespectful to its suppliers. Would that disrespect show up in its ESG report? It could. All Company X would have to do is ask its suppliers how much they agree with this statement: "Company X treats our company with respect."

ESG reporting is incredibly comprehensive, but it is missing the voice of each stakeholder. Here is how companies can systematically listen and report on the voice of each of them.

Listening to Workers

"CEOs make these wonderful flowery statements about people being their greatest assets," Jeff Higgins, founder of the Human Capital Management Institute told *The Wall Street Journal* in 2022. "Why aren't people on the balance sheet if they are the most important asset?"

SEC Chairman Gary Gensler agrees. In a tweet, he said, "Investors want to better understand one of the most critical assets of a company: its people." He further recommended that human capital disclosures "could include a number of metrics, such as workforce turnover, skills and development training, compensation, benefits, workforce demographics including diversity, and health and safety." In fact, many of these metrics are exactly what WEF recommended in 2020.

But while virtually everything is being audited — from pay to workplace accidents — how is the voice of the worker being amplified?

Currently, not well. Gallup finds that 25% of American workers report being totally ignored at work. And, as I previously mentioned, 62% of workers globally are emotionally detached at work, and 18% are downright miserable. But it doesn't have to be this way. The best corporate leaders are listening to their workers and meeting their needs. Gallup finds that in the best-run companies, 73% of workers are emotionally engaged and thriving at work — more than three times the global average of 20%.

Workers have two kinds of basic needs: rational and emotional. A worker's rational needs are exactly what Gensler was outlining — a safe job with good pay and benefits. When a worker's emotional needs are met, they are in a job where they feel recognized, that allows for their development, and that plays to their strengths. The pinnacle of meeting a worker's emotional needs is when they feel cared about. But that isn't happening. In 2022, Gallup found that only 24% of American workers strongly agreed that their organization cared about their wellbeing.

Most workplace management philosophies still treat workers like automatons — simply meet a worker's rational needs and they will turn out a work product. The "S" in ESG metrics understandably tracks the many transactions of life at work (paychecks, hours, work conditions), but it fails to track workers' wellbeing from their perspective.

How can companies fulfill this demand?

They can start with systematic listening, and this is where large-scale scientific surveys help. Surveys that benchmark across the same industry are even better. But a survey alone won't fulfill workers' rational and emotional needs. The people who need to fulfill these demands are, most often, the workers' managers.

The manager is one of the most important factors when it comes to understanding how workers are doing. Seventy percent of what determines a worker's emotional attachment to their job depends on their manager. If you hate your job, it is almost always because of your boss.

And being a "boss" is exactly the problem. Traditional managers operate in a top-down, command-and-control environment. The best managers are coaches. Coaches focus on workers' strengths and development, help them get more opportunities to do what they do best, and help them build strong emotional connections with their colleagues. But most of all, they listen. Great managers have frequent conversations with their team members (at least once per week); the worst managers ignore their workers. In fact, ignoring workers puts them in a worse state of mind than giving them negative feedback.

Organizations that want to take part in the ESG disclosure economy need a metric for the voice of the employee. By increasing workers' wellbeing, employers will also realize a lot of other benefits. Workers who strongly agree that their organization cares about their wellbeing (compared with other workers) are 69% less likely to actively search for a new job, five times more likely to strongly advocate for their company as a place to work, and 71% less likely to report experiencing a lot of burnout.

Listening to Customers

Companies often listen to their customers using satisfaction surveys. But satisfaction surveys fall short of helping companies truly understand how their customers are doing.

Here is an example: Think about buying coffee at your regular coffee shop. When someone asks if you were satisfied with the experience, the question taps into the rational part of your mind — Did they get your order right, and was the coffee hot?

What it does not measure is the *emotional* experience you had at the coffee shop. Did the employees make you feel taken care of? Were you treated with respect? Did anyone recognize you as a regular? Meeting a customer's emotional needs is another level of service — and it is one of the biggest ways companies differentiate themselves from the competition.

Customers' rational needs must be met first. If the coffee is lukewarm or the bathroom is unusable, companies will lose customers.

But if the customers are not treated with respect, then their emotional needs are not being met — and this is where companies are missing out on their biggest opportunities.

While rationally satisfied customers spend slightly more than those who are dissatisfied, Gallup finds that emotionally engaged customers spend a lot more — on average, 23% more. Companies with emotionally engaged customers have seen, on average, 66% higher sales growth, 10% growth in net profit, and a 25% increase in customer loyalty.

Companies that care about their customers listen more. And when they have thousands or millions of customers, they figure out how to listen at scale — usually using surveys. But listening at scale is a science and requires asking exactly the right questions — questions that tap into the emotional mind, not just the rational mind.

In addition to rational satisfaction, Gallup recommends that companies ask their customers to respond to these items, which gauge emotional attachment:

Company always delivers on what they promise.

I feel proud to be a *Company* customer.

Company is the perfect company for people like me.

But some companies are going beyond asking these questions — they are working to improve their customers' lives.

"The objective of our organization is not just to improve our customers' financials, but also their financial wellbeing," the CEO of a financial institution told me. And to know if they are making progress on their customers' financial wellbeing, they measure it.

This CEO isn't alone. Some credit unions and banks are now building strategies to improve the financial wellbeing of their customers. They want to go beyond meeting their customers' rational and emotional needs; they also want to improve their overall lives.

They have their work cut out for them. In the U.S., only about 9% of people strongly agree that their bank puts their financial wellbeing ahead of the interests of the bank, and only about 12% strongly agree their bank helps them reach their financials goals.

But change is possible. Organizations that have been working to improve these metrics have seen large increases in their customers' financial wellbeing. They have even seen a remarkable financial wellbeing resilience during crises. At the onset of the pandemic (March through May 2020), 35% of these institutions' customers were thriving in their financial wellbeing. For the next seven months (June through December 2020), 40% were thriving. In fact, these institutions' customers averaged higher levels of financial wellbeing in the second half of 2020 compared with the months immediately preceding the onset of the pandemic.

Proponents of Friedman's shareholder capitalism might think that meeting customers' emotional needs and improving their overall lives is a distraction from increasing shareholder value. But it's not. Increasing customer engagement and wellbeing also increases shareholder value. In just the financial sector, engaged customers are 39% more likely to sign up for new services, 49% more likely to increase balances, and 32% more likely to seek out financial advice from their financial institution. The return is even higher for financial institutions (or any institution for that matter) that build a strategy to engage their customers *and* improve their wellbeing.

Listening to Suppliers

"We commit to dealing fairly and ethically with our suppliers. We are dedicated to serving as good partners to the other companies, large and small, that help us meet our missions." This is how suppliers were addressed in the Business Roundtable's commitment to stakeholders. The first 10 words of the commitment raise an obvious question: What were companies doing before they signed this document?

Of course, not all companies are unfair or unethical when working with their suppliers. But to systematically engage suppliers in a discussion about how the relationship is going, companies simply have to ask them how much they agree with statements like these:

Company always treats me with respect.

Company is easy to do business with.

Company always does what they say they will do.

When suppliers have an emotional connection to their client, they are 41% more willing to take risks for them, 45% more likely to go the extra mile for them, and 45% more likely to give them best-in-class service.

Strengthening the bond with suppliers starts with listening. And if executives feel that these metrics are not important, consider this: As much as 10% of a company's value can be lost due to supply chain glitches, which are often caused by human error.

Listening to the Community

How is the community doing where you operate your business? Are people's lives getting better or worse?

The best way to improve the wellbeing of your community is first to measure how people's lives are going. In the beginning of this book, I showed wellbeing trends for Tunisia, Egypt, and the U.K. — what if we had those same trends for Austin, Albany, and Richmond in the U.S.?

If a company wanted to truly demonstrate its commitment to its community, it would establish these statistics and provide them to the community. Then everyone could rally around improving them, just like they do now with statistics such as unemployment or GDP.

Stakeholder capitalists agree that improving the welfare of a company's community, employees, customers, and suppliers is also good for business. But most of the indicators they use to gauge progress are objective, such as pay and worker safety. They also need indicators that represent the voice of those stakeholders.

To be clear, I am not advocating for one form of capitalism over another. I am advocating for listening to and meeting the emotional needs of employees, customers, suppliers, and the community, which I believe meaningfully advances all forms of capitalism — stakeholder, customer, state, or even shareholder.

Companies that listen to and emotionally engage their employees see better financial returns. Companies that listen to and engage their customers get more business from them. Companies that listen to and treat their suppliers with respect get better service from them. And companies that listen to their community and improve citizens' lives generate better business conditions for everyone.

Considering the enormity of companies' influence, they have a real opportunity to meaningfully improve billions of lives — regardless of which form of capitalism they subscribe to.

CHAPTER TWENTY
What Public Sector and Private Sector Leaders Can Do Together

I'm afraid there are no more than 1.5 million [people]
in the country, but I can't prove it.

— Apostol Simovski, State Statistical Office
Director, North Macedonia, 2020

In 2020, the North Macedonian government officially reported that the country's population was slightly over 2 million; yet according to the director of the country's statistics office, it was only 1.5 million. Some economists thought the population might be 1.6 million or 1.8 million.

But no one really knew how many people lived in North Macedonia. And the reason no one knew was because North Macedonia had not conducted a census since 2002.[6]

It seems comical that a leader would not know how many people live in their country, but it's not funny. And not having even the most basic statistics is a reality in far too many places. According to the U.N.'s 2019 sustainable development goals report:

> Many national statistical systems across the globe face serious challenges … As a result, accurate and timely information about critical aspects of people's lives is unknown. Numerous groups and individuals remain "invisible," and many development challenges are still poorly understood.

---

6   In October 2021, North Macedonia completed a census. The population is 1,832,696.

If we are going to improve people's lives, the world needs better data everywhere. But too many governments simply cannot afford to produce the statistics necessary for leaders to create informed policy.

According to the same SDG report, only 129 countries in 2018 had implemented a national statistics plan. And of the 129 countries with a plan, only 60% were fully funded. Another study by the World Bank found that while 119 middle- to lower-income countries met the minimum standards to conduct a census, only 41 met the minimum standards to collect vital registration data such as births and deaths.

And the pandemic only exacerbated the world's data collection problems. According to the World Bank in 2020, 65% of National Statistics Offices (NSOs) were partially or fully closed, and 96% had stopped face-to-face data collection. It also said that 90% of NSOs in low- and lower-middle-income countries were "struggling to meet international reporting requirements."

These data collection gaps need to be addressed. If governments cannot address them, then the private sector could — and here's how.

A Company's Purpose and Helping Build the World's Official Statistics for Everything

Most companies articulate what kind of unique value they bring to the world through their mission or purpose statement. As an example, here is what Whole Foods Market says on its website:

> Our purpose is to nourish people and the planet. We're a purpose-driven company that aims to set the standards of excellence for food retailers. Quality is a state of mind at Whole Foods Market.

Nourishing people and the planet is a laudable mission, but what indicators does Whole Foods use to track the nourishment it provides the world?

The world does not have reliable statistics for how well people are nourished (as I discussed in Chapter Eleven). Whole Foods could fix this problem by announcing that it is going to help build the world's official statistics for global nourishment (also known as diet quality). This would not only further demonstrate Whole Foods' commitment to nourishing the planet, it would significantly help the public sector, which badly needs these data.

Two companies are already leading the way in helping produce global statistics that also reflect their companies' missions: Cookpad and Hologic.

Cookpad and the World's Official Statistics for Cooking

Cookpad is a famous Japanese company — so famous that almost half of Japanese adults use its cooking app. The business is a lot like Instagram, except for cooking. When you make a dish, you post a photo of that dish on Cookpad's app and then describe how you made it. People can then re-create your dish and share their own photos and comments.

So what is the purpose of this company? If you had asked Milton Friedman, he would have said "to make money." If you ask Cookpad President and CEO Rimpei Iwata, he says something very different. In 2019, I sat with Rimpei at Cookpad's global headquarters in Tokyo.

"Our goal is to get more people cooking at home. We believe that if they do, they will become more aware of what they are cooking and eating, which will have a positive impact on individual health and also the health of the planet. There's also a wider impact on society as a whole," he told me.

The company's website further articulates its mission: "We believe that cooking is the key to a happier and healthier life for people, communities and the planet."

Cookpad's purpose is clear: Increase home cooking because it will increase people's — and the world's — wellbeing. But how does Cookpad know if its purpose is working? And how does it know if people are cooking more globally?

To quantify these things, Cookpad built the world's official statistics for cooking. Now, in almost every country, every year, Cookpad and Gallup partner to ask people how often they are cooking at home. More specifically, we ask people how often they made lunch and dinner in the past week. Because the official statistics for cooking are on the same survey as the happiness items in the *World Happiness Report*, we can also look at the data to see if cooking is helping make people's lives better.

If Cookpad realizes its purpose, more people will be cooking at home everywhere, which should also improve people's wellbeing.

Hologic and the Global Women's Health Index

With 7,000 employees and a market cap of $20 billion, Massachusetts-based Hologic is a medical device company focused on women's health. But what is its purpose?

According to Hologic, it is "an innovative medical technology company primarily focused on improving women's health and wellbeing through early detection and treatment."

Hologic exists to improve women's health. To better serve that mission, the company wanted to quantify how women's health was faring globally. According to Hologic's CEO Steve MacMillan, "In our ongoing work to support women's health around the world, we've struggled to find comprehensive data that measures progress on key issues like access and quality of care on a global scale."

Instead of sitting back and saying, "The data don't exist for us to really determine how much of an impact we are making in the world," Hologic went out and did something about it. On International Women's Day in 2021, MacMillan said, "Beginning in 2019, we started working to develop the Global Women's Health Index to fill this critical need for a data-driven approach to women's health."

In Hologic's 2021 sustainability report, MacMillan further said:

> For all the products we've made over our Company's lifetime — 3D mammography, the PAP test and HPV test — the data we get from the Hologic Global Women's Health Index may turn out to have the biggest impact on human health of anything we have ever done. Having been at the forefront of so many innovations in women's health, we thought who better to organize and conduct a global effort to obtain answers in our space of healthcare.

In partnership with Johns Hopkins University, George Washington University, RAD-AID, and Popper and Co., among others, Hologic and Gallup built an index to track how women's health is progressing globally.

The results of the 2020 Hologic Global Women's Health Index were sobering — there was not a single country that received a passing grade in women's health. The report ignited a conversation: More needs to be done to improve women's health everywhere.

But imagine if every large company built international statistics like Cookpad and Hologic did. Leaders who believe that their organization has a purpose beyond making money should put that purpose in writing and then help build the world's official statistics around whatever that purpose is. These statistics would not only help them better understand if they are achieving their company's purpose, the resulting data would also help inform public sector leaders who badly need this information.

CONCLUSION
Five Million Conversations

The survey I remember is one I didn't finish. It was with a man, middle-aged, who was sounding somewhat down … I asked him, "Were you happy all day yesterday?" He suddenly began to cry. Not weeping or sniffling, but flat-out sobbing. Then he hung up. I decided not to call back because I could sense his humiliation.

— Gallup interviewer, Omaha, Nebraska, 2010

After conducting 5 million interviews worldwide, it is incredible how many people are surprised when we ask how their lives are going. While hundreds of thousands of people told Gallup how much they enjoyed life, hundreds of thousands of others gave reports just like the man above.

When GDP is released each quarter, it tells us if the economy is growing or shrinking — but it does not report this man's pain. When the U.S. government announces the latest unemployment figure on the first Friday of each month, it does not tell us about this man's sadness. And when the stock market reaches another record high, it does not tell us about this man's misery.

Only this man can tell us these things.

One lasting effect of the global pandemic seems to be how people talk to each other. Before the pandemic, people began business meetings or new encounters by exchanging superficial pleasantries, such as, "How are you?" "Good, and you?"

Now, this conversation actually means something. When someone asks, "How are you?" they are genuinely interested in your wellbeing.

Yet while everyday conversations are changing, the way we monitor global progress is not.

GDP growth, oil prices, and inflation still dominate headlines and captivate leaders' attention. Yet, absent from leadership dashboards is how people feel. This is why the leaders of today are missing the global rise of worry, stress, sadness, anger, and physical pain.

When the leaders of tomorrow are asked, "What indicators do you follow most closely?" — hopefully, many of them will say, "happiness."

APPENDIX

The Birth of the Gallup World Poll

> *Mr. Secretary, there are reports from the region*
> *that support for the Taliban has actually increased*
> *because of the bombing campaign. And if it's fair*
> *to describe the Taliban not just as a collection of*
> *soldiers but as a movement, after you've destroyed*
> *every Taliban tank, won't you have to then go house*
> *to house?*
>
> — Question posed to Secretary of Defense
>   Donald Rumsfeld during a press
>   conference on November 8, 2001

Rumsfeld's answer to this question inspired Gallup to measure the will of the world:

> It seems to me that it's very difficult for you or me ... to go down and do a Gallup poll and try to net out the answer ... And I am not inclined to chase that rabbit.

That day, the Gallup World Poll was born.

Rumsfeld's wry response was his attempt to make light of the fact that not only did he not know the answer, but how *could* he know the answer? It's not like Gallup could conduct a poll in Afghanistan while the U.S. military was bombing the country.

He was right. Conducting face-to-face interviews would have been too dangerous. But Gallup's Chairman and CEO, Jim Clifton, was watching Rumsfeld's press briefing. To him, it was as if Rumsfeld was issuing a challenge to the organization he led.

Jim acted immediately. He called Gale Muller, Gallup's chief methodologist at the time.

"Gale? Can we do a survey in Afghanistan?"

Gale knew it would be too dangerous in the current environment, but he offered an alternative: What if Gallup conducted a massive survey in nine predominantly Muslim countries and asked people what they thought about the war in Afghanistan?

Gallup did just that. Interviewing more than 10,000 people across nine countries (Jordan, Kuwait, Indonesia, Iran, Lebanon, Morocco, Saudi Arabia, Pakistan, and Turkey), we sought not just to answer the reporter's question but also to ask people what they thought of the U.S., 9/11, and a host of other issues.

The results were remarkable. Sixty-two percent of people across seven of the nine countries said that the U.S. military action in Afghanistan could not be justified at all.

The most intriguing finding had to do with how people in predominantly Muslim countries felt about the United States. Officials in the U.S. government had a popular phrase about why terrorists hated America: "They hate us for our freedoms." But was it true?

This statement was directed at the terrorists who committed the atrocities, but some interpreted it as being a sentiment all Muslims felt.

The results of the survey found the exact opposite. People across the predominantly Muslim countries we surveyed not only didn't hate America for its freedoms; freedom was one of the things they admired most about the West. The only thing they admired more was the West's technology.

The main reasons people in these countries gave for why they resented the West had little to do with freedom. Instead, they cited a breakdown in social morals, negative attitudes toward Muslims, corruption, and unfair attitudes about the Palestinian Territories.

Those findings were the biggest headlines from the study. I believe this research helped start a more informed conversation about how people in the Muslim world felt about the U.S. and its leadership. In fact, it later inspired us to do a much larger, more in-depth study of the Muslim world and write a book called *Who Speaks for Islam?*

In that study, politics — not piety or freedom — set the politically radicalized apart from the rest of the Muslim world. The 7% of respondents who didn't like America and said the 9/11 attacks were completely justified were the most likely to say that moderating the West's stance on the Palestinian Territories was a way to improve relations.

But something else happened in that first survey that went almost unnoticed. We also asked people in these nine predominantly Muslim countries how their lives were going.

In Gallup fashion, we asked them to rate their lives on a scale of zero to 10. Just 6% of people reported that their lives were a 10, and 17% said their lives would be a 10 in the next five years.

But these results might make you wonder: Why — in a study about the 9/11 attacks and the war in Afghanistan — did Gallup ask people how their lives were going?

If you recall the conversation between Edward R. Murrow and George Gallup in Chapter Six, you know that Gallup's passion for studying people's happiness started with our founder. Even though George Gallup made his name in political polling, he cared most about how people's lives are going.

This is one reason why we research wellbeing and happiness everywhere, including in predominantly Muslim countries after 9/11. After the positive reception of our discoveries from the post-9/11 study, someone, somewhere at Gallup asked, "Why don't we do this for the entire world?"

It was at that moment we decided we were going to conduct a global study — every year — on every topic that we thought would be most helpful to world leaders.

Jim Clifton went back to Gale Muller and asked him if we could pull off a global study on wellbeing every year. Gale's answer? "I don't see why not."

The Questions We Ask the World

If you do not know how to ask the right question, you discover nothing.

— W. Edwards Deming, American statistician,
educator, and consultant

After Gallup decided to conduct our annual World Poll, we needed to figure out what we were going to ask the world.

We started by using two processes: Conduct a historical review of everything George Gallup had ever asked, and engage global human development experts and behavioral economists.

Conducting a historical review of everything George Gallup ever asked was harder than you might think. Many of the surveys were not stored in neat, structured datasets like virtually everything is today. In fact, Alec Gallup, one of George Gallup's two sons, even stored the old punch cards used in face-to-face interviews in the barn next to his house in Princeton, New Jersey. Because of decay, they were virtually unreadable. Otherwise, we may have started there.

So we began with George Gallup's books, looking at questions he tested all over the world. He asked thousands of questions throughout his life and covered everything. In the 1970s, he asked people in Saudi Arabia and Qatar about their TV watching habits. And in the 1940s and the 1950s, he asked people in Europe about whether they would ever like their countries to unite into one political union.

But perhaps his most famous question — which is now a staple in modern politics — is about the U.S. presidential approval rating.

If you have ever worked in, studied, read about, or argued about politics, you have probably talked about the president's job approval. George Gallup began experimenting with this concept in his first polls. He continued to refine the question throughout Franklin Roosevelt's presidency and finally settled on this wording, just as President Harry Truman took office:

> Do you approve or disapprove of the way [FIRST NAME/ LAST NAME] is handling his job as president?

While this is arguably the most famous question George Gallup ever asked, he asked thousands of other questions that have provided tremendous utility to world leaders. We went through all these questions and added the best ones to the World Poll — mainly questions about various government institutions. Here are some of those questions as we ask them today:

> In this country, do you have confidence in each of the following, or not? How about …
>
> - the military?
> - judicial system and courts?
> - honesty of elections?
>
> In the city or area where you live, do you have confidence in the local police force, or not?
>
> In the city or area where you live, are you satisfied or dissatisfied with …
>
> - the availability of quality healthcare?
> - the educational system or the schools?

The next step was to engage global experts. What should we ask in a global survey? What would help world leaders most?

One of the people we interviewed was Jim Wolfensohn, the former head of the World Bank. He recommended that we put a major emphasis on law and order. Additionally, he encouraged us to quantify people's state of fear in a society — like whether they feel safe in their own communities.

In addition to dozens of stakeholder interviews, we also brought on a group of experts we call Gallup Senior Scientists, including Carol Graham, Deepak Chopra, John Helliwell, Ngozi Okonjo-Iweala, Ed Diener, and Nobel laureates Daniel Kahneman and Angus Deaton.

What Do We Ask?

After our initial research, we developed a behavioral framework for societies. We call it The Gallup World Path.

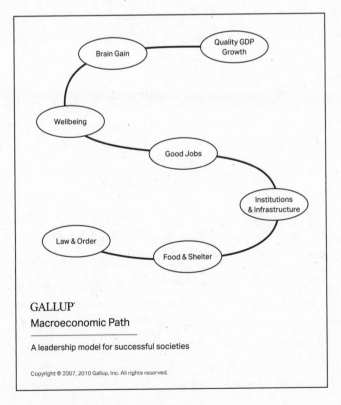

GALLUP
Macroeconomic Path

A leadership model for successful societies

Copyright © 2007, 2010 Gallup, Inc. All rights reserved.

Each of the categories on The Path has a set of corresponding questions that we ask people all over the world.

Step 1: Law and Order

Measuring law and order is more complex than just counting murders and robberies. The best leaders in the world do not just want to make their communities safe — they also want to make people *feel* safe.

From a data perspective, what's the difference?

If you go to the FBI's website to look at U.S. statistics on crime, there are a lot. The website allows you to look through all kinds of data on offenses committed in the U.S., such as violent crime including "four offenses: murder and nonnegligent manslaughter, rape, robbery, and aggravated assault." These data tell us that there were roughly 1.2 million violent crime offenses in the U.S. in 2019 (a 0.5% decrease from 2018).

The FBI collects these data from all participating law enforcement agencies in the United States. Those that do not have complete data make estimates. They also report on all kinds of arrests, police employee data, and even human trafficking.

But all these data are for crimes that were *reported*. In the U.S., many crimes get reported to the police, but does that happen internationally? In some of the poorest countries in the world, do crimes always get reported to the police? And what if the police are in on the crime? Then what does the public record say?

This is where survey data can be incredibly helpful. Instead of relying solely on the number of crimes that have been reported to the police, we can proactively ask people if they have been victims of a crime and report that number. Just like a labor force survey essentially asks, "Do you have a job?", we take a similar approach to crime and ask people if they have been victims of various offenses.

For example, we ask people, "Within the last 12 months, have you been assaulted or mugged?"

Perhaps the most important question we ask with respect to law and order is: "Do you feel safe walking alone at night in the city or area where you live?" No matter how much data you collect on reported crimes, you can never know how safe people feel in their communities unless you ask them.

In addition to personal safety, we also ask people how they feel about their local police. There are about 20 countries where these questions are too sensitive to ask. For example, we have not been able to ask about the police in Egypt since 2016. Someone might consider that fact alone an interesting data point (I sure do).

Here are the questions we ask with respect to law and order:

In the city or area where you live, do you have confidence in the local police force, or not?

Do you feel safe walking alone at night in the city or area where you live?

Within the last 12 months, have you had money or property stolen from you or another household member?

Within the last 12 months, have you been assaulted or mugged?

Since 2018, 6% of adults worldwide have said they were assaulted or mugged in the past year. This translates into about 320 million adults — roughly the population of the entire United States.

Crime is a massive issue in sub-Saharan Africa: Almost every country on the top 10 mugging and assaults list are in this region. Tied for 10th is war-torn Afghanistan, with 17% of people there reporting that they have been assaulted or mugged in the past 12 months.

Where People Are Most Likely to Get Assaulted or Mugged

Rank	Country	Yes
1	Gambia	29%
2	Liberia	28%
3	Sierra Leone	26%
4	Kenya	22%
5	Uganda	21%
6	Cameroon	20%
7	Niger	19%
8	Nigeria	18%
	Congo Brazzaville	18%
10	Afghanistan	17%
	South Africa	17%

Within the last 12 months, have you been assaulted or mugged? Averaged over 2019-2021.
Source: Gallup

In 56 countries — including the U.S. — 3% or less people report being assaulted or mugged in the last 12 months.

Twice as many people said they had money or property stolen in the last 12 months. On average since 2018, 13% — or 680 million people — have reported that they or a household member had been victims of this type of crime.

Where People Are Most Likely to Be Robbed

Rank	Country	Yes
1	Sierra Leone	48%
2	Uganda	45%
3	Gabon	44%
4	Gambia	43%
	Liberia	43%
6	Malawi	41%
	Zambia	41%
8	Botswana	40%
9	Kenya	36%
	Madagascar	36%

Within the last 12 months, have you had money or property stolen from you or another household member? Averaged over 2019-2021.
Source: Gallup

Generally, most people tell us that they are confident in their local police force — 69% of people globally since 2018. A majority of people in 117 countries out of 136 where we asked this question between 2018 and 2020 express confidence in their local police.

Confidence in Police

Most likely to say they have confidence in local police

Rank	Country	Yes
1	Rwanda	94%
2	Singapore	93%
3	Iceland	91%
	Switzerland	91%
5	Luxembourg	90%
6	Finland	89%
7	Norway	88%
8	Austria	87%
	Azerbaijan	87%
10	Portugal	86%
	Germany	86%
	Indonesia	86%

Least likely to say they have confidence in local police

Rank	Country	No
1	Venezuela	72%
2	Afghanistan	71%
3	Bolivia	60%
4	Mexico	58%
5	Gabon	56%
6	Peru	52%
7	Honduras	50%
8	Nigeria	49%
9	Hong Kong S.A.R. of China	48%
	Dominican Republic	48%

In the city or area where you live, do you have confidence in the local police force, or not? Averaged over 2019-2021.
Source: Gallup

The last part of our Law and Order Index involves quantifying fear. As I previously mentioned, great leaders care not just about whether people are safe, they also care about whether people *feel* safe. The United Nations agrees. SDG indicator 16.1.4 specifically encourages governments to focus on the "proportion of population that *feel safe walking alone around the area they live.*" (emphasis added)

Gallup's "feeling safe" indicator is covered earlier in the book. See Chapter Ten for the full results.

Step 2: Food and Shelter

Even in the wealthiest countries, some percentage of the population struggles to meet its basic needs. The next point on the path — Food and Shelter — looks at the prevalence of poverty across nations.

Here are the questions we ask with respect to food and shelter:

Have there been times in the past 12 months when you did not have enough money ...

- to buy food that you or your family needed?
- to provide adequate shelter or housing for you and your family?

Step 3: Institutions and Infrastructure

The third point on the path measures people's confidence in key institutions and evaluates their satisfaction with infrastructure (See Chapter Ten). We also ask about corruption in government and business (See chapters Thirteen and Nineteen).

Here are the questions we ask with respect to institutions and infrastructure:

In the city or area where you live, are you satisfied or dissatisfied with ...

- the public transportation systems?
- the roads and highways?
- the educational system or the schools?
- the quality of air?
- the quality of water?
- the availability of quality healthcare?
- the availability of good affordable housing?

In this country, do you have confidence in each of the following, or not? How about …

- the military?
- judicial system and courts?
- national government?
- financial institutions or banks?
- honesty of elections?

Do you believe that children in (country) are treated with respect and dignity, or not?

Do most children in (country) have the opportunity to learn and grow every day, or not?

Do you have a landline telephone in your home that you use to make and receive personal calls?

Do you have a mobile phone that you use to make and receive personal calls?

Do you have access to the internet in any way, whether on a mobile phone, a computer, or some other device?

Is corruption widespread within businesses located in (this country), or not?

Is corruption widespread throughout the government in (this country), or not?

Step 4: Good Jobs

People's work often shapes their identity and their wellbeing, so it makes sense that Gallup's global surveys show that people who are working full time for an employer — they have good jobs — have higher wellbeing than those who do not. And those who are also engaged and thriving at work have great jobs — and even higher wellbeing.

Here are the questions we ask with respect to good jobs:

Thinking about the job situation in the city or area where you live today, would you say that it is now a good time or a bad time to find a job?

In the city or area where you live, are you satisfied or dissatisfied with the availability of good job opportunities?

Thinking about your work situation over the past 7 days, have you been employed by an employer — even minimally like for an hour or more — from whom you receive money or goods?

(If work for an employer) In a typical week (7 days), how many hours do you work for an employer?

(If do not work 30 hours or more for employer) Again thinking about the last 7 days, were you self-employed, even minimally like for an hour or more? This means working for yourself, freelancing, doing contract work, OR working for your own or your family's business.

(If work for self) In a typical week (7 days), how many hours do you work as a self-employed individual?

(If work less than 30 hours per week) Do you want to work 30 hours or more per week?

(If do not work for employer or self) In the past four weeks, have you actively been looking for employment? "Actively looking" means applying for jobs, searching for jobs, and the like.

(If do not work for employer or self) Would you have been able to begin work had you been offered a job within the last four weeks?

Q01. I know what is expected of me at work.

Q02. I have the materials and equipment I need to do my work right.

Q03. At work, I have the opportunity to do what I do best every day.

Q04. In the last seven days, I have received recognition or praise for doing good work.

Q05. My supervisor, or someone at work, seems to care about me as a person.

Q06. There is someone at work who encourages my development.

Q07. At work, my opinions seem to count.

Q08. The mission or purpose of my company makes me feel my job is important.

Q09. My associates or fellow employees are committed to doing quality work.

Q10. I have a best friend at work.

Q11. In the last six months, someone at work has talked to me about my progress.

Q12. This last year, I have had opportunities at work to learn and grow.

Step 5: Wellbeing

The next point on the path, Wellbeing, measures the interconnected elements that contribute to health, happiness, and productivity, including work, social networks, personal economics, personal health, and citizen engagement. Across countries, measures of wellbeing are strongly related to income, education levels, and reported disease conditions.

Here are the questions we ask with respect to wellbeing:

Are you satisfied or dissatisfied with your standard of living, all the things you can buy and do?

Right now, do you feel your standard of living is getting better or getting worse?

Do you have any health problems that prevent you from doing any of the things people your age normally can do?

Now, please think about yesterday, from the morning until the end of the day. Think about where you were, what you were doing, who you were with, and how you felt.

Did you feel well-rested yesterday?

Were you treated with respect all day yesterday?

Did you smile or laugh a lot yesterday?

Did you learn or do something interesting yesterday?

Did you experience the following feelings during a lot of the day yesterday? How about ...

- enjoyment?
- physical pain?
- worry?
- sadness?

- stress?
- anger?

Please imagine a ladder with steps numbered from zero at the bottom to 10 at the top. The top of the ladder represents the best possible life for you and the bottom of the ladder represents the worst possible life for you.

- On which step of the ladder would you say you personally feel you stand at this time?
- Just your best guess, on which step do you think you will stand in the future, say about five years from now?

Which one of these phrases comes closest to your own feelings about your household's income these days?

- living comfortably on present income
- getting by on present income
- finding it difficult on present income
- finding it very difficult on present income

In the city or area where you live, are you satisfied or dissatisfied with the opportunities to meet people and make friends?

If you were in trouble, do you have relatives or friends you can count on to help you whenever you need them, or not?

Have you done any of the following in the past month? How about …

- donated money to a charity?
- volunteered your time to an organization?
- helped a stranger or someone you didn't know who needed help?

Step 6: Brain Gain

The next point, Brain Gain, reflects a city's or a country's ability to attract and retain talented people whose exceptional gifts and knowledge create new businesses and new jobs to improve the economy.

Here are the questions we ask with respect to brain gain:

Are you satisfied or dissatisfied with the city or area where you live?

In the next 12 months, are you likely or unlikely to move away from the city or area where you live?

Would you recommend the city or area where you live to a friend or associate as a place to live, or not?

Ideally, if you had the opportunity, would you like to move permanently to another country, or would you prefer to continue living in this country? (If yes) To which country would you like to move?

How Gallup Surveys the World

The Gallup World Path is the guiding framework that we use to determine what we ask. In addition to the questions on steps 1-6 of The Path, we ask about topical issues. For example, during the COVID-19 pandemic, we asked people how much they were affected by it and whether they were vaccinated.

So this is *what* we ask. But *how* do we ask these questions to people in over 140 countries?

Many countries have local organizations that do this type of research. If you wanted to conduct a survey in Armenia after the 2020 conflict, there are firms you can hire to do this work. They will charge anywhere between $50,000 and $90,000 (USD) just to drive around the entire country to interview 1,000 randomly selected (probability based) people. You can do some of these projects even cheaper if you ask the firms to conduct a survey in just the capital city or in a few of the biggest cities. In fact, the cost may drop by more than 50% if you do.

But if you conduct surveys in only the biggest cities, do the data represent the entire country? Reputable organizations often do this and not just in the hardest-to-reach places. For example, look at the Rule of Law Index published by the World Justice Project (WJP). To measure the rule of law, the WJP relies on two datasets: one that collects expert opinions and one that comes from a public opinion survey.

The methodology is detailed in the back of the report. They go through each individual country, how many people they surveyed, how they conducted the surveys, and where they conducted the surveys. For example, they conduct a study in Belize each year. The study involves 1,000 face-to-face interviews, and the sample is nationally representative. This means that the people who participated were selected from the entire country (including urban and rural areas).

Their methodology for China is different. There, the WJP conducted roughly 500 interviews in Shanghai, Beijing, and Guangzhou. Now, imagine using that approach in the U.S. You conduct surveys in Los Angeles; New York; and Washington, D.C. Do those data represent the entire U.S.? The second-largest economy in the world probably warrants a better methodology.

The World Justice Project has publicly committed to doing better:

> Toward this end, nationally representative polls have been conducted in 63 countries and jurisdictions covered in the WJP Rule of Law Index 2020. Nationally representative polls will be conducted in the remaining countries and jurisdictions in future editions of the Index.

I don't blame the WJP for what they did. A global survey using a gold standard methodology is not cheap. Previously, I mentioned that a national survey can cost tens of thousands of dollars. Do the math on how much it costs if you use the highest standard of methodology in 140 countries. That is just what you outsource; it does not include the people you need to clean, vet, analyze, and report on the data. Gallup's longtime Chief Financial Officer, Jim Krieger, once publicly disclosed that Gallup had spent over $100 million on the World Poll.

So to understand how people's lives are going, Gallup calls people in roughly 40 countries and conducts face-to-face interviews in another 100 countries, and all of it is really expensive. But how do we actually identify the people we talk to?

In-person Interviews

For face-to-face interviews, we use a process called a multistage stratified cluster sample. Here is what that means in non-survey language: We take a map of every country and break it up into states, provinces, or governorates using the country's most recent census. In some cases, we use geographic imaging because the census is so dated. The entire breakdown is called a sampling frame.

Within each state, province, or governorate, we randomly select neighborhoods or villages where we go to survey (what we call Primary Sampling Units or PSUs). We select about 100 PSUs across the country. Here is an example of PSUs selected for Kenya.

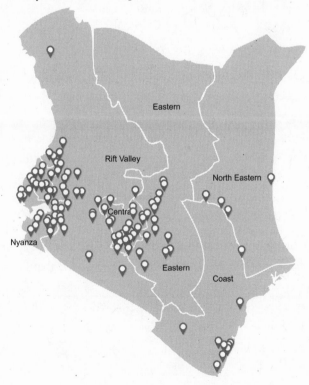

We interview between eight and 12 people in each of these PSUs. They are selected using a process as random as possible. For example, if there is a community in a small town in Kenya, the interviewer will use a starting point, which might be a school, a church, or a postal building. From there, they identify the nearest residential street. After that, they are given specific instructions on how to randomly select a house or apartment.

Technology has made interviewing a lot easier. In 2006, we conducted all face-to-face interviews using paper and pencil. In some communities, the interviewers had to conceal the documents. Otherwise, they were perceived as government workers who might be viewed unfavorably. Now, in almost all countries, interviewers use a handheld device to select the household member to interview and to type in the respondents' answers.

These handheld devices allow for faster surveys and GPS tracking. GPS lets us see where interviewers went and how long they were there. Once, someone's GPS coordinates indicated that they were on top of a lake, and we were understandably concerned. We found out later they were not conducting an interview — they were fishing. We were glad the interviewer was safe, but when we find out that an interviewer is falsifying data, we discontinue working with them and throw out all their work.

Sometimes the household member selected to do the survey is unavailable (for example, they may be at work). If that happens, the interviewer will revisit the household another time. If the selected respondent will be unavailable for the rest of the survey period or refuses to be interviewed, the interviewer selects a different household.

Cultural restrictions can also add challenges to the selection process. In a few Middle Eastern and Asian countries where the culture dictates that the gender of the interviewer and the respondent must be the same, respondents are randomly selected among all eligible adults of the same gender.

Telephone Interviews

In countries where we conduct interviews by telephone, Gallup calls people using random digit dialing (RDD) or a nationally representative list of phone numbers. Gallup typically uses a dual sampling frame, which means we select people randomly from landline and mobile telephone samples. In some countries, the sampling frame is mobile telephone only (like in Finland, for example).

If we are contacting people on landline telephones, we select respondents within the household one of two ways: We ask to speak to the person who has the next birthday, or we list all eligible household members and let the computer-assisted telephone interview (CATI) program choose the respondent.

Over different days and times of day, interviewers make at least five attempts to reach a person and complete an interview in each household.

Once the respondent is selected, telephone interviews last approximately 30 minutes, while face-to-face interviews last between 45 minutes to one hour.

REFERENCES

This book covers a wide range of research. For more details about Gallup's research and other studies referenced in the book's text, please see this expanded reference section. For some references, we have included additional notes. Please note that any statistics not cited stem from Gallup research and studies.

Introduction

Notes

Best and Worst Life Ratings

Percentage of people who rated their lives a 10 (best life) and those who rated their lives a zero (worst life)

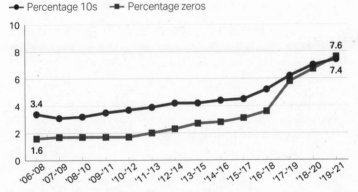

Wellbeing scores for people who rated their lives a 10 (best life) and those who rated their lives a zero (worst life) from 2006-2021. Wellbeing scores range from 0-10.

Source: Gallup

References

Clifton, J. (2019, May 7). *It's the manager.* Gallup. https://www.gallup.com/workplace/251642/manager.aspx

Clifton, J., & Harter, J. (2019). *It's the manager.* Gallup Press.

Clifton, J., & Harter, J. (2021). *Wellbeing at Work.* Gallup Press.

Gallup. *How does the Gallup World Poll work?* Gallup. https://www.gallup.com/178667/gallup-world-poll-work.aspx

Viviani, S., & Ray, J. (2021, August 12). *World headed in wrong direction on hunger.* Gallup. https://news.gallup.com/opinion/gallup/353150/world-headed-wrong-direction-hunger.aspx

Overview

References

Chavez, D. (2020, April 28). *Nearly half of global workforce at risk as job losses increase due to COVID-19: UN labour agency.* United Nations. https://news.un.org/en/story/2020/04/1062792

FAO, IFAD, UNICEF, WFP and WHO. (2021). *The state of food security and nutrition in the world 2021. Transforming food systems for food security, improved nutrition and affordable healthy diets for all.* FAO. https://doi.org/10.4060/cb4474en

The pandemic may be encouraging people to live in larger groups. (2020, December 5). *The Economist.* https://www.economist.com/international/2020/12/05/the-pandemic-may-be-encouraging-people-to-live-in-larger-groups

Part I: The Leadership Blind Spot: Happiness and Wellbeing

Chapter One: What Economic Models Miss

Notes

Human Development Index: The entire series of Human Development Index (HDI) values and rankings are recalculated every year using the most recent (revised) data and functional forms. The HDI rankings and values in the 2014 Human Development Report cannot therefore be compared directly to indices published in previous Reports. Please see hdr.undp.org for more information.

The HDI was created to emphasize that people and their capabilities should be the ultimate criteria for assessing the development of a country, not economic growth alone. The HDI can also be used to question national policy choices, asking how two countries with the same level of GNI per capita can end up with different human development outcomes.

http://hdr.undp.org/en/indicators/137506#

References

The 1992 campaign; Clinton hub is Little Rock. (1992, May 14). *The New York Times*. https://www.nytimes.com/1992/05/14/us/the-1992-campaign-clinton-hub-is-little-rock.html

Alexander, R. (2013, July 16). *Counting crowds: Was Egypt's uprising the biggest ever?* BBC News. https://www.bbc.com/news/magazine-23312656

Ali Baba gone, but what about the 40 thieves? (2011, January 20). *The Economist*. https://www.economist.com/briefing/2011/01/20/ali-baba-gone-but-what-about-the-40-thieves

Beaumont, P. (2011, January 20). Mohammed Bouazizi: The dutiful son whose death changed Tunisia's fate. *The Guardian*. https://www.theguardian.com/world/2011/jan/20/tunisian-fruit-seller-mohammed-bouazizi

Carden, D. L. (2019). *Mapping ASEAN: Achieving peace, prosperity, and sustainability in Southeast Asia.* Indiana University Press.

Carvin, A. (2011, January 13). *Online reports detail chaos, deaths in Tunisia; add yours.* NPR. https://www.npr.org/sections/thetwo-way/2011/01/13/132888992/tunisia-protests-social-media

Carvin, A. (2011, January 16). *Sidi Bou Zid: A Jasmine Revolution in Tunisia.* https://web.archive.org/web/20131211214152/http://storify.com/acarvin/sidi-bou-zid-a-jasmine-revolution-in-tunisia

Clifton, J. (2017, October 20). *Is your country ready for change?* Gallup. https://news.gallup.com/opinion/gallup/220712/country-ready-change.aspx

Clifton, J., & Morales, L. (2021, February 2). *Egyptians', Tunisians' well-being plummets despite GDP gains.* Gallup. https://news.gallup.com/poll/145883/Egyptians-Tunisians-Wellbeing-Plummets-Despite-GDP-Gains.aspx

Data Commons. (n.d.). *Tunisia.* [Data set]. Data Commons. https://datacommons.org/place/country/TUN?utm_medium=explore&mprop=amount&popt=EconomicActivity&cpv=activitySource%2CGrossDomesticProduction&hl=en

de Soto, H. (2011, December 16). The real Mohamed Bouazizi. *Foreign Policy.* https://foreignpolicy.com/2011/12/16/the-real-mohamed-bouazizi/

Division of Economic Research of the Bureau of Foreign and Domestic Commerce. (1943, January 4). *National income, 1929–32. Letter from the acting secretary of commerce transmitting in response to senate resolution No. 220 (72d Cong.) A report on national income, 1929–32.* National Bureau of Economic Research. https://fraser.stlouisfed.org/files/docs/publications/natincome_1934/19340104_nationalinc.pdf

Doing business 2010: Reforming through difficult times. (2009). Palgrave Macmillan, International Finance Corporation, and The World Bank. https://www.doingbusiness.org/en/reports/global-reports/doing-business-2010

Doucet, L. (2011, January 11). *Tunisia celebrates press freedom after 'Jasmine Revolution'* [Video]. BBC News. https://www.bbc.com/news/av/world-africa-12251117

Human Development Reports. (2019-2020). *Human Development Index (HDI)* [Data set]. United Nations Development Programme. http://hdr.undp.org/en/indicators/137506#

Klein, P. A. (1993, June). *Federal elections 92: Election results of the U.S. President, the U.S. Senate and the U.S. House of Representatives.* Federal Election Commission. https://www.fec.gov/resources/cms-content/documents/federalelections92.pdf

Kuznets, S. (1934, June). *National income, 1929-1932.* National Bureau of Economic Research. https://www.nber.org/system/files/chapters/c2258/c2258.pdf

Riley, R. L. (n.d.). *Bill Clinton: Campaigns and elections.* The Miller Center. https://millercenter.org/president/clinton/campaigns-and-elections

Robinson, K. (2020, December 3). *The Arab Spring at ten years: What's the legacy of the uprisings?* Council on Foreign Relations. https://www.cfr.org/article/arab-spring-ten-years-whats-legacy-uprisings

Schwab, K. (2010). *The global competitiveness report 2010-2011.* World Economic Forum. https://www3.weforum.org/docs/WEF_GlobalCompetitivenessReport_2010-11.pdf

U.S. Bureau of Economic Analysis. (2018, February 5). What is the value of household work? *The BEA Wire, BEA.* https://www.bea.gov/news/blog/2012-06-11/what-value-household-work

The World Bank. (n.d.). *GDP growth (annual %) - Tunisia.* [Data set]. The World Bank. https://data.worldbank.org/indicator/NY.GDP.MKTP.KD.ZG?locations=TN

Chapter Two: Unhappiness and Elections

Notes

Shifts in Life Satisfaction in 2016 U.S. Presidential Election Relative to 2012 Election

	Number of counties	Current life satisfaction 7-10	Future life optimism 8-10
Democratic shift of:			
10+ percentage pts.	46	73%	72%
5 to <10 percentage pts.	140	69%	69%
0 to <5 percentage pts.	490	67%	67%
Republican shift of:			
10+ percentage pts.	328	61%	58%
5 to <10 percentage pts.	851	62%	60%
0 to <5 percentage pts.	1,257	64%	64%

Placement on imaginary ladder with 10 steps, where top step is best possible life, today and five years from now.

Source: Gallup

India: Thriving and GDP per Capita

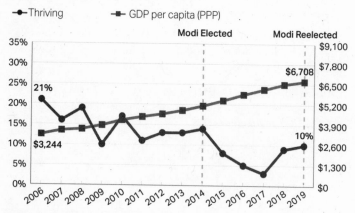

GDP per capita (PPP) estimates are from the International Monetary Fund's World Economic Outlook database, April 2021. Purchasing power parity; 2017 international dollars.

Source: Gallup and International Monetary Fund

References

Abramson, Alana. (2016, December 22). *Hillary Clinton officially wins popular vote by nearly 2.9 million.* ABC News. https://abcnews. go.com/Politics/hillary-clinton-officially-wins-popular-vote-29-million/story?id=44354341

Aisch, G., Pearce, A., & Russell, K. (2016, June 24). How Britain voted in the E.U. referendum. *The New York Times.* https://www.nytimes.com/interactive/2016/06/24/world/europe/how-britain-voted-brexit-referendum.html

Alabrese, E., Becker, S. O., Fetzer, T., & Novy, D. (2019, January). Who voted for Brexit? Individual and regional data combined. *European Journal of Political Economy, 56*, 132-150.

Arora, A., Spatz, E., Herrin, J., Riley, C., Roy, B., Kell, K., Coberley, C., Rula, E., & Krumholz, H. M. (2016). Population well-being measures help explain geographic disparities in life expectancy at the county level. *Health Affairs (Project Hope), 35*(11), 2075-2082. https://doi.org/10.1377/hlthaff.2016.0715

Ashcroft, M. (2016, June 24). *How the United Kingdom voted on Thursday… and why.* Lord Ashcroft Polls. https://lordashcroftpolls.com/2016/06/how-the-united-kingdom-voted-and-why/

Bowman, B. (2016, October 12). *Whether Trump wins or not, America's Brexit moment is coming.* The Conversation. https://theconversation.com/whether-trump-wins-or-not-americas-brexit-moment-is-coming-65386

Britain stuns world by voting to leave the European Union. (2016, June 24). Democracy Now! https://www.democracynow.org/2016/6/24/headlines

Cameron likens Brexit to putting 'bomb under economy.' (2016, June 6). BBC News. https://www.bbc.com/news/uk-politics-eu-referendum-36459451

Clifton, J. (2017, October 20). *Is your country ready for change?* Gallup. https://news.gallup.com/opinion/gallup/220712/country-ready-change.aspx

Eurobarometer Data Service. (1973-2021). *Life satisfaction* [Data set]. Leibniz Institute for the Social Sciences. https://www.gesis.org/en/eurobarometer-data-service/search-data-access/eb-trends-trend-files/list-of-trends/life-satisf

Fidler, M. (2016, June 24). How newspapers covered Brexit – in pictures. *The Guardian*. https://www.theguardian.com/politics/gallery/2016/jun/24/newspapers-brexit-front-pages-eu

Gallup. (2017). *What happiness today tells us about the world tomorrow*. Gallup. https://news.gallup.com/reports/220601/what-happiness-today-tells-us-about-the-world-tomorrow.aspx

Grynbaum, M. M. (2020, September 29). 84 million is the number to beat for tonight's debate to set a ratings record. *The New York Times*. https://www.nytimes.com/2020/09/29/us/84-million-is-the-number-to-beat-for-tonights-debate-to-set-a-ratings-record.html

Human Development Report 2020. (n.d.). *The next frontier: Human development and the Anthropocene* [Briefing note for countries on the 2020 Human Development Report: United Kingdom]. United Nations Development Programme. http://hdr.undp.org/sites/default/files/Country-Profiles/GBR.pdf

Human Development Reports. (1990-2019). *United Kingdom: Human Development Indicators* [Data set]. United Nations Development Programme. http://hdr.undp.org/en/countries/profiles/GBR#

Inglehart, R. F., & Norris, P. (2016, August). *Trump, Brexit, and the rise of populism: Economic have-nots and cultural backlash.* [Draft paper]. Faculty Research Working Paper Series. https://research.hks.harvard.edu/publications/getFile.aspx?Id=1401

Jahan, S. (2016). *Human development report 2016: Human development for everyone.* United Nations Development Programme. http://hdr.undp.org/sites/default/files/2016_human_development_report.pdf

Kottasova, I. (2016, June 24). *The pound is crashing on U.K. vote for Brexit.* CNN. https://money.cnn.com/2016/06/24/investing/pound-crash-eu-referendum/

Labour market statistics time series (LMS). (2021, December 14). *Unemployment rate (aged 16 and over, seasonally adjusted)* [Data set]. Office for National Statistics. https://www.ons.gov.uk/employmentandlabourmarket/peoplenotinwork/unemployment/timeseries/mgsx/lms

Lee, T. B. (2016, June 25). *Brexit: the 7 most important arguments for Britain to leave the EU.* Vox. https://www.vox.com/2016/6/22/11992106/brexit-arguments

October 28, 1980 Debate Transcript. (n.d.). The Commission on Presidential Debates. https://www.debates.org/voter-education/debate-transcripts/october-28-1980-debate-transcript/

Rees, K. (2016, June 30). *FTSE ends June on 2016 high.* Reuters. https://www.reuters.com/article/us-britain-stocks/ftse-ends-june-on-2016-high-idUSKCN0ZG2GC

Shea, C. (2011, September 23). Asking about politics ruins people's sense of well-being. *The Wall Street Journal.* https://www.wsj.com/articles/BL-IMB-2660

Understanding How Gallup Uses the Cantril Scale. (n.d.). Gallup. https://news.gallup.com/poll/122453/understanding-gallup-uses-cantril-scale.aspx

University of Essex, Institute for Social and Economic Research. (2021). *Understanding Society.* UK Data Service. SN: 6614. https://www.understandingsociety.ac.uk/about/about-the-study

Ward, G. (2015, April). *Is happiness a predictor of election results?* [CEP Discussion Paper No 1343]. Centre for Economic Performance. http://cep.lse.ac.uk/pubs/download/dp1343.pdf?utm_source=link_newsv9&utm_campaign=item_206468&utm_medium=copy

Ward, G. (2019). Happiness and voting behavior. In Helliwell, J. F., Layard, R., & Sachs, J. D. (Eds.), *World happiness report 2019* (pp. 26-65). Sustainable Development Solutions Network. https://worldhappiness.report/ed/2019/happiness-and-voting-behavior/

Ward, G. (2020). Happiness and voting: Evidence from four decades of elections in Europe. *American Journal of Political Science, 64*(3), 504-518. https://onlinelibrary.wiley.com/doi/10.1111/ajps.12492

Which presidential debates drew the biggest TV audiences? (2020, October 1). Statista https://www.statista.com/chart/23075/estimated-tv-viewership-of-presidential-debates/

Witters, D., & Liu, D. (2018, April 25). *Poor well-being associated with shift to Trump in 2016.* Gallup. https://news.gallup.com/poll/232448/poor-associated-shift-trump-2016.aspx

Part II: Addressing the Blind Spot: Measuring Happiness and Wellbeing

References

Cave, J. (2014, April 22). *Is Alvin Wong, 2010's 'happiest man in America,' still happy?* HuffPost. https://www.huffpost.com/entry/alvin-wong-happiest-man-america_n_5122548

Rampell, C. (2011, March 5). Discovered: The happiest man in America. *The New York Times.* https://www.nytimes.com/2011/03/06/weekinreview/06happy.html

Strachan, M. (2017, December 6). 'The Happiest Man In America' Lives In Hawaii, Owns His Own Business (VIDEO). HuffPost. https://www.huffpost.com/entry/the-happiest-man-in-the-w_n_833098

Wong, A. (n.d.). *My philosophy.* Alvin Wong. http://www.alvin-wong.com/my-philosophy/

Chapter Three: The Happiest People in the World?

Notes

Why so many countries? There are 156 countries in the 2019 *World Happiness Report,* yet Gallup only conducts surveys in roughly 140 countries annually. The difference is because the *WHR* uses a three-year average of data (which I also often do in this book). And Gallup doesn't always conduct surveys in the same 140 countries every year (we may not include a country because of safety concerns or budgetary restraints).

For example, the 2019 *WHR* uses Gallup World Poll data from 2016-2018. We did surveys in the Democratic Republic of Congo in 2016 and 2017 only. The *WHR* averaged those two years to represent DRC's happiness score for the 2019 report. But in the 2021 report, the DRC does not appear because Gallup has not conducted a survey in the DRC since 2017 (and the *WHR* aggregated 2018-2020 for that report).

References

Helliwell, J. F., Huang, H., & Wang, S. (2015). Chapter 2. The geography of world happiness. In Helliwell, J., Layard, R., & Sachs, J. (Eds.), *World happiness report 2015* (pp. 12-41). Sustainable Development Solutions Network. https://s3.amazonaws.com/happiness-report/2015/WHR15_Sep15.pdf

Helliwell, J., Layard, R., Sachs, J. D., de Neve, J.-E., Aknin, L., Huang, H., Wang, S., & Paculor, S. (2020). *World happiness report 2020*. Sustainable Development Solutions Network. https://worldhappiness.report/ed/2020/

Helliwell, J. F., & Wang, S. (2012). Chapter 2. The state of world happiness. In Helliwell, J., Layard, R., & Sachs, J. (Eds.), *World happiness report 2012* (pp. 10-57). Sustainable Development Solutions Network. https://s3.amazonaws.com/happiness-report/2012/World_Happiness_Report_2012.pdf

Hosie, R. (2020, March 20). *I stopped 10 people on the streets of Finland, the happiest country in the world, to find out what their secret is*. Insider. https://www.insider.com/finnish-people-share-secret-to-happiness-finland-why-happiest-country-2020-2#2-its-not-an-outward-happiness-honna-2

Leaver, K. (2018, June 18). *Why the Finns don't want to be happy*. BBC Travel. https://www.bbc.com/travel/article/20180617-why-the-finns-dont-want-to-be-happy

Martela, F. (2018, May 11). Finland is the happiest country in the world, and Finns aren't happy about it. *Observations*. https://blogs.scientificamerican.com/observations/finland-is-the-happiest-country-in-the-world-and-finns-arent-happy-about-it/

Methodology Center. Gallup. https://www.gallup.com/178685/methodology-center.aspx

Oxford Languages. (n.d.). Happiness. Definition from *Oxford Languages* dictionary.

Savolainen, J. (2021, April 28). *The grim secret of Nordic happiness*. Slate. https://slate.com/news-and-politics/2021/04/finland-happiness-lagom-hygge.html?via=rss_socialflow_facebook&fbclid=IwAR0LI7utgIfmV6g5VfYstwOM3DLNoUWEeMDEQvsdNu-C3AmcsQgr2M391wyU

Seligman, M. E. P. (2011). *Flourish: A visionary new understanding of happiness and well-being.* Free Press.

Chapter Four: How on Earth Do You Measure Happiness?

Notes

Subjective wellbeing — a brief history: Nobel laureate Daniel Kahneman and University of Illinois professor Ed Diener were influential in conceiving the contemporary views of subjective wellbeing. In the journal article "Guidelines for National Indicators of Subjective Well-Being and Ill-Being," Diener defines subjective wellbeing as "all of the various types of evaluations, both positive and negative, that people make of their lives. It includes reflective cognitive evaluations, such as life satisfaction and work satisfaction, interest and engagement, and affective reactions to life events, such as joy and sadness."

Similarly, in the book *The Science of Well-Being: Integrating Neurobiology, Psychology, and Social Science,* Kahneman makes note of the distinction between "experienced well-being" and "evaluative well-being." Experienced wellbeing is concerned with momentary affective states and the way people feel about experiences in real time, while evaluative wellbeing is the way they remember their experiences after they are over. Experienced wellbeing seeks to bypass the effects of judgment and memory and has historically been measured using the experience sampling method or the day reconstruction method — both of which seek to capture feelings and emotions as close to the subject's immediate experience as possible. Inspired by the work of Kahneman and his colleagues, Gallup adapted these methods to a large-scale survey environment by framing a series of experience and emotion questions within the context of the past 24 hours.

Eudaimonia: Most wellbeing researchers recommend including a third construct in the overall definition of wellbeing, which we do not include: *eudaimonia.* Aristotle used this word to describe the pinnacle of a great life — that someone has a sense of meaning and purpose in life and is "flourishing." (2012 *WHR*)

Researchers are attempting to measure eudaimonia. Using the framework from the Organisation for Economic Co-operation and Development, the U.K.'s Office of National Statistics measured life evaluation, life affect (positive and negative), and eudaimonia throughout the entire country. According to the 2012 *World Happiness Report,* "The results show that the eudaimonic answers are correlated with both emotional measures, but more closely to life satisfaction than to either emotion."

Figuring out a measure for this remains important because most people know they have a purpose in life. We once asked the world, "Do you feel your life has an important purpose?" Globally, 90% of people said yes. Because the rate was so high and the country-level responses so uniform, we sunsetted the question.

The importance of having purpose is evident across many studies. In a Gallup study of U.S. college graduates, respondents were asked to reflect on their first good job and to describe what made it a good job. The No. 1 reason? "Mission and purpose of the job." "Pay" was No. 2.

But arriving at one question to determine whether people are realizing their purpose has proved elusive. According to the *WHR,* "… although notions of meaning or purpose in life are a crucial part of eudaimonia, it is unclear as to whether a single question of this sort adequately captures all of the relevant aspects of eudaimonia."

Instead, the *WHR* identifies a potential link between eudaimonia and wellbeing at work: "An important school of thought focuses on the importance of intrinsic motivation at work — and related to that the importance of the intrinsic features of the job (rather than pay) as sources of satisfaction: eudaimonic returns associated with human flourishing."

Gallup explores how well the world is doing at work in Chapter Eight. The closest we have come to capturing eudaimonia is asking people to respond to this statement: "At work, I have the opportunity to do what I do best every day."

We ask workers to rate this statement on a 5-point scale, and we find that one-third of workers believe they do have the opportunity to do what they do best every day. In the future, a metric could be developed that applies more broadly and includes people who are not in the workforce.

A shorter ladder question: We split our survey samples in 60 countries and tested to see if a shorter version of the Cantril ladder question would yield the same results. We asked half of the people the exact Cantril ladder question, and we asked the other half a shorter version. We found that shortening the question does not change how people respond to it.

These findings may be unremarkable to some, but they are remarkable to us. In survey research, you do not have much time with a respondent. In phone studies, you have about 15 to 30 minutes. Asking shorter questions means you have more time for other questions.

References

Bradburn, N. (1969). *The structure of psychological well-being.* Aldine.

Cantril, H. (1966). *The pattern of human concerns.* Rutgers University Press.

Clifton, J. (2019, April 25). *Does money buy happiness?* Gallup. https://news.gallup.com/opinion/gallup/249116/money-buy-happiness.aspx

Clifton, J., & Harter, J. (2021). *Wellbeing at Work.* Gallup Press.

Diener, E. (1984). Subjective well-being. *Psychological Bulletin, 95*(3), 542–575. https://doi.org/10.1037/0033-2909.95.3.542

Diener, E. (2005). Guidelines for national indicators of subjective wellbeing and ill-being. *Journal of Happiness Studies, 7,* 397-404.

Diener, E. (2009). *The science of well-being: The selective works of Ed Diener.* Springer.

Gallup. *Gallup Global Emotions 2021.* (2021). Gallup. https://www.gallup.com/analytics/349280/gallup-global-emotions-report.aspx

Helliwell, J., Layard, R., & Sachs, J. (2012). *World happiness report.* Sustainable Development Solutions Network. https://s3.amazonaws.com/happiness-report/2012/World_Happiness_Report_2012.pdf

Helliwell, J., Layard, R., & Sachs, J. (2013). *World happiness report 2013.* Sustainable Development Solutions Network. https://s3.amazonaws.com/happiness-report/2013/WorldHappinessReport2013_online.pdf

Huber, B. R. (2014, January 13). *Americans with and without children at home report similar life satisfaction.* Princeton University. https://www.princeton.edu/news/2014/01/13/americans-and-without-children-home-report-similar-life-satisfaction

Kahneman, D., Diener, E., & Schwarz, N. (Eds.). (1998). *Wellbeing: The foundations of hedonic psychology.* Russell Sage Foundation.

Kahneman, D., & Riis, J. (2005). Living and thinking about it: Two perspectives on life. In F. Huppert, N. Baylis, & B. Kaverne (Eds.), *The science of wellbeing: Integrating neurobiology, psychology, and social science* (pp. 285-304). Oxford University Press.

Lloyd's Register Foundation. (2020). *The Lloyd's Register Foundation World Risk Poll: Full report and analysis of the 2019 poll.* Lloyd's Register Foundation. https://wrp.lrfoundation.org.uk/

Marken, S. (2020, July 1). *Purpose and pay define a 'good job' for college grads.* Gallup. https://news.gallup.com/poll/312623/purpose-pay-define-good-job-college-grads.aspx

Moore, C. (2021, July 12). *What is eudaimonia? Aristotle and eudaimonic well-being.* PositivePsychology.com. https://positivepsychology.com/eudaimonia/

Oxford Languages. (n.d.). Love. Definition from *Oxford Languages* dictionary.

Stone, A. A., & Deaton, A. (2014). Evaluative and hedonic wellbeing among those with and without children at home. *Proceedings of the National Academy of Sciences of the United States of America, 111*(4), 1328-1333. https://doi.org/10.1073/pnas.1311600111

Tomyn, A. J. (2017). Hadley Cantril: A pioneer in public opinion research. *Applied Research in Quality of Life, 12*, 1033-1034. https://doi.org/10.1007/s11482-017-9569-9

Tortora, B., Kluch, K., & Kluch, S. (2015). *Current and future life evaluation: Results of experiments in the Gallup World Poll to reduce the length of the question wording* [PowerPoint slides]. American Association for Public Opinion Research. https://www.aapor.org/AAPOR_Main/media/AnnualMeetingProceedings/2015/D4-3-Tortora.pdf

Wilkinson, W. (2007, April 11). *In pursuit of happiness research: Is it reliable? What does it imply for policy?* Policy Analysis. https://www.cato.org/sites/cato.org/files/pubs/pdf/pa590.pdf

The World Factbook. (2021). *Country comparisons — Real GDP per capita* [Data set]. Central Intelligence Agency. https://www.cia.gov/the-world-factbook/field/real-gdp-per-capita/country-comparison

Chapter Five: Do People Know How Happy They Are?

References

International Labour Organization. (2017, July 25). *Labour Force Surveys* [Data set]. International Labour Organization. https://www.ilo.org/dyn/lfsurvey/lfsurvey.list?p_lang=en

Office of the Law Revision Counsel: United States Code. (n.d.). *50 USC Ch. 53: Trading with the enemy*. U.S. House of Representatives. https://uscode.house.gov/view.xhtml?path=/prelim@title50/chapter53&edition=prelim

U.S. Bureau of Labor Statistics. (2015, October 8). *How the government measures unemployment*. United States Department of Labor. https://www.bls.gov/cps/cps_htgm.htm#definitions

U.S. Bureau of Labor Statistics. (2020, February 10). *Monthly employment situation report: Quick guide to methods and measurement issues*. United States Department of Labor. https://www.bls.gov/bls/empsitquickguide.htm

Zumbrun, J. (2016, July 26). U.S. jobless picture offers room for interpretation. *The Wall Street Journal*. https://www.wsj.com/articles/u-s-jobless-picture-offers-room-for-interpretation-1469577415

Chapter Six: Behavioral Economics and Measuring a Great Life
References

America's Founding Documents. (n.d.). *Declaration of Independence: A Transcription* [Transcription of original]. National Archives. https://www.archives.gov/founding-docs/declaration-transcript (Original work published July 4, 1776)

Bodnar, A. (2011, December 1). Psychologist wins Nobel Prize. *New England Psychologist.* https://www.nepsy.com/articles/columnists/psychologist-wins-nobel-prize/

Dickinson, E. (2011, January 3). GDP: A brief history. *Foreign Policy.* https://foreignpolicy.com/2011/01/03/gdp-a-brief-history

French, P. (2009, April 13). Enter the dragon king. *Vanity Fair.* https://www.vanityfair.com/culture/2009/05/bhutan-king200905

Froh, J. J. (2004). The history of positive psychology: Truth be told. *NYS Psychologist, 16*(3), 18-20.

Gallenkamp, M. (2010). *Democracy in Bhutan: An analysis of constitutional change in a Buddhist monarchy.* (IPCS Research Papers). Institute of Peace and Conflict Studies. https://www.files.ethz.ch/isn/113886/RP24-Marian-Bhutan.pdf

GOV.UK. (2010, November 25). *Britain's wellbeing to be measured.* Government Digital Service. https://www.gov.uk/government/news/britains-wellbeing-to-be-measured

Gross National Happiness Institute. (n.d.). The Gross National Happiness Origin. Gross National Happiness Institute. http://gnh.institute/gross-national-happiness-gnh-origin.htm

Harris, G. (2013, October 4). Index of happiness? Bhutan's new leader prefers more concrete goals. *The New York Times.* https://www.nytimes.com/2013/10/05/world/asia/index-of-happiness-bhutans-new-leader-prefers-more-concrete-goals.html

High-Level Expert Group on the Measurement of Economic Performance. (n.d.). *Measurement of economic performance and social progress: About.* Organisation for Economic Co-operation and Development. https://www.oecd.org/statistics/measuring-economic-social-progress/aboutthehigh-levelexpertgroup.htm

Kagan, J. (2021, October 5). *Gross National Happiness (GNH).* Investopedia. https://www.investopedia.com/terms/g/gnh.asp

Kahneman, D. (2015). *Thinking, fast and slow.* Farrar, Straus and Giroux.

Karan, P. P. (n.d.). Bhutan: Government and society. *Encyclopædia Britannica.* Britannica Group, Inc. https://www.britannica.com/place/Bhutan/Government-and-society

Kelly, A. (2012, December 1). Gross national happiness in Bhutan: The big idea from a tiny state that could change the world. *The Guardian.* https://www.theguardian.com/world/2012/dec/01/bhutan-wealth-happiness-counts

Kennedy, R. F. (n.d.). *Remarks at the University of Kansas, March 18, 1968* [Speech transcript]. John F. Kennedy Presidential Library and Museum. https://www.jfklibrary.org/learn/about-jfk/the-kennedy-family/robert-f-kennedy/robert-f-kennedy-speeches/remarks-at-the-university-of-kansas-march-18-1968 (Original speech given March 18, 1968)

Kessler, J. B., & Roth, A. E. (2014). *Don't take 'no' for an answer: An experiment with actual organ donor registrations* (NBER Working Paper No. 20378). National Bureau of Economic Research. https://www.nber.org/system/files/working_papers/w20378/w20378.pdf

Manson, M. (2020). *Everything is f*cked: A book about hope.* HarperCollins Publishers.

Maslow, A. H. (1954). *Motivation and personality.* Harpers.

NobelPrize.org. (2022, January 19). *Daniel Kahneman – Facts.* Nobel Prize Outreach. https://www.nobelprize.org/prizes/economic-sciences/2002/kahneman/facts/

OECD. (2013). *OECD guidelines on measuring subjective well-being.* OECD Publishing. https://read.oecd-ilibrary.org/economics/oecd-guidelines-on-measuring-subjective-well-being_9789264191655-en#page267

OECD Better Life Index. (n.d.). *What's the Better Life Index?* Organisation for Economic Co-operation and Development. https://www.oecdbetterlifeindex.org/about/better-life-initiative/#question3

Office for National Statistics. (2018, September 28). *Surveys using our four personal well-being questions: A guide to what surveys include the four ONS personal well-being questions.* Office for National Statistics. https://www.ons.gov.uk/peoplepopulationandcommunity/wellbeing/methodologies/surveysusingthe4officefornationalstatisticspersonal wellbeingquestions

Oxford Languages. (n.d.). Behavioral economics. Definition from *Oxford Languages* dictionary.

Oxford Poverty & Human Development Initiative. (n.d.). Bhutan's Gross National Happiness Index. University of Oxford. https://ophi.org.uk/policy/gross-national-happiness-index/

Psychology Today. (n.d.). Priming. In *Psychology Today Basics.* Retrieved January 19, 2022, from https://www.psychologytoday.com/us/basics/priming

Roy, E. A. (2019, May 29). New Zealand 'wellbeing' budget promises billions to care for most vulnerable. *The Guardian.* https://www.theguardian.com/world/2019/may/30/new-zealand-wellbeing-budget-jacinda-ardern-unveils-billions-to-care-for-most-vulnerable

Schaffner, F. J. (Director). (1956, April 13). Interview with George Gallup (3, 33) [TV series episode]. In Aaron, J. A., & Zousmer, J. (Producers), *Person to person.* CBS.

Seligman, M. E. P. (2002). *Authentic happiness: Using the new positive psychology to realize your potential for lasting fulfillment.* Free Press.

Shonk, K. (2021, December 20). What is anchoring in negotiation? Learn how to defuse the anchoring bias and make smart first offers. *Program on Negotiation, Harvard Law School, Daily Blog.* https://www.pon.harvard.edu/daily/negotiation-skills-daily/what-is-anchoring-in-negotiation/

Stratton, A. (2010, November 14). David Cameron aims to make happiness the new GDP. *The Guardian.* https://www.theguardian.com/politics/2010/nov/14/david-cameron-wellbeing-inquiry

Thaler, R. H. (2009, September 26). Opting in vs. opting out. *The New York Times.* https://www.nytimes.com/2009/09/27/business/economy/27view.html

Thaler, R. H., & Sunstein, C. R. (2009). *Nudge: Improving decisions about health, wealth, and happiness.* Penguin Books.

UAE. (2021, July 7). *Happiness.* UAE government. https://u.ae/en/about-the-uae/the-uae-government/government-of-future/happiness

United Nations General Assembly. (2011, August 25). *Happiness: Towards a holistic approach to development.* [Resolution adopted by the General Assembly on 19 July 2011]. United Nations Secretary-General. https://www.un.org/ga/search/view_doc.asp?symbol=A/RES/65/309

The World Factbook. (2021). *Country comparisons — Real GDP per capita* [Data set]. Central Intelligence Agency. https://www.cia.gov/the-world-factbook/field/real-gdp-per-capita/country-comparison

Part III: What Makes a Great Life?

References

Lewis-Beck, M. S., Bryman, A., & Futing Liao, T. (2004). *The SAGE encyclopedia of social science research methods* (Vols. 1-0). Sage Publications, Inc. https://doi.org/10.4135/9781412950589

Chapter Seven: The Five Elements of a Great Life

References

Azar, B. (2010, May). Are your findings 'WEIRD'? *Monitor on Psychology, 41*(5). http://www.apa.org/monitor/2010/05/weird

Clifton, J., & Harter, J. (2021). *Wellbeing at work.* Gallup Press.

Diego-Rosell, P., Tortora, R., & Bird, J. (2018). International determinants of subjective well-being: Living in a subjectively material world. *Journal of Happiness Studies: An Interdisciplinary Forum on Subjective Well-Being, 19*(1), 123-143. https://doi.org/10.1007/s10902-016-9812-3

Diener, E. (2009). *Culture and well-being: The collected works of Ed Diener.* Springer.

Fontane Pennock, S. (2021, December 7). *The hedonic treadmill — are we forever chasing rainbows?* PositivePsychology.com. https://positivepsychology.com/hedonic-treadmill/

Gallup, G., & Hill, E. (1959, August 15, 22, 29). The secrets of long life. *The Saturday Evening Post.* http://www.saturdayeveningpost.com/wp-content/uploads/satevepost/the-secret-of-a-long-life.pdf

Hanel, P. H., & Vione, K. C. (2016). Do student samples provide an accurate estimate of the general public? *PLoS ONE, 11*(12), e0168354. https://doi.org/10.1371/journal.pone.0168354

Harter, J. (2010). *Wellbeing: The five essential elements.* Gallup Press.

Henrich, J., Heine, S. J., & Norenzayan, A. (2010). The weirdest people in the world? *Behavioral and Brain Sciences, 33*(2-3), 61-83. https://doi.org/10.1017/S0140525X0999152X

Lickerman, A. (2013, April 21). *How to reset your happiness set point.* Psychology Today. https://www.psychologytoday.com/us/blog/happiness-in-world/201304/how-reset-your-happiness-set-point

Morin, A. (2018, June 18). Loneliness is as lethal as smoking 15 cigarettes per day. Here's what you can do about it. *Inc.* https://www.inc.com/amy-morin/americas-loneliness-epidemic-is-more-lethal-than-smoking-heres-what-you-can-do-to-combat-isolation.html

Newman, K. M. (2020, February 18). How much of your happiness is under your control? *Greater Good.* https://greatergood.berkeley.edu/article/item/how_much_of_your_happiness_is_under_your_control

Rauch, J. (2019). *The happiness curve: Why life gets better after 50.* Picador.

Raypole, C. (2020, February 24). *Don't underestimate the stress of student loan debt.* GoodTherapy. https://www.goodtherapy.org/blog/dont-underestimate-the-stress-of-student-loan-debt-0224207

Røysamb, E., Nes, R.B., Czajkowski, N. O., Vassend, O. (2018). Genetics, personality and wellbeing. A twin study of traits, facets and life satisfaction. *Scientific Reports 8*(12298), 1-13. https://doi.org/10.1038/s41598-018-29881-x

Silver, L., van Kessel, P., Huang, C., Clancy, L., & Gubbala, S. (2021, November 18). *What makes life meaningful? Views from 17 advanced economies.* Pew Research Center. https://www.pewresearch.org/global/2021/11/18/what-makes-life-meaningful-views-from-17-advanced-economies/

University College London. Student loan debt has negative consequences in later life, review by IOE researchers suggests. (2018, June 11). University College London. https://www.ucl.ac.uk/ioe/news/2018/jun/student-loan-debt-has-negative-consequences-later-life-review-ioe-researchers-suggests

Chapter Eight: The Global Great Jobs Crisis
Notes

GDP per Capita (PPP) and Unemployment

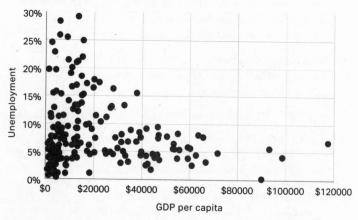

Data are from World Bank database (https://data.worldbank.org/indicator). 2020 unemployment percentage among workforce from International Labour Organization, ILOSTAT database. Data retrieved February 8, 2022. GDP (in international dollars) from International Comparison Program, World Bank, World Development Indicators database, World Bank, Eurostat-OECD PPP Programme. Unemployment with GDP per capita (PPP): Pearson -0.192 (sig at 0.05), 175 countries. Additionally, unemployment with the log of GDP PPP: Pearson -0.204 (Sig at 0.01), 175 countries.

Source: International Labour Organization and World Bank

References

Brenan, M. (2021, July 14). *Americans' confidence in major U.S. institutions dips.* Gallup. https://news.gallup.com/poll/352316/americans-confidence-major-institutions-dips.aspx

Campbell, L. (2017, October 18). *We've broken down your entire life into years spent doing tasks.* HuffPost. https://www.huffpost.com/entry/weve-broken-down-your-entire-life-into-years-spent-doing-tasks_n_61087617e4b0999d2084fec5

Clifton, J. (2018, May 1). *Real global unemployment is 33%, not 6%.* Gallup. https://news.gallup.com/opinion/gallup/233459/billion-worldwide-looking-great-jobs.aspx

Clifton, J., & Marlar, J. (2011). *Good jobs: The new global standard.* Gallup.

Clifton, J., & Marlar, J. (2011, March 15). *Worldwide, good jobs linked to higher well-being.* Gallup. https://news.gallup.com/poll/146639/worldwide-good-jobs-linked-higher-wellbeing.aspx

FAO, IFAD, UNICEF, WFP, and WHO. (2021). *The state of food security and nutrition in the world 2021. Transforming food systems for food security, improved nutrition and affordable healthy diets for all.* FAO. https://doi.org/10.4060/cb4474en

Gallup. (2016). *First, break all the rules: What the world's greatest managers do differently.* Gallup Press.

Gammarano, R. (2019). *Quick guide on interpreting the unemployment rate.* International Labour Organization Department of Statistics' Data Production and Analysis Unit. https://ilo.org/wcmsp5/groups/public/---dgreports/---stat/documents/publication/wcms_675155.pdf

Gomis, R., Kapsos, S., Kühn, S., & Liepmann, H. (2020). *World employment and social outlook: Trends 2020.* International Labour Organization. https://www.ilo.org/wcmsp5/groups/public/---dgreports/---dcomm/---publ/documents/publication/wcms_734479.pdf

Grant, A. (Host). (2021, March 16). Taken for granted: Daniel Kahneman doesn't trust your intuition [Audio podcast episode]. In *Taken for granted.* TED Audio Collective. https://podcasts.apple.com/us/podcast/taken-for-granted-daniel-kahneman-doesnt-trust-your/id1346314086?i=1000513174086

Harter, J. (2012, July 23). *Mondays not so "blue" for engaged employees.* Gallup. https://news.gallup.com/poll/155924/mondays-not-blue-engaged-employees.aspx

Harter, J., & Agrawal, S. (2011, March 30). *Workers in bad jobs have worse well-being than jobless.* Gallup. https://news.gallup.com/poll/146867/workers-bad-jobs-worse-wellbeing-jobless.aspx

In developing countries, many people cannot afford not to work. (2018, June 7). *The Economist.* https://www.economist.com/finance-and-economics/2018/06/07/in-developing-countries-many-people-cannot-afford-not-to-work

The Investopedia Team. (2022, January 10). *Unemployment rate.* Investopedia. https://www.investopedia.com/terms/u/unemploymentrate.asp

Jobs, S. (2005, June 14). *Commencement address delivered by Steve Jobs* [Speech transcript]. Stanford University. https://news.stanford.edu/2005/06/14/jobs-061505/ (Original speech given June 12, 2005)

Lloyd's Register Foundation. (2020). *The Lloyd's Register Foundation World Risk Poll: Full report and analysis of the 2019 poll.* Lloyd's Register Foundation. https://wrp.lrfoundation.org.uk/

Mendes, E. (2012, June 11). *For Americans, Mondays aren't all that bad.* Gallup. https://news.gallup.com/opinion/thrive/172370/americans-mondays-aren-bad.aspx

O'Neill, A. (2021, August 3). *Global unemployment rate from 2010 to 2020.* [Data set]. Statista. https://www.statista.com/statistics/279777/global-unemployment-rate/

Reuters staff. (2020, January 20). *ILO sees end to falling global unemployment rate.* Reuters. https://www.reuters.com/article/us-un-economy/ilo-sees-end-to-falling-global-unemployment-rate-idUSKBN1ZJ27D

Stone, A. A., Schneider, S., & Harter, J. K. (2012). Day-of-week mood patterns in the United States: On the existence of 'Blue Monday', 'Thank God it's Friday' and weekend effects, *The Journal of Positive Psychology, 7*(4), 306-314. https://doi.org/10.1080/17439760.2012.691980

Udall, A. T., & Sinclair, S. (1982). The 'luxury unemployment' hypothesis: A review of recent evidence. *World Development, 10*(1), 49-62. https://doi.org/10.1016/0305-750X(82)90079-1

United Nations. (n.d.). *Global issues: Water.* United Nations. https://www.un.org/en/global-issues/water

United Nations. (2020). *The sustainable development goals report 2020.* United Nations. https://unstats.un.org/sdgs/report/2020/The-Sustainable-Development-Goals-Report-2020.pdf

United Nations Statistics Division. (n.d.) *Make cities and human settlements inclusive, safe, resilient and sustainable.* United Nations Department of Economic and Social Affairs. https://unstats.un.org/sdgs/report/2019/goal-11/

WESO Data Finder: World Employment and Social Outlook. (2022). *Rate %, Unemployment, World* [Data set]. International Labour Organization. https://www.ilo.org/wesodata

The World Bank. (2021, June 15). *Unemployment, total (% of total labor force) (modeled ILO estimate)*. [Data set]. The World Bank. https://data.worldbank.org/indicator/SL.UEM.TOTL.ZS?most_recent_year_desc=true

The World Bank. (2021, June 15). *Unemployment, total (% of total labor force) (modeled ILO estimate) – Canada, Niger, France*. [Data set]. The World Bank. https://data.worldbank.org/indicator/SL.UEM.TOTL.ZS?end=2019&locations=CA-NE-FR&most_recent_value_desc=false&start=1991

Chapter Nine: Does Money Buy Happiness?

Notes

Income Difficulties and Income Inequality

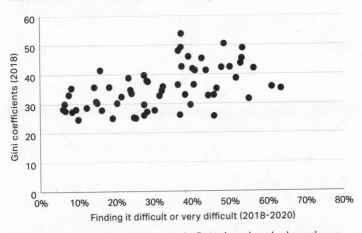

This chart illustrates the relationship between the Gini index and people who say they are finding it difficult to get by on their current incomes. Results are shown for 62 countries where both sets of numbers were available. The Gini index is a summary measure of income inequality. The correlation between income difficulties and income inequality (Gini) is 0.524 and 0.514 Spearman and Pearson, respectively.

Gini coefficients from World Bank, Development Research Group. Data are based on primary household survey data obtained from government statistical agencies and World Bank country departments. For more information and methodology, please see PovcalNet (http://iresearch.worldbank.org/PovcalNet/index.htm).

Source: Gallup and World Bank

Income Difficulties and Median Income

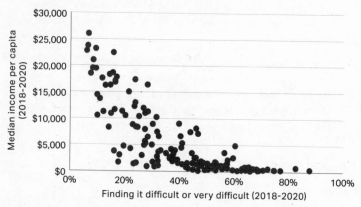

This chart illustrates the relationship between median income per capita (in international dollars) and people who say they are finding it difficult or very difficult on their current incomes. Results are shown for 147 countries where both sets of numbers were available. The correlation between income difficulties and median income in international dollars is -0.856 and -0.772 Spearman and Pearson, respectively.

Source: Gallup

References

Cantril, H. (1966). *The pattern of human concerns.* Rutgers University Press.

Deaton, A. (2008, February 27). *Worldwide, residents of richer nations more satisfied.* Gallup. https://news.gallup.com/poll/104608/worldwide-residents-richer-nations-more-satisfied.aspx

Dugan, A., & Marken, S. (2014, August 7). *Student debt linked to worse health and less wealth.* Gallup. https://news.gallup.com/poll/174317/student-debt-linked-worse-health-less-wealth.aspx

Easterlin, R. (1974). Does economic growth improve the human lot?: Some empirical evidence. In David, P. A. & Reder, M. W. (Eds.), *Nations and households in economic growth: Essays in honor of Moses Abramovitz* (pp. 89-125). Academic Press.

Feldman, K. (2015, September 24). The best quotes from legendary broad-caster Vin Scully. *New York Daily News.* https://www.nydailynews.com/sports/baseball/best-quotes-legendary-broadcaster-vin-scully-article-1.2373233

Graham, C. (2012). *The pursuit of happiness: An economy of well-being.* Brookings Institution Press.

Jebb, A. T., Tay, T., Diener, E., & Oishi, S. (2018). Happiness, income satiation and turning points around the world. *Nature Human Behaviour, 2*, 33-38.

Kela. (2020, June, 5). *Results of Finland's basic income experiment: Small employment effects, better perceived economic security and mental wellbeing*. Kela. https://www.kela.fi/web/en/news-archive/-/asset_publisher/lN08GY2nIrZo/content/results-of-the-basic-income-experiment-small-employment-effects-better-perceived-economic-security-and-mental-wellbeing

Kesebir, S. (2016, April 25). When economic growth doesn't make countries happier. *Harvard Business Review*. https://hbr.org/2016/04/when-economic-growth-doesnt-make-countries-happier

Might the pandemic pave the way for a universal basic income? (2021, March 2). *The Economist*. https://www.economist.com/finance-and-economics/2021/03/02/might-the-pandemic-pave-the-way-for-a-universal-basic-income

Neubert, A. P. (2018, February 13). *Money only buys happiness for a certain amount*. Purdue University. https://www.purdue.edu/newsroom/releases/2018/Q1/money-only-buys-happiness-for-a-certain-amount.html

Norton, M., & de Neve, J.-E. (2014, October 8). *Busts hurt more than booms help: New lessons for growth policy from global wellbeing surveys*. VoxEU.org. https://voxeu.org/article/wellbeing-research-recessions-hurt-more-booms-help

OECD. (2011). *Society at a glance 2011: OECD social indicators*. OECD Publishing. http://dx.doi.org/10.1787/soc_glance-2011-en

Palmer, H. S., & Momand, A. R. (Directors). (1915). *Keeping up with the Joneses (Men's styles)* [Film]. Mutual Film Corporation.

Robison, J. (2011, November 17). *Happiness is love — and $75,000*. Gallup. https://news.gallup.com/businessjournal/150671/happiness-is-love-and-75k.aspx

Smith C. (2014). Easterlin paradox. In Michalos, A. C. (Ed.), *Encyclopedia of Quality of Life and Well-Being Research*. Springer. https://doi.org/10.1007/978-94-007-0753-5_802

Stevenson, B., & Wolfers, J. (2013). *Subjective well-being and income: Is there any evidence of satiation?* (CAMA Working Paper 21/2013). SSRN. https://ssrn.com/abstract=2265690

Chapter Ten: The World's Broken Communities
Notes

Do You Trust Your Neighbors?

Country	Very likely	Somewhat likely	Not likely at all
Most likely to trust neighbors			
Netherlands	85%	14%	1%
Norway	84%	13%	2%
Finland	79%	19%	3%
Austria	77%	15%	6%
Germany	76%	16%	6%
Sweden	76%	21%	3%
Ireland	74%	19%	6%
Australia	73%	23%	3%
Denmark	73%	24%	3%
New Zealand	73%	22%	5%
Switzerland	73%	19%	7%
Least likely to trust neighbors			
Rwanda	12%	39%	47%
Sierra Leone	28%	27%	44%
Eswatini	26%	27%	44%
Lithuania	18%	34%	44%
Laos	18%	29%	43%
Ecuador	17%	38%	43%
Madagascar	10%	47%	43%
Gabon	19%	35%	42%
Nicaragua	15%	40%	42%
Bolivia	13%	43%	42%

Suppose you lost a small bag that contained items of great financial value to you that had your name and address written on it. If it were found by a neighbor, how likely is it that it would be returned to you with all of its contents? 2019.

Source: Gallup

Do You Trust Strangers?

Country	Very likely	Somewhat likely	Not likely at all
Most likely to trust strangers			
Algeria	17%	48%	30%
Norway	16%	69%	15%
Iran	15%	63%	20%
Kuwait	12%	51%	29%
Netherlands	11%	62%	25%
Finland	10%	61%	28%
Austria	10%	60%	28%
New Zealand	8%	65%	26%
Germany	8%	60%	30%
Australia	7%	64%	28%
Canada	7%	61%	30%
Least likely to trust strangers			
Nicaragua	3%	11%	84%
Madagascar	2%	14%	83%
Cambodia	2%	10%	83%
Ecuador	4%	13%	82%
Thailand	2%	10%	82%
Laos	3%	7%	81%
Afghanistan	3%	17%	80%
Venezuela	5%	13%	80%
Myanmar	8%	10%	78%
El Salvador	5%	16%	77%

Suppose you lost a small bag that contained items of great financial value to you that had your name and address written on it. If it were found by a stranger, how likely is it that it would be returned to you with all of its contents? 2019.

Source: Gallup

References

Cohn, A., Maréchal, M. A., Tannenbaumand, D., & Lukas Zünd, C. L. (2019). Civic honesty around the globe. *Science, 365*(6448), 70–73. https://doi.org/10.1126/science.aau8712

Egypt President Abdul Fattah al-Sisi: Ruler with an iron grip. (2020, December 1). BBC News. https://www.bbc.com/news/world-middle-east-19256730

English, C., & Steele, E. (2015, May 15). *Evaluating country development using local citizen ratings of community basics* [PowerPoint slides]. American Association for Public Opinion Research. https://www.aapor.org/AAPOR_Main/media/AnnualMeetingProceedings/2015/E5-4-English.pdf

Harter, J. (2010). *Wellbeing: The five essential elements.* Gallup Press.

Helliwell, J. F., Huang, H., Wang, S., & Norton, M. (2021). Happiness, trust, and deaths under COVID-19. In Helliwell, J. F., Layard, R., Sachs, J. D., & de Neve, J.-E. (Eds.), *World happiness report 2021* (pp. 13–56). Sustainable Development Solutions Network. https://worldhappiness.report/ed/2021/happiness-trust-and-deaths-under-covid-19/

Hessler, P. (2019, June 19). Mohamed Morsi, who brought the Muslim Brotherhood to the Egyptian presidency. *The New Yorker.* https://www.newyorker.com/news/news-desk/mohamed-morsi-who-brought-the-muslim-brotherhood-to-the-egyptian-presidency

Hopper, E. (2020, July 29). Want to be happier? Try volunteering, study says. *Washington Post.* https://www.washingtonpost.com/lifestyle/2020/07/29/volunteer-happy-mental-health/

Kennedy, M. (2019, June 20). *What dropping 17,000 wallets around the globe can teach us about honesty.* NPR. https://www.npr.org/2019/06/20/734141432/what-dropping-17-000-wallets-around-the-globe-can-teach-us-about-honesty

Kirkpatrick, D. D. (2012, June 24). Named Egypt's winner, Islamist makes history. *The New York Times.* https://www.nytimes.com/2012/06/25/world/middleeast/mohamed-morsi-of-muslim-brotherhood-declared-as-egypts-president.html

United Nations Statistics Division. (2020). *SDG Indicators: Metadata repository.* [Data set]. United Nations Department of Economic and Social Affairs. https://unstats.un.org/sdgs/metadata/?Text=&Goal=16&Target=16.1

Chapter Eleven: The Global Hunger Crisis

References

Angelidi, A. M., Belanger, M. J., Kokkinos, A., Koliaki, C. C., & Mantzoros, C. S. (2021). Novel noninvasive approaches to the treatment of obesity: From pharmacotherapy to gene therapy, *Endocrine Reviews.* https://doi.org/10.1210/endrev/bnab034

Baraniuk, C. (2019, April 29). *The long-term effects of going hungry.* BBC Future. https://www.bbc.com/future/article/20190429-why-food-poverty-is-a-health-time-bomb

Belluz, J. (2017, June 19). *Obesity now kills more people worldwide than car crashes, terror attacks, and Alzheimer's combined.* Vox. https://www.vox.com/science-and-health/2017/6/19/15819808/obesity-global-epidemic

Division of Nutrition, Physical Activity, and Obesity. *Overweight & obesity: Adult obesity causes & consequences.* (2021, March 22). Centers for Disease Control and Prevention. https://www.cdc.gov/obesity/adult/causes.html

Endocrine Society. (2021, October 26). *Over 4 million deaths per year worldwide caused by obesity.* Endocrine Society. https://www.endocrine.org/news-and-advocacy/news-room/2021/over-4-million-deaths-per-year-worldwide-caused-by-obesity

FAO, IFAD, UNICEF, WFP, and WHO. (2019). *In brief: The state of food security and nutrition in the world. Safeguarding against economic slowdowns and downturns.* FAO. https://www.unicef.org/media/55926/file/SOFI-2019-in-brief.pdf

FAO, IFAD, UNICEF, WFP, and WHO. (2019). *The state of food security and nutrition in the world. Safeguarding against economic slowdowns and downturns.* FAO. https://www.fao.org/3/ca5162en/ca5162en.pdf

FAO, IFAD, UNICEF, WFP, and WHO. (2020). *The state of food security and nutrition in the world 2020. Transforming food systems for affordable healthy diets for all.* FAO. https://doi.org/10.4060/ca9692en

FAO, IFAD, UNICEF, WFP, and WHO. (2021). *The state of food security and nutrition in the world 2021. Transforming food systems for food security, improved nutrition and affordable healthy diets for all.* FAO. https://doi.org/10.4060/cb4474en

Food and Agriculture Organisation. (n.d.). *Voices of the hungry: The Food Insecurity Experience Scale.* United Nations. http://www.fao.org/in-action/voices-of-the-hungry/fies/en/

Food and Agriculture Organisation. (n.d.). *Voices of the hungry: Frequently asked questions.* United Nations. https://www.fao.org/in-action/voices-of-the-hungry/faq/en/

Food and Agriculture Organisation. (2021, February 1). *SDG indicator metadata.* United Nations. https://unstats.un.org/sdgs/metadata/files/Metadata-02-01-02.pdf

Frongillo, E. A., Nguyen, H. T., Smith, M. D., & Coleman-Jensen, A. (2017). Food insecurity is associated with subjective well-being among individuals from 138 countries in the 2014 Gallup World Poll. *The Journal of Nutrition, 147*(4), 680-687. https://doi.org/10.3945/jn.116.243642

Fryar, C. D., Carroll, M. D., & Afful, J. (2020). *Prevalence of overweight, obesity, and severe obesity among adults aged 20 and over: United States, 1960–1962 through 2017–2018.* NCHS Health E-Stats. National Center for Health Statistics. https://www.cdc.gov/nchs/data/hestat/obesity-adult-17-18/obesity-adult.htm

Hales, C. M., Carroll, M. D., Fryar, C. D., & Ogden C. L. (2020). *Prevalence of obesity and severe obesity among adults: United States, 2017–2018.* NCHS Data Brief, No. 360. National Center for Health Statistics.

Hall, L. (2012, January 12). *A closer look at who benefits from SNAP: State-by-state fact sheets.* Center on Budget and Policy Priorities. https://www.cbpp.org/research/food-assistance/a-closer-look-at-who-benefits-from-snap-state-by-state-fact-sheets#Alabama

Herforth, A., Beal, T., & Rzepa, A. (2020, October 16). *Global diet quality project aims to bridge data gap.* Gallup. https://news.gallup.com/opinion/gallup/321968/global-diet-quality-project-aims-bridge-data-gap.aspx

Jones, A. D. (2017). Food insecurity and mental health status: A global analysis of 149 countries. *American Journal of Preventive Medicine, 53*(2), 264-273. https://doi.org/10.1016/j.amepre.2017.04.008

National Center for Health Statistics. (2021, September 10). *Obesity and overweight.* Centers for Disease Control and Prevention. https://www.cdc.gov/nchs/fastats/obesity-overweight.htm

Orner, M. (2014, July 1). *The effects of hunger.* The Borgen Project. https://borgenproject.org/effects-hunger/

Research Program on Climate Change, Agriculture and Food Security. (n.d.) *Food security: Undernourishment and obesity.* CGIAR. https://ccafs.cgiar.org/bigfacts/#theme=food-security&subtheme=undernourishment

United Nations. (2021, March 11). *'If you don't feed people, you feed conflict', UN chief tells Security Council.* United Nations. https://news.un.org/en/story/2021/03/1087032

Viviani, S., & Ray, J. (2021, August 12). *World headed in wrong direction on hunger.* Gallup. https://news.gallup.com/opinion/gallup/353150/world-headed-wrong-direction-hunger.aspx

Waite, T., & Thoelke, O. (2021, May 18). *3 devastating effects of hunger on the body.* Feeding America. https://www.feedingamerica.org/hunger-blog/3-ways-hunger-affects-your-body

Why Food Is Everything. (2015, April 15). *National Geographic.* https://www.nationalgeographic.com/culture/article/150415-jose-andres-three-questions-food-spanish

World Food Program USA. (2021, April 6). *Scale of acute hunger in the Democratic Republic of the Congo "staggering," FAO, WFP warn.* United Nations World Food Programme. https://www.wfpusa.org/news-release/scale-of-hunger-in-drc-staggering/

World Health Organization. (n.d.). *The double burden of malnutrition.* World Health Organization. https://www.who.int/nutrition/double-burden-malnutrition/infographic_print.pdf

World Health Organization. (n.d.). *Obesity.* World Health Organization. https://www.who.int/health-topics/obesity#tab=tab_1

World Health Organization. (2021, June 9). *Obesity and overweight.* World Health Organization. https://www.who.int/news-room/fact-sheets/detail/obesity-and-overweight

Chapter Twelve: A Lonely Planet

References

Bernstein, E. (2016, April 18). The science of making friends. *The Wall Street Journal.* https://www.wsj.com/articles/the-science-of-making-friends-1460992572

Birnstengel, G. (2020, January 17). *What has the U.K.'s minister of loneliness done to date?* Next Avenue. https://www.nextavenue.org/uk-minister-of-loneliness/

Cox, D. A. (2021, June 8). *The state of American friendship: Change, challenges, and loss.* Survey Center on American Life. https://www.americansurveycenter.org/research/the-state-of-american-friendship-change-challenges-and-loss/

Cox, D. A. (2021, June 29). *Men's social circles are shrinking.* Survey Center on American Life. https://www.americansurveycenter.org/why-mens-social-circles-are-shrinking/

de Neve, J.-E. (2018). Work and well-being: A global perspective. In Sachs, J. D., Bishr, A. B., de Neve, J.-E., Durand, M., Diener, E., Helliwell, J. F., Layard, R., Seligman, M., Achor, S., Alshugairi, A., Bokova, I., Ura, D. K., Kingo, L., Lyubomirsky, S., & O'Donnell, G. (Eds.), *Global happiness policy report 2018* (pp. 74-127). Sustainable Development Solutions Network. https://s3.amazonaws.com/ghc-2018/GHC_Ch5.pdf

Department for Digital, Culture, Media and Sport and Office for Civil Society. (2018). *A connected society: A strategy for tackling loneliness.* Department for Digital, Culture, Media and Sport; Office for Civil Society Prime Minister's Office, 10 Downing Street; Tracey Crouch MP; and The Rt Hon Jeremy Wright QC MP. https://assets.publishing.service.gov.uk/government/uploads/system/uploads/attachment_data/file/936725/6.4882_DCMS_Loneliness_Strategy_web_Update_V2.pdf

Frame, S. (2017, October 18). *Julianne Holt-Lunstad probes loneliness, social connections.* American Psychological Association. https://www.apa.org/members/content/holt-lunstad-loneliness-social-connections

Friedman, R. (2014, December 2). *You need a work best friend.* The Cut. https://www.thecut.com/2014/12/you-need-a-work-best-friend.html

GOV.UK. (2018, January 17). *PM commits to government-wide drive to tackle loneliness.* Government Digital Service. https://www.gov.uk/government/news/pm-commits-to-government-wide-drive-to-tackle-loneliness

Holt-Lunstad, J., Smith, T. B., Layton, J. B. (2010). Social relationships and mortality risk: A meta-analytic review. *PLoS Medicine, 7*(7), 1-20. https://doi.org/10.1371/journal.pmed.1000316

Kennedy, R. F. (n.d.). *Remarks at the University of Kansas, March 18, 1968* [Speech transcript]. John F. Kennedy Presidential Library and Museum. https://www.jfklibrary.org/learn/about-jfk/the-kennedy-family/robert-f-kennedy/robert-f-kennedy-speeches/remarks-at-the-university-of-kansas-march-18-1968 (Original speech given March 18, 1968)

Kodama, S. (2021, February 13). *Japan appoints 'minister of loneliness' to help people home alone.* Nikkei Asia. https://asia.nikkei.com/Spotlight/Coronavirus/Japan-appoints-minister-of-loneliness-to-help-people-home-alone

London, T. J. (2018, April 25). How the world's first loneliness minister will tackle 'the sad reality of modern life.' *Time.* https://time.com/5248016/tracey-crouch-uk-loneliness-minister/

OECD. (n.d.). *Suicide rates.* [Data set]. Organisation for Economic Co-operation and Development. https://data.oecd.org/healthstat/suicide-rates.htm

Osaki, T. (2021, February 21). As suicides rise amid the pandemic, Japan takes steps to tackle loneliness. *The Japan Times.* https://www.japantimes.co.jp/news/2021/02/21/national/japan-tackles-loneliness/

The pandemic may be encouraging people to live in larger groups. (2020, December 5). *The Economist.* https://www.economist.com/international/2020/12/05/the-pandemic-may-be-encouraging-people-to-live-in-larger-groups

Pandey, E. (2021, February 3). *Why your "work bestie" matters.* Axios. https://www.axios.com/pandemic-work-friend-85b59702-af80-4b7b-9bbb-5405463ec419.html

Ryall, J. (2021, April 23). *Japan: 'Minister of loneliness' tackles mental health crisis*. Deutsche Welle. https://www.dw.com/en/japan-minister-of-loneliness-tackles-mental-health-crisis/a-57311880

Sachs, J. D., Bishr, A. B., de Neve, J.-E., Durand, M., Diener, E., Helliwell, J. F., Layard, R., Seligman, M., Achor, S., Alshugairi, A., Bokova, I., Ura, D. K., Kingo, L., Lyubomirsky, S., & O'Donnell, G. (2018). *Global happiness policy report 2018*. Sustainable Development Solutions Network. https://www.happinesscouncil.org/report/2018/global-happiness-policy-report

Skopeliti, C. (2021, February 25). Japan appoints 'Minister for Loneliness' after rise in suicides. *The Independent*. https://www.independent.co.uk/news/world/asia/japan-minister-loneliness-suicides-tetsushi-sakamoto-b1807236.html

Suicides in Japan hit a 20-year low. (2017, June 28). *The Economist*. https://www.economist.com/graphic-detail/2017/06/28/suicides-in-japan-hit-a-20-year-low

Surprisingly, suicide has become rarer during the pandemic. (2021, April 24). *The Economist.* https://www.economist.com/graphic-detail/2021/04/24/surprisingly-suicide-has-become-rarer-during-the-pandemic

Chapter Thirteen: The Serious Outcomes of Unhappiness

References

Case, A., & Deaton, A. (2020). *Deaths of despair and the future of capitalism*. Princeton University Press.

English, C., & Steele, E. (2015, May 15). *Evaluating country development using local citizen ratings of community basics* [PowerPoint slides]. American Association for Public Opinion Research. https://www.aapor.org/AAPOR_Main/media/AnnualMeetingProceedings/2015/E5-4-English.pdf

Institute for Economics and Peace. (2021). *Global Peace Index 2021: Measuring peace in a complex world*. Institute for Economics and Peace. https://www.visionofhumanity.org/wp-content/uploads/2021/06/GPI-2021-web-1.pdf

Institute for Economics and Peace. (2021). *Global peace index 2021: Overview and key findings* [PowerPoint slides]. Institute for Economics and Peace. https://www.visionofhumanity.org/resources/global-peace-index-2020-presentation-2/

Kallehauge, K. (2021, June 25). *Global Peace Index 2021 — A year of civil unrest*. Impakter. https://impakter.com/global-peace-index-2021-a-year-of-civil-unrest/

Strohecker, K. (2021, July 28). *Analysis: Pandemics & protests: Unrest grips developing countries*. Reuters. https://www.reuters.com/world/pandemics-protests-unrest-grips-developing-countries-2021-07-28/

United Nations. (n.d.). Ageing. United Nations. https://www.un.org/en/global-issues/ageing

Ward, G. (2020). Happiness and voting: Evidence from four decades of elections in Europe. *American Journal of Political Science, 64*(3), 504-518.

Ward, G., Collins, H., Norton, M. I., & Whillans, A. V. (2020). *Work values shape the relationship between stress and (un)happiness.* (Harvard Business School Working Paper No. 21-044). Harvard Business School. https://www.hbs.edu/ris/Publication%20Files/21-044_f5a41dc5-0489-46c1-9338-d93165f09434.pdf

Ward, G., Schwartz, H. A., Giorgi, S., Menges, J., & Matz, S. C. (2021). *The role of negative affect in shaping populist voting: Converging evidence from the field.* [Unpublished paper].

Part IV: Four Unanswered Questions

Chapter Fourteen: How Are Women's Lives Going?

Notes

Percentage of Women and Men in the Workplace by Number of Children in Household

Employment status	Women number of children				Men number of children			
	0	1	2	3+	0	1	2	3+
Good job (full time for an employer)	23%	23%	17%	10%	33%	37%	36%	27%
Self-employed	9%	11%	12%	14%	14%	19%	21%	25%
Part time do not want full time	7%	7%	7%	7%	6%	5%	5%	6%
Part time want full time	6%	9%	9%	9%	7%	7%	8%	8%
Unemployed	6%	8%	10%	10%	7%	9%	9%	12%
Out of workforce	48%	43%	46%	50%	32%	23%	21%	21%

Averaged over 2019-2021.

Source: Gallup

References

Belser, P., Maitre, N., Vazquez-Alvarez, R., Maman Waziri, K., Xu, D., & Zarkou, A. (2020, December 2). *Global wage report 2020-21: Wages and minimum wages in the time of COVID-19.* International Labour Organization. https://www.ilo.org/global/publications/books/WCMS_762534/lang--en/index.htm

Catalyst. (2021, February 11). *Women in the workforce — global: Quick take.* Catalyst. https://www.catalyst.org/research/women-in-the-workforce-global/

Clifton, J., & Ray, J. (2015, March 4). *Nearly 2 billion women worldwide are struggling, suffering.* Gallup. https://news.gallup.com/poll/181790/nearly-billion-women-worldwide-struggling-suffering.aspx

DailyMail.com. (2021, March 4). *Father cuts off 17-year-old daughter's head and carries it through the streets because he did not approve of her boyfriend*. DailyMail.com. https://www.dailymail.co.uk/news/article-9325637/Dad-cuts-17-year-old-daughters-head-carries-streets-didnt-like-boyfriend.html

FAO, IFAD, UNICEF, WFP, and WHO. (2020). *The state of food security and nutrition in the world 2020. Transforming food systems for affordable healthy diets for all*. FAO. https://doi.org/10.4060/ca9692en

Graham, C., & Chattopadhyay, S. (2013). Gender and well-being around the world. *International Journal of Happiness and Development, 1*(2), 212-232. https://doi.org/10.1504/IJHD.2013.055648

Hologic. (2021). *2020 global report: The Hologic Global Women's Health Index: Pathways to a healthy future for women*. Hologic. https://hologic.womenshealthindex.com/Hologic_2020-Global-Women%27s-Health-Index_Full-Report.pdf

OECD. (n.d.). *Gender wage gap*. [Data set]. Organisation for Economic Co-operation and Development. https://data.oecd.org/earnwage/gender-wage-gap.htm

Ray, J., Esipova, N., & Pugliese, A. (2017). *Towards a better future for women and work: Voices of women and men*. International Labour Organization and Gallup. https://www.ilo.org/wcmsp5/groups/public/---dgreports/---dcomm/---publ/documents/publication/wcms_546256.pdf

Research Papers in Economics. (2021). *Top 10% female economists, as of December 2021*. Research Papers in Economics. https://ideas.repec.org/top/top.women.html

Schaeffer, K. (2020, October 5). *Key facts about women's suffrage around the world, a century after U.S. ratified 19th Amendment*. Pew Research Center. https://pewrsr.ch/3izs8X9

Sidner, S., & Udas, S. (2012, June 19). *Indian police: Man chops off daughter's head, citing her 'indecent behavior'*. CNN. https://www.cnn.com/2012/06/18/world/asia/india-daughter-beheaded

Some ideas for reducing violence against women. (2021, March 13). *The Economist.* https://www.economist.com/leaders/2021/03/13/some-ideas-for-reducing-violence-against-women

Specia, M. (2019, June 24). Saudi Arabia granted women the right to drive. A year on, it's still complicated. *The New York Times.* https://www.nytimes.com/2019/06/24/world/middleeast/saudi-driving-ban-anniversary.html

UNdata. (2019). *Gender Inequality Index.* [Data set]. United Nations Development Programme. http://data.un.org/DocumentData.aspx?id=415

UNICEF's Data & Analytics team. (2021). *Attitudes and social norms on violence.* UNICEF. https://data.unicef.org/topic/child-protection/violence/attitudes-and-social-norms-on-violence/

Walk Free Foundation. (2018). *The Global Slavery Index 2018.* Walk Free Foundation. https://www.globalslaveryindex.org/

White, D. (2021, March 4). *Beheaded by dad: Horrific moment dad calmly carries daughter's severed head through the streets after 'beheading her in honour killing'.* The U.S. Sun. https://www.the-sun.com/news/2450027/dad-carries-daughters-severed-head-streets-beheading-honour-killing/

The World Bank. (2021, June 15). *Labor force participation rate, male (% of male population ages 15+) (modeled ILO estimate) – India.* [Data set]. The World Bank. https://data.worldbank.org/indicator/SL.TLF.CACT.MA.ZS?locations=IN

World Health Organization. (2021, March 9). *Devastatingly pervasive: 1 in 3 women globally experience violence.* World Health Organization. https://www.who.int/news/item/09-03-2021-devastatingly-pervasive-1-in-3-women-globally-experience-violence

World Health Organization. (2022, January 21). *Female genital mutilation.* World Health Organization. https://www.who.int/news-room/fact-sheets/detail/female-genital-mutilation

Chapter Fifteen: The Emotionless Society

References

Bell, J. (2021, September 21). *Singaporeans drowning in hours of unpaid overtime*. Human Resources Director Asia. https://www.hcamag.com/asia/specialisation/mental-health/singaporeans-drowning-in-hours-of-unpaid-overtime/310737

Bradburn, N. M. (1969). *The structure of psychological well-being*. Aldine Publishing Company.

Chee Tung, L. (2013, September 30). *Singaporeans are still emotionally stressed*. Gallup. https://news.gallup.com/businessjournal/164642/singaporeans-emotionally-stressed.aspx

Chin, N. C. (2012, November 23). Emotions not taking over? *TODAY*, 4.

EmotionlessSporean. (2013). *Emotionless Singaporean: A fun day at Orchard Road* [Video] YouTube. https://www.youtube.com/watch?v=Hhq8mwmOTTk&t=2s

Gallup. (2017). *State of the global workplace*. Gallup.

Gallup. (2021). *State of the global workplace: 2021 report*. Gallup. https://www.gallup.com/workplace/349484/state-of-the-global-workplace.aspx

Goh, M. (2019, August 7). *No condos and country clubs, here are the new 5Cs defined by Singaporeans*. AsiaOne. https://www.asiaone.com/lifestyle/no-condos-and-country-clubs-here-are-new-5cs-defined-singaporeans

Ho, D. (2012, November 23). Strong feelings over 'emotionless S'poreans'. *The Straits Times*, A3.

Hodal, K. (2012, November 21). Singapore is world's least emotional country, poll finds. *The Guardian*. https://www.theguardian.com/world/2012/nov/21/singapore-least-emotional-country-poll

Human Development Reports. (2020). *Latest Human Development Index Ranking* [Data set]. United Nations Development Programme. http://hdr.undp.org/en/content/latest-human-development-index-ranking

Lim, J. (2018, December 14). *Singapore residents working fewer hours since 2010: MOM report*. TODAY. https://www.todayonline.com/singapore/singapore-residents-working-fewer-hours-2010-mom-report

Michel, C. (2015, March 30). Lee Kuan Yew's Singapore as a model for Kazakhstan. *The Diplomat*. https://thediplomat.com/2015/03/lee-kuan-yews-singapore-as-a-model-for-kazakhstan/

Ministry of Manpower. (2020, November 18). *Hours of work, overtime and rest day*. Ministry of Manpower. https://www.mom.gov.sg/employment-practices/hours-of-work-overtime-and-rest-days#normal-hours-of-work

Mustafa, F. (2021, April 8). *Singapore's endless pursuit of cleanliness*. BBC Travel. https://www.bbc.com/travel/article/20210407-singapores-endless-pursuit-of-cleanliness

O'Neill, A. (2021, July 15). *Unemployment rate in Singapore 2020*. Statista. https://www.statista.com/statistics/378643/unemployment-rate-in-singapore/

Singapore profile – Timeline. (2018, May 10). BBC News. https://www.bbc.com/news/world-asia-15971013

Strong feelings over 'emotionless Singaporeans'. (2012, November 24). If *Only Singaporeans Stopped to Think*. https://ifonlysingaporeans.blogspot.com/2012/11/strong-feelings-over-emotionless.html

Tang, L. (2018, December 26). *The big read: breaking Singapore's workaholic culture*. TODAY. https://www.todayonline.com/big-read/big-read-breaking-singapore-workaholic-culture

The World Bank. (n.d.). *GDP per capita, PPP (current international $) – Singapore*. [Data set]. The World Bank. https://data.worldbank.org/indicator/NY.GDP.PCAP.PP.CD?locations=SG

Chapter Sixteen: A Letter to Rwandan President Paul Kagame

References

Address by President Kagame at World Leaders Forum, Columbia University, 26 September 2019. (2019, September 26). Paul Kagame. https://www.paulkagame.com/address-by-president-kagame-at-world-leaders-forum-columbia-university-26-september-2019/

Biracyaza, E., & Habimana, S. (2020). Contribution of community-based sociotherapy interventions for the psychological well-being of Rwandan youths born to genocide perpetrators and survivors: Analysis of the stories telling of a sociotherapy approach. *BMC Psychology, 8*(102), 1-15. https://doi.org/10.1186/s40359-020-00471-9

Fareed Zakaria GPS. (n.d.). *Interview with Rahm Emanuel; Interview with Paul Kagame* [Speech transcript]. CNN. http://www.cnn.com/TRANSCRIPTS/1206/10/fzgps.01.html (Original interview June 10, 2012)

Fidèle, K., & de Laminne de Bex, A. (2011). *Innovation developed in Rwanda to support social protection interventions.* International Labour Organization. https://www.social-protection.org/gimi/gess/RessourcePDF.action;jsessionid=XWahaHbfy-bWhmC_p3eJrl9ZGZT2po7hSt2F-H_SDdn9XM47PF7q!-1398058155?id=23180

IRIN News. (2005, March 10). *Gacaca courts begin operations.* The New Humanitarian. https://www.thenewhumanitarian.org/report/53358/rwanda-gacaca-courts-begin-operations

Nforngwa, E. (2019, April 8). *How Rwanda genocide victim, perpetrator became friends.* Voice of America. https://www.voanews.com/a/rwanda-s-genocide-victims-perpetrators-turned-neighbors-friends-/4866397.html

Rieder, H., & Elbert, T. (2013). Rwanda – Lasting imprints of a genocide: Trauma, mental health and psychosocial conditions in survivors, former prisoners and their children. *Conflict and Health, 7*(6), 1-13. https://doi.org/10.1186/1752-1505-7-6

Rwanda genocide: 100 days of slaughter. (2019, April 4). BBC News. https://www.bbc.com/news/world-africa-26875506

Schaal, S., Weierstall, R., Dusingizemungu, J.-P., & Elbert, T. (2012). Mental health 15 years after the killings in Rwanda: Imprisoned perpetrators of the genocide against the Tutsi versus a community sample of survivors. *Journal of Traumatic Stress, 25*(4), 446-453. https://doi.org/10.1002/jts.21728

Seay, L. (2017, June 2). Rwanda's gacaca courts are hailed as a post-genocide success. The reality is more complicated. *Washington Post.* https://www.washingtonpost.com/news/monkey-cage/wp/2017/06/02/59162/

Skok, S. (n.d.). *What impact did the Belgian presence in Rwanda have to spark further conflict?* Seattlepi.com. https://education.seattlepi.com/impact-did-belgian-presence-rwanda-spark-further-conflict-5558.html

Swart, M. (2020, June 7). *'Music to kill to': Rwandan genocide survivors remember RTLM.* Al Jazeera. https://www.aljazeera.com/features/2020/6/7/music-to-kill-to-rwandan-genocide-survivors-remember-rtlm

Vásquez, I., & McMahon, F. (2020). *The Human Freedom Index 2020: A global measurement of personal, civil, and economic freedom.* Cato Institute and the Fraser Institute. https://www.cato.org/sites/cato.org/files/2020-12/human-freedom-index-2020.pdf

What happened in Rwanda's 1994 genocide? (2020, May 16). Reuters. https://www.reuters.com/article/france-rwanda-arrest-genocide/what-happened-in-rwandas-1994-genocide-idINKBN22S0M6

The World Bank. (2021, October 7). *The World Bank in Rwanda.* The World Bank. https://www.worldbank.org/en/country/rwanda/overview#1

Chapter Seventeen: How the Global Pandemic Shaped Happiness

References

2014-2016 Ebola outbreak in West Africa. (2019, March 8). Centers for Disease Control and Prevention. https://www.cdc.gov/vhf/ebola/history/2014-2016-outbreak/index.html

Helliwell, J. F., Huang, H., Wang, S., & Norton, M. (2021). Happiness, trust, and deaths under COVID-19. In Helliwell, J. F., Layard, R., Sachs, J. D., & de Neve, J.-E. (Eds.), *World happiness report 2021* (pp. 13-56). Sustainable Development Solutions Network. https://worldhappiness.report/ed/2021/happiness-trust-and-deaths-under-covid-19/

Himelein, K. (2015, April 15). *The socio-economic impacts of Ebola in Liberia.* Liberia Institute of Statistics, World Bank Group, & Gallup. https://www.worldbank.org/content/dam/Worldbank/document/Poverty%20documents/Socio-Economic%20Impacts%20of%20Ebola%20in%20Liberia%2C%20April%2015%20(final).pdf

Holbrook, A. L., Green, M. C., & Krosnick, J. A. (2003). Telephone versus face-to-face interviewing of national probability samples with long questionnaires: Comparisons of respondent satisficing and social desirability response bias. *Public Opinion Quarterly, 67*(1), 79-125. https://doi.org/10.1086/346010

IMF: Global economy to shrink for first time in 60 years. (2009, March 20). CNN. http://edition.cnn.com/2009/BUSINESS/03/20/imf.global.economy/index.html

IMF lifts China's GDP to 8.4 %, but Gita Gopinath says growth unbalanced. (2021, April 7). The Economic Times. https://economictimes.indiatimes.com/news/international/world-news/imf-lifts-chinas-gdp-to-8-4-but-gita-gopinath-says-growth-unbalanced/articleshow/81953286.cms?from=mdr

International Monetary Fund. (2021, January). *World economic outlook update: Policy support and vaccines expected to lift activity.* International Monetary Fund. https://www.imf.org/en/Publications/WEO/Issues/2021/01/26/2021-world-economic-outlook-update

Keeter, S. (2015, May 13). *From telephone to the web: The challenge of mode of interview effects in public opinion polls.* Pew Research Center. https://www.pewresearch.org/methods/2015/05/13/from-telephone-to-the-web-the-challenge-of-mode-of-interview-effects-in-public-opinion-polls/

The pandemic's true death toll: Our daily estimate of excess deaths around the world. (2022, March 1). *The Economist.*

Ray, J. (2021, May 3). *COVID-19 put more than 1 billion out of work.* Gallup. https://news.gallup.com/poll/348722/covid-put-billion-work.aspx

Reinhart, RJ. (2021, May 3). *COVID-19 affected people's lives everywhere.* Gallup. https://news.gallup.com/poll/348716/covid-affected-people-lives-everywhere.aspx

Surprisingly, suicide has become rarer during the pandemic. (2021, April 24). *The Economist.* https://www.economist.com/graphic-detail/2021/04/24/surprisingly-suicide-has-become-rarer-during-the-pandemic

The World Bank. (n.d.). *GDP growth (annual %).* [Data set]. The World Bank. https://data.worldbank.org/indicator/NY.GDP.MKTP.KD.ZG?end=2020&start=1961

Wuhan coronavirus: From silent streets to packed pools. (2020, August 18). BBC News. https://www.bbc.com/news/world-asia-china-53816511

Part V: What Leaders Can Do to Improve How People's Lives Are Going

Chapter Eighteen: What Public Sector Leaders Can Do
References

Abidi, A. (2021, January 29). *Tunisia's new uprising: A return of the police state?* openDemocracy. https://www.opendemocracy.net/en/north-africa-west-asia/tunisias-new-uprising-a-return-of-the-police-state/

BBC News. (2021, January 19). *Tunisia protests: More than 600 hundred arrested.* BBC News. https://www.bbc.com/news/av/world-55718868

Department of Economic and Social Affairs Sustainable Development. (2021). *3: Ensure healthy lives and promote well-being for all at all ages.* United Nations. https://sdgs.un.org/goals/goal3

Feuer, S. (2021, January 22). *Riots erupt in Tunisia.* The Washington Institute for Near East Policy. https://www.washingtoninstitute.org/policy-analysis/riots-erupt-tunisia

Price, N. (2021, July 26). *Situation in Tunisia: Press statement.* U.S. Department of State. https://www.state.gov/situation-in-tunisia/

Yee, V. (2021, July 27). In Tunisia, some wonder if the revolution was worth it. *The New York Times.* https://www.nytimes.com/2021/01/19/world/middleeast/tunisia-protests-arab-spring-anniversary.html

Chapter Nineteen: What Private Sector Leaders Can Do
References

Always Right. (2009, November 6). Drucker Institute. https://www.drucker.institute/thedx/110609-always-right/

Bebchuk, L. & Tallarita, R. (2020, August 12). *Was the Business Roundtable statement on corporate purpose mostly for show? – (1) Evidence from lack of board approval.* Harvard Law School Forum on Corporate Governance. https://corpgov.law.harvard.edu/2020/08/12/was-the-business-roundtable-statement-on-corporate-purpose-mostly-for-show-1-evidence-from-lack-of-board-approval/

Brenan, M. (2022, February 7). *Low satisfaction with U.S. gov't regulation of businesses.* Gallup. https://news.gallup.com/poll/389519/low-satisfaction-gov-regulation-businesses.aspx

Business Roundtable. (2019, August 19). *Business Roundtable redefines the purpose of a corporation to promote 'an economy that serves all Americans'.* Business Roundtable. https://www.businessroundtable.org/business-roundtable-redefines-the-purpose-of-a-corporation-to-promote-an-economy-that-serves-all-americans

CEO activism in America is risky business. (2021, April 14). *The Economist.* https://www.economist.com/business/2021/04/14/ceo-activism-in-america-is-risky-business

Clifford, T. (2020, January 16). *Capitalism 'will fundamentally be in jeopardy' if business does not act on climate change, Microsoft CEO Satya Nadella says.* CNBC. https://www.cnbc.com/2020/01/16/microsoft-ceo-capitalism-is-in-jeopardy-if-we-do-not-act-on-climate-change.html

Denning, S. (2020, January 5). Why stakeholder capitalism will fail. *Forbes.* https://www.forbes.com/sites/stevedenning/2020/01/05/why-stakeholder-capitalism-will-fail/?sh=291f569785a8

Denning, S. (2021, May 2). Why business must shift from value extraction to value creation. *Forbes.* https://www.forbes.com/sites/stevedenning/2021/05/02/why-business-must-shift-from-value-extraction-to-value-creation/?sh=1dc18ad469f0

Fleming, J. H., Coffman, C., & Harter, J. K. (2005). Manage your Human Sigma. *Harvard Business Review.* https://www.nova.edu/ie/ice/forms/human_sigma.pdf

Francis, T. (2017, April 6). Why you probably work for a giant company, in 20 charts. *The Wall Street Journal.* https://www.wsj.com/graphics/big-companies-get-bigger/

Friedman, M. (1970, September 13). A Friedman doctrine-- The social responsibility of business is to increase its profits. *The New York Times.* https://www.nytimes.com/1970/09/13/archives/a-friedman-doctrine-the-social-responsibility-of-business-is-to.html

Gallup. (n.d.). *Consulting expertise: Customer centricity.* Gallup. https://www.gallup.com/workplace/311870/customer-centricity.aspx

Gallup. (2021). *State of the global workplace: 2021 report*. Gallup. https://www.gallup.com/workplace/349484/state-of-the-global-workplace.aspx

Gensler, G. [@GaryGensler]. (2021, August 18). *Investors want to better understand one of the most critical assets of a company: its people.* [Tweet]. Twitter. https://twitter.com/garygensler/status/1428022885889761292?lang=en

Global 500. (n.d.). *Fortune*. https://fortune.com/global500/?utm_content=invest&tpcc=gfortune500&gclid=Cj0KCQiAi9mPBhCJARIsAHchl1w0bwFI4iGQ8DPXrntzRjbJ1lmY4jmOmEaeXXMQdyM8uKi_ocQp_n4aAh-cEALw_wcB

Harter, J. (2021, July 29). *U.S. employee engagement holds steady in first half of 2021*. Gallup. https://www.gallup.com/workplace/352949/employee-engagement-holds-steady-first-half-2021.aspx

How Japan's stakeholder capitalism is changing. (2021, March 18). *The Economist*. https://www.economist.com/business/2021/03/18/how-japans-stakeholder-capitalism-is-changing

Lapham, K., Verwey, J., Singh, M., Unadkat, A. (2021). Breaking down the new EU ESG disclosure regulation: One month to go. *The National Law Review, XI*(41). https://www.natlawreview.com/article/breaking-down-new-eu-esg-disclosure-regulation-one-month-to-go

Masercola, N. (2022, January 12). *The JUST Report: Meet the 2022 JUST 100 leaders*. JUST Capital. https://justcapital.com/news/the-just-report-meet-the-2022-just-100-leaders/

Mayer, C., Strine, L. E., Jr., & Winter, J. (2020, September 13). 50 years later, Milton Friedman's shareholder doctrine is dead. *Fortune*. https://fortune.com/2020/09/13/milton-friedman-anniversary-business-purpose/

More investors want companies to report human capital data. (2022, February 22). Nasdaq. https://www.nasdaq.com/articles/more-investors-want-companies-to-report-human-capital-data

Nink, M., Rowlands, L., & Robison, J. (2020, October 22). *The weak link in your value chain: Disengaged suppliers*. Gallup. https://www.gallup.com/workplace/321995/weak-link-value-chain-disengaged-suppliers.aspx

Ping, D. X. (2006). *Selected works of Deng Xiaoping: Volume I (1938–1965)*. Foreign Languages Press. https://oregondigital.org/downloads/oregondigital:df72k239v

The rise of state capitalism. (2012, January 21). *The Economist*. https://www.economist.com/leaders/2012/01/21/the-rise-of-state-capitalism

Robertson, A., & Griffiths, J. (2019, November 27). *Credit unions & banks: The financial wellbeing proposition*. Gallup. https://www.gallup.com/workplace/268220/credit-unions-banks-financial-wellbeing-proposition.aspx

Rowlands, L. & Fleming, J. H. (2015). *Creating strategic advantage through superior supplier engagement*. Gallup. https://www.gallup.com/services/176399/creating-strategic-advantage-superior-supplier-engagement.aspx

Saad, L. (2019, November 25). *Socialism as popular as capitalism among young adults in U.S.* Gallup. https://news.gallup.com/poll/268766/socialism-popular-capitalism-among-young-adults.aspx

Salesforce. (n.d.). *Stakeholder capitalism: The time to build a better future is now*. Salesforce. https://www.salesforce.com/company/stakeholder-capitalism/

Schwab, K., & Vanham, P. (2021, January 26). *What is the difference between stakeholder capitalism, shareholder capitalism and state capitalism?* World Economic Forum. https://www.weforum.org/agenda/2021/01/what-is-the-difference-between-stakeholder-capitalism-shareholder-capitalism-and-state-capitalism-davos-agenda-2021/

Shum, A., & McClune, D. (2020, December 15). *Give with Microsoft Bing*. Medium. https://medium.com/microsoft-design/give-with-microsoft-bing-db5598a07153

Sinek, S. [@simonsinek]. (2009, October 28). *100% of customers are people. 100% of employees are people. If you don't understand people, you don't understand business.* [Tweet]. Twitter. https://twitter.com/simonsinek/status/5232157344?lang=en

Sorenson, S. (n.d.). *How employees' strengths make your company stronger.* Gallup. https://www.gallup.com/workplace/231605/employees-strengths-company-stronger.aspx

Squawk Box. (2022, January 11). CNBC Transcript: Billionaire investor & JUST Capital co-founder Paul Tudor Jones and Accenture chair & CEO Julie Sweet speak with CNBC's "Squawk Box" Today [Speech transcript]. CNBC. https://www.cnbc.com/2022/01/11/cnbc-transcript-billionaire-investor-just-capital-co-founder-paul-tudor-jones-and-accenture-chair-ceo-julie-sweet-speak-with-cnbcs-squawk-box-today.html

Squawk Box. (2022, January 12). *Nasdaq CEO Adena Friedman on ESG: We are a disclosure economy.* CNBC. https://www.cnbc.com/video/2022/01/12/nasdaq-ceo-adena-friedman-on-esg-we-are-a-disclosure-economy.html

Statement on the purpose of a corporation. (2020). Business Roundtable. https://s3.amazonaws.com/brt.org/BRT-StatementonthePurposeofaCorporationOctober2020.pdf

The truth about dirty assets. (2022, February 12). *The Economist.* https://www.economist.com/leaders/2022/02/12/the-truth-about-dirty-assets

The visible hand. (2012, January 21). *The Economist.* https://www.economist.com/special-report/2012/01/21/the-visible-hand

Vuong, A. (2021, January 13). *Why financial wellbeing is critical to member success.* CreditUnions.com. https://www.creditunions.com/articles/why-financial-wellbeing-is-critical-to-member-success/#ixzz6zvg43hbD

What happens when firms have to stump up for good causes. (2021, January 9). *The Economist.* https://www.economist.com/business/2021/01/09/what-happens-when-firms-have-to-stump-up-for-good-causes

Wirz, M., & Kiernan, P. (2022, February 17). Investors seek more information about companies' struggles to hire, retain staff. *The Wall Street Journal.* https://www.wsj.com/articles/investors-seek-more-information-about-companies-struggles-to-hire-retain-staff-11645045610?st=w06mbws55vg1yle&reflink=desktopwebshare_twitter

World Economic Forum, Deloitte, EY, KPMG, & PwC. (2020 September). *Measuring stakeholder capitalism towards common metrics and consistent reporting of sustainable value creation: White paper.* World Economic Forum. https://www3.weforum.org/docs/WEF_IBC_Measuring_Stakeholder_Capitalism_Report_2020.pdf

Younis, M. (2019, May 20). *Four in 10 Americans embrace some form of socialism.* Gallup. https://news.gallup.com/poll/257639/four-americans-embrace-form-socialism.aspx

Zaveri, P. (2020, January 14). *Microsoft CEO Satya Nadella said that a book published last year by Oxford professor Colin Mayer inspired him to think differently about capitalism.* Insider. https://www.businessinsider.com/microsoft-satya-nadella-book-colin-mayer-capitalism-2019-2020-1

Chapter Twenty: What Public Sector and Private Sector Leaders Can Do Together

References

Badiee, S., Jütting, J., Appel, D., Klein, T., & Swanson, E. (2017). The role of national statistical systems in the data revolution. In *Development Co-operation Report 2017: Data for Development* (pp. 55-75). OECD Publishing. https://read.oecd-ilibrary.org/development/development-co-operation-report-2017/the-role-of-national-statistical-systems-in-the-data-revolution_dcr-2017-8-en#page1

Cookpad and Gallup. (n.d.). *Making everyday cooking fun and measuring global home cooking habits with Cookpad.* Cookpad and Gallup. https://www.gallup.com/analytics/345410/cookpad-success-story.aspx

Cookpad: Our mission make everyday cooking fun. (n.d.). Cookpad. https://www.cookpadteam.com/

Gallup. (2009). Customer engagement: What's your engagement ratio? Gallup.

Gallup (2014). *State of the American consumer: Insights for business leaders.* Gallup. https://www.gallup.com/services/176282/state-american-consumer.aspx

Hologic announces multi-year initiative to improve quality of life and life expectancy of women worldwide. (2021, March 8). Business Wire. https://www.businesswire.com/news/home/20210308005128/en/Hologic-Announces-Multi-year-Initiative-to-Improve-Quality-of-Life-and-Life-Expectancy-of-Women-Worldwide

Judah, T. (2020, May 14). *Wildly wrong: North Macedonia's population mystery.* Reporting Democracy. https://balkaninsight.com/2020/05/14/wildly-wrong-north-macedonias-population-mystery/

Krishna, P. (2021, April 26). With no frills or celebrities, Cookpad is a global go-to for recipes. *The New York Times.* https://www.nytimes.com/2021/04/26/dining/cookpad-recipe-site.html

No one knows how many people live in North Macedonia. (2020, May 14). *The Economist.* https://www.economist.com/europe/2020/05/14/no-one-knows-how-many-people-live-in-north-macedonia

OECD. (2017). *Development Co-operation Report 2017: Data for Development.* OECD Publishing. https://doi.org/10.1787/dcr-2017-en

Statistical Office. (2021, October 1). Address by the director of the State Statistical Office on the occasion of the completion of the census 2021. Organization of the census. [Translated using Google Translate]. https://popis2021.stat.gov.mk/

Survey of National Statistical Offices (NSOs) during COVID-19. (2020, July 6). The World Bank. https://www.worldbank.org/en/research/brief/survey-of-national-statistical-offices-nsos-during-covid-19

United Nations. (2019). *The sustainable development goals report 2019.* United Nations. https://unstats.un.org/sdgs/report/2019/The-Sustainable-Development-Goals-Report-2019.pdf

Whole Foods Market. (n.d.). *Mission and values.* Whole Foods Market. https://www.wholefoodsmarket.com/mission-values

Appendix

The Birth of the Gallup World Poll

References

CNN Live Event/Special. (n.d.). *General Tommy Franks and Sec. of Defense Rumsfeld give Pentagon briefing* [Speech transcript]. CNN. https://transcripts.cnn.com/show/se/date/2001-11-08/segment/04 (Original speech November 8, 2001)

Gallup. (2008, March 27). Islam and the West: Clash or coexistence? In John Esposito, J., & Mogahed, D. (Authors), *Who Speaks for Islam?* (pp. 142-144). Gallup. https://news.gallup.com/poll/105700/Islam-West-Clash-Coexistence.aspx

Rumsfeld, D. (2001). *Public statements of Donald H. Rumsfeld, secretary of defense, 2001*. Historical Office of the Office of the Secretary of Defense.

Washington Post. (2001, September 20). Text: President Bush Addresses the Nation [Speech transcript]. *Washington Post.* https://www.washingtonpost.com/wp-srv/nation/specials/attacked/transcripts/bushaddress_092001.html

The Questions We Ask the World

Uniform Crime Reporting Program. (2019). *2019 crime in the United States.* Federal Bureau of Investigation. https://ucr.fbi.gov/crime-in-the-u.s/2019/crime-in-the-u.s.-2019/topic-pages/violent-crime

Uniform Crime Reporting Program. (2019). *Crime in the United States by Volume and Rate per 100,000 Inhabitants, 2000-2019.* [Data set]. Federal Bureau of Investigation. https://ucr.fbi.gov/crime-in-the-u.s/2019/crime-in-the-u.s.-2019/tables/table-1

United Nations Statistics Division. (n.d.) *SDG indicators: Metadata repository.* United Nations Department of Economic and Social Affairs. https://unstats.un.org/sdgs/metadata/?Text=&Goal=16&Target=16.1

How Gallup Surveys the World

World Justice Project. (2020). *World Justice Project Rule of Law Index 2020.* World Justice Project.

ABOUT GALLUP

Gallup is a global analytics, advisory and learning firm that helps leaders solve their organizations' biggest problems.

Gallup knows more about the will of employees, customers, students and citizens than any other organization in the world. We offer solutions, transformations and services in many areas, including:

- Culture change
- Leadership development
- Manager development
- Strengths-based coaching and culture
- Strategies for organic growth
- "Boss-to-coach" software tools
- Attracting and recruiting star team members
- Succession planning
- Performance management system and ratings
- Refining performance metrics
- Reducing defects and safety risks
- Evaluating internal programs
- Employee engagement and experience
- Predictive hiring assessments
- Retention forecasting
- Creating agile teams
- Improving the customer experience (B2B)
- Diversity and inclusion
- Wellbeing initiatives

To learn more, please contact Gallup at https://www.gallup.com/contact.

ABOUT THE AUTHOR

Jon Clifton is the CEO of Gallup. His mission is to help 7 billion citizens be heard on their most pressing work and life issues through the Gallup World Poll, a 100-year initiative spanning over 150 countries.

Clifton is a nonresident senior fellow at Baylor University's Institute for Studies of Religion. He serves on the boards of directors for Gallup and Young Professionals in Foreign Policy, and he previously served on the boards for three nonprofits and a startup — Meridian International Center, StreetWise Partners, Chess Challenge in DC, and Findyr.

Because of his expertise, Clifton has been interviewed on BBC News, Axios, C-SPAN's "Washington Journal," and Al-Jazeera, and he has testified in front of the U.S. Congress on the state of American small business and entrepreneurship. He is a frequent contributor on Gallup.com and has written for *The Hill*, *The Diplomatic Courier*, and *The Global Action Report*.

Clifton received a bachelor's degree in political science and history from the University of Michigan and a Juris Doctor in international law from the University of Nebraska. He was also awarded an honorary doctorate in humane letters from Midland University.

ACKNOWLEDGMENTS

Nobel laureate Daniel Kahneman was once asked about his own happiness. According to *Quartz*, Kahneman said there were "periods when he worked alone on writing that were 'terrible,' when he felt 'miserable.'" Every author probably knows exactly what he meant.

But Kahneman also said that we feel happiness primarily in the company of others. This is what I felt in the company of editors Geoff Brewer and Kelly Henry and designer Samantha Allemang when writing this book. They spent countless hours with me reviewing every word, data point, and graph to make sure each was perfect.

This book would not have happened without the encouragement of my dad, Jim Clifton. Using his Activator theme, Jim encouraged me to spend every weekend writing a book that reflected the best insights from Gallup's World Poll. He read dozens of versions of every chapter and patiently listened to me ruminate about the most minute details of this book. I am indebted to him for his coaching and encouragement.

Gallup books don't happen without Seth Schuchman, who leads Gallup Press. He guided us from a simple outline to what you are reading right now. I am also thankful to Ambassador Robin Renee Sanders, Carol Graham, Shauna Olney, Julie Ray, and Sir Angus Deaton for their valuable advice and opinions that enriched the content in *Blind Spot*. This book was also possible because of the around-the-clock work of James Scissom, who helped with everything from research to scheduling time with stakeholders to producing charts. Also thank you to Ashley Anderson for her contributions to marketing and communications and to our Gallup Press coordinator, Christy Trout.

I am grateful to *Blind Spot*'s peer-review committee — otherwise known as the "suicide squad" — who read the book's earliest versions and provided detailed commentary. This group included Pablo Diego-Rosell, Larry Emond, Faith Gaines, Jim Harter, Taek Lee, Stephanie Marken, Jane Miller, Lymari Morales, Matt Mosser, Steve O'Brien, Julie Ray, Ilana Ron-Levey, Andrew Rzepa, Lydia Saad, Pa Sinyan, Priscilla Standridge, Chris Stewart, Anson Vuong, and Mohamed Younis. I am eternally grateful to them for the time they spent reviewing and sharing their deep expertise.

As with most Gallup content, this book is full of data. To produce each trend, correlation, and segmentation analysis, I needed the brilliance and technical expertise of Dato Tsabutashvili, Anna Zelaya, Robert Bird, Jenny Marlar, and Stafford Nichols. And thank you to Trista Kunce for checking, rechecking, and checking again every data point, white paper, quotation, and reference in this book.

Blind Spot most certainly would not have been possible without the Gallup World Poll team — past and present. This group empowered leaders everywhere to systematically listen to how people feel in almost every country in the world. The list of contributors to the World Poll is long, but there are a few who I have been lucky to work with closely and who have helped make the World Poll into what it is today. Thank you to Zach Bikus, Patrick Bogart, Richard Burkholder, Marc Carpenter, Anna Chan, Manas Chattopadhyay, Steve Crabtree, Joe Daly, Cynthia English, Neli Esipova, Jihad Fakhreddine, Alec Gallup, Johanna Godoy, Jerry Hansen, Kris Hodgins, Alison Hunter, Sara Huston, Elizabeth Keating, Ken Kluch, Sofia Kluch, Jim Krieger, Jay LaMontagne, Jay Loschky, Chris McCarty, Dalia Mogahed, Nicole Naurath, Armand Ngnecheko, Kiki Papachristoforou, Rachel Penrod, Anita Pugliese, John Reimnitz, Magali Rheault, Jesus Rios, Chayanun

Saransomrurtai, Rajesh Srinivasan, Nadiia Sydorenko, Bob Tortora, Ahmed Younis, Galina Zapryanova, and Julie Zeplin.

Almost everyone on the Gallup World Poll team was mentored by the late Gale Muller, including me. He led the World Poll from the day we started until the day he died. The World Poll would not have been possible without his leadership, and all of us are better at our jobs and simply better people because of him. Gale was remarkably kind (he led with Harmony), brilliant, and fun — but most of all, he was inspirational.

Two days before Gale lost his life to cancer, he called to tell me about a pattern in the data that had him perplexed. Knowing his condition, I asked him if it was a good idea for him to be working. What he said back to me is something I will never forget. He said, "Jon, I want to make a contribution until my last day." And that he did — and he continues to make an impact through all of us to this day.

Lastly, there are thousands of Gallup World Poll interviewers all over the planet who knock on doors and call people in their homes simply to have a conversation with everyday people about their lives. They are truly changing the world because they do what all of us need to do more of, which is listen. To the thousands of interviewers who have worked on this project, thank you for listening and reporting on how the world feels. I hope leaders everywhere are paying attention to your work.

Gallup Press exists to educate and inform the people who govern, manage, teach and lead the world's 7 billion citizens. Each book meets Gallup's requirements of integrity, trust and independence and is based on Gallup-approved science and research.